▼ CRITICAL ISSUES IN CHILD WELFARE

▼ # CRITICAL ISSUES IN CHILD WELFARE

Nora S. Gustavsson
Elizabeth A. Segal

SAGE Publications
International Educational and Professional Publisher
Thousand Oaks   London   New Delhi

For information address:

 SAGE Publications, Inc.
2455 Teller Road
Thousand Oaks, California 91320

SAGE Publications Ltd.
6 Bonhill Street
London EC2A 4PU
United Kingdom

SAGE Publications India Pvt. Ltd.
M-32 Market
Greater Kailash I
New Delhi 110 048 India

Printed in the United States of America

Library of Congress Cataloging-in-Publication Data

Gustavsson, Nora S.
    Critical issues in child welfare / authors, Nora S. Gustavsson,
Elizabeth A. Segal.
        p. cm.
    Includes bibliographical references and index.
    ISBN 0-8039-4504-3 (cl). — ISBN 0-8039-4505-1 (pb)
    1. Child welfare—United States. I. Segal, Elizabeth A.
II. Title.
HV741.G87 1994
362.7'0973—dc20   93-46436
                                                                              CIP

94 95 96 97 10 9 8 7 6 5 4 3 2

Sage Production Editor: Rebecca Holland

Contents

Acknowledgments

The authors would like to acknowledge the assistance of Michael J. McCreight. His careful reading of the manuscript and attention to detail are much appreciated. While this book included the research and work of others, the authors take sole responsibility for its content.

Preface

Recent social and political events combined with demographic changes raise new concerns regarding the survival of today's children. Childhood has become a passage fraught with peril for many of America's children. The services and policies designed to protect children are inconsistent and at times ineffective. This book addresses these issues.

In this text, the authors combine information from various disciplines such as education, medicine, psychology, child development, economics, sociology, and political science in a highly readable form. The multidisciplinary approach provides the basis for the analyses presented in the book.

Few texts offer students such a multidisciplinary analysis. This text is designed to broaden the perspective of students and incorporates an ecological focus. Traditional texts in the child welfare field use a residual focus and emphasize policies and services that substitute for or support the abilities of parents to care for their children. Although these important topics are discussed, this text critically analyzes issues often ignored by traditional texts that touch the lives of children. The related social policies and programs are also analyzed.

Undergraduate students in human service and social science fields will find this book particularly helpful. They will be exposed to the major social issues confronting children today. The ecological perspective will help graduate students in human service fields expand their view of child welfare services from a reactive perspective to a proactive and preventive approach.

The book is organized into four sections. The first section establishes broad parameters for viewing child welfare. Chapter 1 looks at the Rights of Children. The precarious legal status of children contributes to their marginalization and complicates advocacy efforts. The legal and social rights of children are discussed in detail. The second chapter reviews the physical and mental health of America's children. This chapter introduces the student to the importance of prevention as a policy approach. The third chapter identifies some of the major issues in education and the obstacles to achieving a quality education.

The second part of the text examines the residual nature of child welfare policies and programs in this country. Chapter 4 provides students with an analysis of the economic welfare of children and the perils of growing up in poverty. Chapter 5 presents the issue of child abuse and neglect and discusses the growing awareness and extent of the problem. Chapter 6 looks at how children fare when the state becomes their primary caretaker. Foster care and adoption are core child welfare services and consume significant resources. These services are analyzed.

The third section highlights recent threats to the survival of children. Chapter 7 examines the assumptions, politics, and facts about drug use and the family. The connection between HIV infection, children, and drugs is explained. Chapter 8 presents the issue of homelessness among children and families, the fastest growing group among the homeless. Chapter 9 considers the impact of violence on children and the newly emerging consequences of increasing exposure to violence in communities.

The last section of the book takes the reader into topics that at first glance may seem unrelated to the themes usually associated with child welfare. Chapter 10 looks at the field of child development as a major contributor to the expanding knowledge base in child welfare. Chapter 11 examines the role of research in children's issues. The need for more methodologically sound designs, neglected areas, and research ethics are explained. Chapter 12 stresses the need for prevention. The costs and benefits of taking a preventive approach in response to the problems that threaten the safety and security of children are outlined.

This book can be used as a primary text in undergraduate or graduate courses in the social sciences. It can also be used as a supplementary text. The chapters and sections can stand alone, making the text useful for multiple courses. Instructors can select specific sections of the text to match their course objectives.

PART I

Caring for America's Children

Part I surveys the current status of children. Legal rights, health status, and education are vital components and the common experience for all America's children. Chapter 1 explores the value conflict in our society and analyzes what rights children do have and should have. The body politic has failed to resolve the children's rights issue. This conflict has resulted in a precarious balancing act among the rights of the state, the rights of parents, and the rights of children. This chapter establishes the framework for this book.

Chapter 2 discusses both the physical and emotional well-being of America's children. It includes an analysis of the policies and programs designed to support the health needs of children. The third chapter examines the public school experience. It assesses the educational system's ability to meet the needs of a changing and diverse youth population.

1

The Rights of Children

Questions about what policies and services children should have are difficult to answer. Some of the difficulty is due to disagreements about children's rights. Social policies to support children will continue to be fragmented until there is agreement about children's rights.

This chapter outlines the basic issues in the debate about children's rights. The potential conflicts between parents and children as well as the role of the state are explained. The role of the judicial system in defining and enforcing rights is explored.

The failure to resolve fundamental issues concerning the rights of children and the role of the state has contributed to the marginal status of children. For example, social policies to protect children's rights to health care, nutrition, housing, education, financial support, and adequate parenting are inconsistent and inadequate. Chapter 1 provides the foundation for understanding the conflicts and the patchwork of social policies which have resulted from these unresolved issues.

The vulnerable and dependent nature of childhood influences the debate about children's rights. Children have multiple and changing needs that must be met over a long period of time in order to help them become productive members of society. In addition, the roles, rights, and obligations of parents and the state in meeting the needs of children are subject to ongoing debate. Political and social factors also play a role both in how children are perceived and how their needs are met.

Needs and rights are intimately related. For example, there is agreement that children need adequate nutrition and health care in order to thrive. However, there is little agreement about the right of children to receive this care and how the care should be provided. If parents fail to provide such care the state may intervene and at substantial cost remove the children and place them in foster care. However, the state has failed to consistently support parents' abilities to care for their children. Some American families do not have the resources to obtain health care, nutrition, and housing.

Children have few rights and there is no consensus on what rights they should have. Part of the difficulty in trying to establish agreed-upon rights for children is due to the nature of childhood and the ambiguities associated with the label of child. Children must depend on the wisdom and benevolence of their caretakers in order to mature physically, emotionally, socially, and intellectually. Children have markedly varying capacities and abilities, however, including the capacity for judgment. A 6-month-old child is rapidly learning but has limited communication skills. A 15-year-old is also defined as a child yet possess the capacity of independent thought and an ability to articulate needs and wishes. The 6-month-old does not yet appreciate First Amendment guarantees of free speech. The 15-year-old not only can appreciate the guarantee but may desire to exercise this right.

Children's rights are viewed as zero sum or finite. This idea reflects the view that as the rights of one party increase, the rights of another party decrease. In addition to parents and children, the state plays a role in defining rights and obligations. The state may assume the role of mediator in conflicts between parents and children. For example, parents have the right to select a religion for their child. The state can interfere with this right when the life of the child is endangered. The state may disregard the rights of the parents in cases where a child needs medical care and the parents object to such care due to religious views. The last few decades have witnessed the emergence of a children's liberation movement that asserts the need for independent legal rights for children and a reluctance to rely on parents or the state to act in the best interests of children (Hegar, 1989). The liberationist view is adversarial and a reflection of the zero sum concept.

There is no consensus on what rights children should have. The legacy of this lack of consensus is a patchwork of rights that are incoherent and inconsistent. This chapter examines the limited rights afforded selected groups of children and highlights the implications of these rights for social policy development.

Legal and Social Rights of Children

Legal rights are by definition enforceable. Adults denied the right to vote, for example, may seek redress through the courts. Social rights emerge from needs and provide a framework for social policy development. As problems faced by vulnerable children become more visible, social policies emerge. For example, the Runaway and Homeless Youth Act of 1978 authorized a national switchboard and crisis and referral services. Early childhood education programs, day care, and compulsory immunizations are examples of the state responding to social needs. However, children do not have an enforceable right to these services.

Children are afforded few rights. Their legal rights, when accused of a crime, are similar to the rights of adults. Other rights guaranteed by the Constitution, such as the right to the free exercise of religion and speech, are restricted. There is some consensus on social rights, enforceable through the courts, such as the right to an education and the right to financial support. However, there is disagreement on the content of these rights.

There is no mention of children in the Constitution. This is not surprising because physical survival was a major concern for residents of the new republic and the labor of children was needed. It was not until the early 20th century that the notion of childhood as a unique developmental phase began to gain widespread support.

After World War II, knowledge about the abilities and needs of children increased dramatically. The fields of child psychology and education grew. The judicial system began to struggle with questions about children's rights. A number of factors contributed to these changes. Industrialization and immigration were progressing and there was less need for the labor of young children. The population was beginning to shift from rural to urban, thus minimizing the need for selected groups of children to work in the fields. The philosophy of the Progressive Era was supportive of a caring attitude toward children. The prominent reformers of the time, such as Jane Addams and the Abbott sisters, were champions of children's rights.

Legal Rights

Courts serve a social policy role and have delineated the legal rights of children. However, courts are by definition reactive institutions in that they do not actively seek causes of action or solicit cases. They respond only when an action is filed. Courts have been a major contributor to the patchwork rights of children.

The courts have been most active in identifying the rights of children accused of criminal acts. Juvenile courts were first established in the early 20th century and were based on a well-intentioned but paternalistic notion that adults knew what was best for children and would take proper action to insure the rehabilitation of young people in trouble with law enforcement or their parents. This principle of rehabilitation lasted until the 1960s, when the Supreme Court extended limited civil rights to youngsters accused of criminal behavior (*In re Gault*, 1967). Juvenile court was now clearly adversarial and based in part on due process principles. Children are generally denied two fundamental rights available to adults, the right to a trial by jury and the right to bail, although some states have extended these rights.

The abandonment of the old model of the juvenile court may be regarded as a victory for those who support the enfranchisement of children. Children have some due process rights. However, there has been a price to the extension of legal rights for juveniles. Young people can be tried as adults (*Kent v. United States*, 1966). If convicted of a capital offense, young people may become eligible for the death penalty. Advocates for children view execution as a violation of the Eighth Amendment. The Supreme Court has ruled on the applicability of the death penalty for children and has said that it is not a violation of the Eighth Amendment. The Court has restricted the execution of children who were younger than 16 when they committed the capital offense, particularly in states whose legislatures have not established a minimum age for execution (*Thompson v. Oklahoma*, 1988).

It is still permissible for the state to execute 16- and 17-year-olds (*Stanford v. Kentucky*, 1989). The notion that an adolescent can be rehabilitated and returned to the community is not popular. There is consistent public support for the use of the death penalty for people (including adolescents) convicted of capital crimes. This may be a reflection of a number of factors including growing community intolerance of violent criminal behavior (especially activities associated with the illicit drug trade), racism as evidenced by the exceedingly large numbers of young black males arrested and/or incarcerated (U.S. Department of Justice, 1987a), and a seeming inability to effectively alter the destructive behaviors of offenders. The high recidivism rates of offenders (both adult and juvenile) are used to support punitive solutions as opposed to treatment-oriented interventions.

Right to Financial Support

Children are unable to support themselves. Labor laws, a development of the 20th century, restrict the ability of young people to obtain employment. Parents are responsible for support, and courts have consistently affirmed the obligation of both parents to provide financial support for their children. The marital status of the parents is irrelevant. Federal laws such as the 1984 Child Support Enforcement Amendments represent an attempt to force parents to support their children. In spite of these intentions, children remain the poorest group of Americans (see Chapter 4 for discussion of child support issues and the juvenilization of poverty).

While the government and courts have been quick to try to force parents to provide financial support for children, there has been hesitancy on the part of government to support poor children. The primary federal program that supports poor children is Aid to Families with Dependent Children (AFDC), a residual, means-tested program that can be characterized as meager. Some children are supported by Social Security funds. The death of a parent who had paid into Social Security and parental or child disability are two ways of qualifying for Social Security benefits. These benefits are generally more generous than AFDC benefits and carry less of a stigma.

These two supplemental income programs are funded by the federal government, and states supplement AFDC benefits. States administer the programs and some states have attempted to deny children these limited financial benefits. A few states instituted "suitable home" sections in their AFDC regulations but failed to define clearly what constituted *suitable*. In the early 1960s, states such as Louisiana used the suitable home section to deny thousands of children benefits by using this vague section to justify termination of benefits. The 1962 Amendments to the Social Security Act limited the right of states to terminate or deny benefits to children based on the suitable home section. The amendments require states to make efforts to improve the home or place the children in substitute care if improvement is not possible.

During the 1980s, states again attempted to deny needy children financial support based on the status of their parents. In 1986, the U.S.

Court of Appeals for the Seventh Circuit ruled that children who are U.S. citizens are eligible for AFDC even if their parents are undocumented (*Doe v. Reivitz*, 1987). At issue was a regulation from the state of Wisconsin that denied AFDC benefits to children if their parents did not register for the Work Incentive Program (WIN). The children of undocumented parents such as migrant workers, are especially vulnerable to poverty, poor health, substandard housing, and inadequate education (see Chapter 3 for a discussion of attempts to deny migrant children the right to attend public schools).

The right to financial support is limited. Children remain the poorest group of Americans, and there is no consensus on how to address poverty among children. Other nations, such as France, Canada, and Sweden, provide a children's allowance as part of their effort to support children and help them to grow up to become productive, contributing members of society. American income support programs remain depriving and stigmatizing.

Right to Education

There is consensus that children have a right to an education. Compulsory school attendance laws represent an attempt to force this right upon children. Compulsory school attendance laws are a phenomenon of the 20th century and were enacted during a time when the need for child labor was decreasing.

If education is a right, then it is a coercive right. Children who fail to exercise this right are subject to sanction. The California Supreme Court has upheld the incarceration of truant children (*In re Michael G.*, 1988). If adults fail to exercise their First Amendment rights, for example, there is no state sponsored punishment. The right to an education can be tied to financial support in some states and is commonly referred to as "learn-fare." If children are receiving AFDC benefits and fail to exercise their right to an education, the AFDC grant is reduced. Wisconsin was the first state to institute learnfare. Education is a right that the state must try to force upon its poorest citizens. There is no learnfare program for the nonpoor. This is, indeed, a strange concept of a "right."

There is no agreement about the elements that should be included in an education program. Parents may decide to educate their children at home. States vary in the minimal criteria parents must meet for home instruction. Parents have the right to remove their children from school for religious reasons. In *Wisconsin v. Yoder* (1972), the Supreme Court ruled that Amish parents may remove their children from school after the children complete the elementary grades and that this action does not constitute a violation of compulsory school attendance laws. This decision is a reflection of the notion that there is an assumed identity of interests between parents and children. In the Yoder case, some of the children were not asked if they wanted to be removed from school. Perhaps this is a reflection of the concept of identity of interests; the wishes of the children are assumed to be identical to the wishes of the parents, so there is no need to ask the children about their wishes.

Courts continue to define the rights of children in educational settings. Handicapped children, as a result of the Education for the Handicapped Act of 1975, P.L. 94-142, receive special attention from the courts. For example, the Supreme Court in *Honig v. Doe* (1988) restricted the ability of school districts to suspend handicapped students. If a school district wants to remove a child for more than 10 days, then it must follow special regulations. Handicapped children are educationally at risk. Federal law has attempted to force school districts to meet the educational needs of handicapped children, but there remains much confusion about what constitutes an education and what educational services must be provided (see Chapter 3 for a discussion of the special needs of handicapped children).

Balancing the Rights of Parents, Children, and the State

Society assumes that parents are in the best position to meet the needs of their children and it is the responsibility of parents to meet the physical, emotional, intellectual, and spiritual needs of their children. The state may intervene in the relationship between parents and children when parents violate community standards of minimum care. These standards vary considerably among states. For example, children living in a large city in New England without electricity, water, or more than 2 days of food in the home might be considered neglected by their parents and subject to placement in foster care. These same conditions exist in migrant farm camps in other parts of the country, yet it is highly unlikely that the children of migrant workers would be removed and placed in foster care (see Chapter 5 for a discussion of child maltreatment).

Advocates for children view health care as a basic right. Unfortunately, the health needs of a significant number of children, especially poor children, are unmet. Even basic, inexpensive preventive care such as immunizations is not routinely provided (see Chapter 2 for a discussion of the health status of children). Parents whose employers do not provide health insurance, unemployed parents not eligible for publicly financed health care, or parents in rural areas without health care providers and facilities, are unable to obtain consistent, quality medical care for their children. Large cities are finding it increasingly difficult to meet the health care needs of their residents as the need for services exceeds the available resources.

There is no right to health care for any group of Americans. The state has been unable or unwilling to meet the health care needs of children. However, the state will intervene and prosecute parents for failing to meet the health needs of their children. States are beginning to charge parents with violations of criminal statutes if the parent fails to obtain medical care for a sick child. Several states are prosecuting parents for relying on prayer to heal their children. This presents an interesting challenge to the First Amendment guarantees of free exercise of religion.

The laws governing the reporting of suspected instances of child abuse generally exclude children who suffer harm due to their parents' religious beliefs or the use of spiritual means for medical care. Under these reporting laws, parents who rely on prayer for healing cannot lose permanent custody of their children. However, parents are being charged with felonies such as manslaughter when children die as a result of relying solely on prayer to heal the child. A California mother has been charged with child endangerment and involuntary manslaughter in the death of her 4-year-old daughter. The mother is a Christian Scientist and used prayer to try to heal her daughter when the child developed symptoms of meningitis. The mother petitioned the Supreme Court and requested the Court order the state not to prosecute her. The Court has refused to stop the criminal trial (*Walker v. Superior Court*, 1989).

It is unclear if the prosecution of parents represents an extension of the rights of children. It appears that parents may exercise their First Amendment rights, but if their child dies as a result of exercising these rights, parents may be prosecuted. The prosecutions do little to protect the children already injured by their parents' religious beliefs. However, these prosecutions may eventually influence other parents and encourage them to seek medical help for their sick children.

Advances in medical technology have created potential conflicts between the rights of parents and the rights of children. For example, courts are struggling with questions such as whether parents have the right to use one child as an organ donor for another child. Organ donations from relatives offer the best chance for survival for children in need of kidneys or bone marrow. These medical procedures can be complicated, painful, and can reduce the life chances of the donating child. The wishes of young children cannot be ascertained. Older children can understand the potential costs and benefits, however, and questions about the right of older children to refuse to donate their organs to their siblings have yet to be resolved. Courts have not forced unwilling adults to donate their organs.

Children have restricted access to health care, especially in the area of sexuality. Approximately 37 states have enacted parental notification laws that require that a minor must first notify her parents before she obtains an abortion. The Supreme Court has declared unconstitutional some of these regulations. Parental permission laws are not constitutional; however, parental notification laws are legal if they include a procedure for allowing the minor to petition a court for permission for an abortion without first notifying her parents (*Bellotti v. Baird,* 1979). Two recent Supreme Court rulings indicate that it may become increasingly difficult for minors to terminate their pregnancies. In *Hodgson v. Minnesota* (1990), the Court upheld a Minnesota law that requires a minor to wait 48 hours after notifying both of her parents before she may proceed with an abortion. The Hodgson case represents the first time the Court has upheld state laws requiring that both parents be notified and that requires a minor to wait 48 hours after notifying her parents before proceeding with the abortion. Again, this regulation is constitutional as long as the minor also has the right to petition a court for authorization to proceed with an abortion. In *Ohio v. Akron Center for Reproductive Health* (1990), the Court upheld an Ohio law requiring minors wishing court authorization for an abortion to meet certain conditions:

1. prove at least one parent had abused her, or
2. establish she has the maturity to make her own decision, or
3. prove that notifying a parent would not be in her best interest.

Recent Court rulings continue to place restrictions on access to abortion. In 1992, the Court upheld a Pennsylvania law requiring the informed consent of one parent with a judicial bypass option (*Planned Parenthood of Southeastern Pennsylvania v. Casey*, 1992).

The rights of young people to obtain mental health counseling without parental permission are limited. The Supreme Court has not ruled in this area, therefore each state has established its own regulations. In Illinois, for example, a person under the age of 18 may receive a maximum of five mental health counseling sessions, each no more than 45 minutes in duration. If the young person wishes a sixth session, parental permission is required.

Parents exercise a great deal of control in the mental health area. Not only can they restrict mental health services for their children, they can also commit their children to psychiatric hospitals. Formal commitment proceedings are required in most states in order to admit an adult to a psychiatric hospital against his or her will. This is a right the Supreme Court has refused to extend to children. However, the Court has required post-commitment reviews (*Parham v. J. R.*, 1979). Each state differs in the length of time a child spends as a psychiatric in-patient before the hearing is held. Also, states vary in the standards required to continue the involuntary commitment of children. Generally, standards for children are less stringent than standards for adults, making it relatively easy for parents to keep their children in psychiatric hospitals. The past decade has witnessed a significant increase in the number of adolescents admitted to private psychiatric hospitals.

Fetal Rights: New Challenges

Improvements in medical technology have made it possible to monitor the development of the fetus and determine with some degree of accuracy when maternal conduct has a negative impact on the developing fetus. The past decade has witnessed the establishment of a new class of criminals: pregnant women. The doctrine of assumed identity of interests between parent and child is no longer valid when the pregnant woman engages in behavior that may harm the fetus and violates community standards. It is unclear if the criminalization of maternal conduct and subsequent elevation of fetal rights represents an expansion of children's rights. It has been interpreted as an attempt to treat pregnant women as fetal containers with limited rights to privacy (Maier, 1989). The interests in the right of the fetus to be born at term and without exposure to harmful substances while in utero is specific to the prenatal state. There seems to be less interest in the rights of children already born. The elevation of fetal rights may also represent an attempt to influence the abortion debate and challenge one of the major assumptions in *Roe v. Wade* (1973) that the fetus is not a person entitled to full Fourteenth Amendment protections.

Maternal Chemical Dependency and the Fetus

Chemically dependent pregnant women are especially vulnerable to sanctions. By 1990, most states had modified their definitions of neglect and/or abuse to include infants born with illicit chemicals in their blood or urine. Hospitals in these states must notify child welfare agencies whenever they observe such a condition in an infant or be subject to sanction for violating the reporting law. This new reporting requirement raises questions about the nature of the doctor-patient relationship, the role of informed consent, and the reliability and validity of drug testing. Medical facilities are struggling with issues such as whether they should routinely test all newborns for drugs and whether to inform pregnant women that their bodily fluids will be tested for illicit chemicals. In some states, women have been prosecuted for felonies such as delivery of drugs to a minor, child abuse, and manslaughter when their infants are born with evidence of prenatal chemical exposure and subsequently experience a negative event (see Chapter 7 for a discussion of the issues associated with chemical dependency).

Illicit chemicals such as cocaine have attracted attention, and medical research indicates that these chemicals may contribute to negative outcomes such as low birth weight, small head circumference, prematurity, organ malformations, and death (Chasnoff, Burns, & Burns, 1987; Regan, Ehrlich, & Finnegan, 1987). However, there are serious methodological problems in much of the medical research, such as a lack of control groups and small sample sizes. Also, there are few longitudinal studies, making it difficult to determine if problems observed at birth persist. In order to develop policies and practices that will help these infants to thrive, additional research is urgently needed.

It is interesting to note that there are a number of commonly used but legal chemicals that clearly present a threat to the physical and mental well-being of the developing fetus. Cigarette packages, for example, carry a warning about the possible consequences of smoking during pregnancy. Products that contain alcohol also post warnings about the use of this chemical while pregnant. As medical knowledge expands, even more noxious agents that may present a threat to the developing fetus will be identified. The legislators and courts will have to decide how to balance concerns about the health of the fetus with the rights of the mother. Because of the large numbers of women using tobacco and alcohol, punitive policies such as incarceration will be expensive to implement both financially and politically.

Invasive Medical Procedures and the Fetus

The mother need not engage in behavior that violates community standards in order to face challenges to her right to privacy. Hospitals have been seeking court orders in an effort to force pregnant women to undergo treatments and procedures. In addition to forcing unwanted procedures on the mother, advances in surgical techniques make it possible to operate on the fetus. Hospitals may seek court orders in an attempt to force parents to submit the fetus to what are thought to be lifesaving surgical procedures.

The use of court orders may be a defensive action on the part of the medical community. Fears of lawsuits when children suffer morbidity or mortality that might have possibly been avoided if the hospital and physician had taken some additional action, encourage invasive procedures. These actions help to establish the notion that the fetus is a person with rights and when those rights are in conflict with the rights of the parent, and in these cases it is always the mother, courts may intervene and order invasive, unwanted procedures, against the wishes of the mother.

A particularly distressing example of the elevation of fetal rights occurred in 1987. A hospital sought a court order to force a terminally ill woman to undergo a caesarean section in an attempt to save the life of her 26-week-old fetus. In making his decision, the judge indicated that because the woman was going to die anyway, her wishes were irrelevant and the right of the fetus to survive should be primary. Medical testimony indicated that the caesarean would hasten the death of the mother but could offer a better chance of survival for the fetus. The caesarean was ordered and within 3 days of the procedure, both mother and child were dead (*In re A. C.*, 1987).

Fetal rights represents an arena for debate and litigation. It may provide a basis for expanding the rights of children while restricting the rights of the parent. If unborn children are to be afforded limited rights and safe environments, then precedents may be established that can be used to extend these same rights to children already born. The definition of the harmful agent may also be expanded from the pregnant woman in the fetal rights cases to professionals, agencies, politicians, and communities in the case of children already born but living in harmful situations (see Chapter 8 for a discussion of one type of harmful situation—homelessness).

The *Parens Patriae* Power of the State

Parents may lose custody of their children for failing to provide adequate protection and care. The state exercises *parens patriae* power whenever it intervenes to protect children. This doctrine is used to justify state actions such as licensing of day care, child abuse reporting laws, and the authority of juvenile courts to hear cases. Chemical use by pregnant women or disagreeing with medical authorities about the necessity of certain procedures can result in court action and a loss of the decision-making authority of the parent. The state may then assume the role of parent and supervise the care provided by the parent or provide care directly for the child (the *parens patria* power of the state). However, the state is held to a different standard of care than are parents.

Parents can harm their children through overt or covert means. Unfortunately, the state may also maltreat children under its supervision, especially children in placements such as foster homes, group homes, residential facilities, detention centers, and psychiatric hospitals. When harmed, children have limited rights to seek damages. Courts have been reluctant to hold the state responsible for harm to children unless the children were harmed under specific conditions, such as when the children are in the care and custody of the state.

In a six to three decision, the Supreme Court has held that the due process clause of the Fourteenth Amendment does not require states to protect children from harm inflicted by their families (*DeShaney v. Winnebago County Department of Social Services*, 1989). The facts of this case are instructive and reveal the lack of rights for children as well as a lack of state responsibility to protect children known to be at risk for serious injury.

Joshua DeShaney was born in 1979 and lived with his father after his parents divorced in 1980. In January 1983 Joshua was seen at a hospital emergency room covered with bruises. A report of suspected child abuse was made and Joshua was temporarily removed from his father's custody. Three days later it was decided that there was insufficient evidence to keep Joshua, so he was returned to his father's care with a written agreement (signed by the father) stipulating that Joshua would enroll in Head Start and the father would receive counseling. A few months later, Joshua was again treated at the hospital for suspicious injuries. The family was visited by a public child welfare worker for the next 6 months. During these visits the worker noted bumps and bruises on Joshua. Joshua had not been enrolled in Head Start.

Joshua was seen again in November at the hospital for a cut head, bruises, bloody nose, and swollen ear. The hospital reported their suspicion of child abuse to the child welfare agency. No action was taken by the agency. The child welfare worker made two additional visits to the DeShaney home following the November incident. On both of these occasions, she was told that Joshua was too ill to be seen. The day following her second visit in March 1984, Joshua was beaten so severely that he sustained permanent brain damage and is expected to spend the rest of his life in an institution for the profoundly retarded. Joshua's father is serving a prison term for inflicting these injuries. Joshua's mother sued the child welfare agency for failing to protect her son, for violating his Fourteenth Amendment rights, and other violations of federal law.

A factor that seemed to have considerable influence in the decision of the Court was custody. Joshua was not in the physical custody of the state when he was injured. Because he was being cared for by his father, the Court ruled the state did not have an obligation to protect Joshua from harm inflicted in the home. In a dissenting opinion, Justice Brennan concluded the child welfare agency had failed Joshua in that the agency had undertaken the vital duty of protecting children and had failed to perform this duty. The decision of the Court limits the liability of child welfare workers. They may not be successfully sued for violations of the Fourteenth Amendment when children known to the state but not in the custody of the state are injured.

State laws may allow non-custodial parents to sue on behalf of their injured children if child welfare agencies and their employees fail to meet their legal responsibilities under reporting laws or laws establishing child welfare services. These same agencies and workers may also be liable for damages under federal laws when children in the care and custody of the state are injured. The state uses a number of different types of placements, such as foster homes, group homes, and residential treatment facilities (see Chapter 6 for a discussion on the state sponsored placements available to children removed from the care and custody of their parents). Children injured in these settings have successfully sued child welfare agencies in the federal court system where damage awards can be considerably higher than awards ordered in state courts (*Taylor By and Through Walker v. Ledbetter*, 1989).

The Needs of Children

There is no consensus in America on the basic needs of children and this is an essential component in defining the rights of children. Children of all ages need to be cared for, nurtured, intellectually stimulated, loved, and taught values if they are to feel good about themselves and become contributing members of society. There is consensus, even among politically diverse groups, that the family provides the best environment for meeting the needs of children. The consensus collapses when specific strategies on how best to support families in their difficult task of child rearing are discussed.

Needs and rights are intimately connected. Individuals have great difficulty exercising rights if their basic needs are not met. Children are no exception to this axiom. Debates about what rights children should have hold little meaning when newborn infants in selected rural and urban areas are dying at an alarmingly high rate. The basic right to survival is threatened in many parts of America when murder becomes the leading cause of death for young black males (see Chapter 9 for a discussion of the effects of violence). If the basic needs of children are not being met, then a discussion of children's rights is superfluous.

Role of the Family in Meeting Needs

The primary purpose of the state is not child rearing. This is the task of the family. The state can be a neglectful and inadequate caretaker. A more appropriate role for the state is that of supporting the ability of parents to meet the needs of their children. Parents are charged with difficult tasks that can challenge their resources. These tasks include:

1. providing for health care and nutritional needs,
2. locating affordable and quality day care,
3. obtaining education to prepare children for the changing and complex nature of work,
4. providing affordable and safe housing in neighborhoods free of violence that allow children to feel connected to the community.

Social policies are needed in order to help parents accomplish these goals. For example, there is little parents can do to increase the supply of affordable housing. This is a task for government (see Chapter 12 for a discussion of policies that can support families).

There continues to be much debate about the best way to support families. For example, child care as a social need has become less of a partisan issue in the past few years. Day-care legislation has been an item for congressional action and there is agreement on the need for child care. Conflict develops when specific strategies are suggested for addressing day-care needs. One group wants the federal government to play the major role in developing, monitoring, and financing day care. Another group opposes this and wants the private and sectarian sector to meet day-care needs with little government supervision. Neither group can agree on how to finance day care. There are other groups that view public funding of day care as a threat to the integrity of the family and want tax credits for dependents increased so mothers can stay home and care for their own children. While these groups fight about defining and financing day care, millions of families struggle with trying to locate affordable, reliable, quality day care.

While parents have the primary responsibility for meeting the needs of their children, the state has an important role to play. Children's rights can be grouped into a few categories (Soobiah, 1990). Children need nurturing and protection from exploitation. The state can assist parents in meeting the nutritional and health needs of children. Children need safe environments. The state can serve a protective function and regulate child labor, the physical environment, and guard the safety of children. This can be accomplished by reducing or eliminating environmental risks such as lead paint and by restricting the types of punishment administered to children.

The role of the state becomes more active in cases where the freedom of the child is at risk or when there is conflict between the parent and child. As children become subject to harsh treatment in the criminal justice system, full due process rights must be extended. Young people hospitalized against their wishes or who are expected to donate their organs may need the state to protect them.

Summary

Thanks to the efforts of developmentalists and other specialists, knowledge about children, particularly young children, has increased significantly. Children have social and cognitive skills that vary by developmental phase and that enable children to understand and appreciate rights. The 20th century has been characterized by both a recognition and an expansion of children's rights. Most of the rights have been won through court actions. This is a slow method for extending rights to children because courts are reactive institutions not known for making quick decisions. As children have gained legal rights normally afforded adults they have also been subject to the harsh penalties administered to adults. This seems to be part of the trade-off in the quest for legal rights. As children reject paternalism and seek due process, they become eligible for the sanctions prescribed for adults.

There are many challenges to the dynamic balance of rights among parents, children, and the state. While parents continue to assume the primary responsibility for children and therefore the greatest share of rights, the doctrine of assumed identity of interests between parents and children is under attack. This is most clearly evidenced in the emerging area of fetal rights. The state is expanding its *parens patriae* role in an attempt to force parents to provide safe environments or submit to medical procedures the state determines are necessary for fetal viability. Perhaps the state will expand this role and provide for infant and child viability.

In spite of the potential conflicts of interests between parents and children, the family offers the most appropriate environment for meeting the needs of children. However, due to factors that are often beyond the control of parents, these needs are becoming increasingly difficult to meet. Families need support from their communities in order to meet the needs of their children. The role of the state in helping families is subject to ongoing debate and is a reflection of long-standing political and value conflicts. These conflicts often paralyze the political process. Political interest groups disagree on the roles of government and the private sector in meeting needs, methods of financing such as using general tax revenues or user fees, and the efficiency and freedom in methods of financing such as providing parents with tax credits and vouchers or government directly paying for the services.

The issues associated with the rights and needs of children and the obligations and roles of parents and the state are difficult to conceptualize. Political, social, religious, and economic forces interact and create a maze of inconsistent, contradictory, and fragmented policies. Advocates for children continue to identify core needs and seek to support institutions such as the family, schools, and health organizations that should be meeting the nurturing and protective needs of children.

2

The Health of America's Children

All of society is affected by the physical and mental health of this nation's children. Health care in this country is provided reactively. The result is a patchwork system designed to address symptoms of disease. Preventive measures, even though proven to be effective, are limited, particularly for children living in poverty. The overall health of a child is multidimensional and includes physical, emotional, and cognitive development. Therefore, this chapter examines both the physical and mental health care of children and the implications for our nation's future.

Nothing is more important in guaranteeing a productive future for a person than good health. Proper cognitive, physical, social, and emotional development all require care and nurturing throughout childhood. Good developmental outcomes enhance the opportunities for young people to develop into productive adults. Today's children are the future of our nation. In spite of this obvious point, the care and well-being of children in the United States is inadequate and often ignored as an important social issue. The result is generations of children who grow up in poor health at a significant cost to society and themselves. Discussion of children's health includes both the physical and mental realms. Often, these areas are considered as separate concerns and are treated as such. However, children develop physically, mentally, and emotionally in a concurrent way. It is important to consider the overall health of a child as the confluence of physical and mental well-being. This chapter therefore looks at both the physical and mental health of children in the 1990s.

Health Status of Children

It is difficult to measure health. Rather, most studies and data reflect the incidence of illness and disease, and consider health to be the absence of them. Our nation's health care system follows this principle of absence. Most care is offered only after the detection of a health-related problem. However, there are a number of preventive measures designed to safeguard a person from illness. For children, preventive health care is especially important. The longer a child is free of illness, the greater the potential for stronger development.

The life expectancy of a child born today is almost 75 years of age, compared to 71 years in 1970 (Select Committee on Children, Youth & Families, 1989d). The rate of life expectancy has increased significantly over the past 50 years. This increase is considered to be a reflection of improved health for children and technological advances in medical care. Although this is true overall, there are subgroups of our population where the improvements in health are not as significant.

A number of areas related to the health of children are cause for national concern. Two significant issues, aside from a lack of adequate preventive programs, are the spread of pediatric AIDS and the growth in the numbers of chemically exposed children born. These two problems are creating new demands on an already stressed health care system. The needs of these special children will continue for years and years to come and will continue to tax our overburdened health system. Chapter 7 covers the issues of pediatric AIDS and chemically exposed infants in greater detail. Although much progress has been made in this country, other health-related problems face today's children.

Infant Mortality

The need for preventive health care for poor women and their children is crucial. Poor women tend to receive inadequate prenatal care, resulting in a greater proportion of complicated births and a higher incidence of infant mortality. Infant mortality, the rate of "babies who are born alive but die before their first birthday" (National Commission to Prevent Infant Mortality, 1988b, p. 2) provides a valuable indicator of the general health of the nation. This country prides itself on progress and state-of-the-art medical care. However, for children, particularly poor children, overall health status could be greatly improved.

The United States falls behind 21 other industrialized nations in the rate of infant mortality. The overall rate of infant mortality in 1988 was more than 10 deaths per 1,000 live births, and for black children the rate was almost 18 deaths (U.S. Department of Health and Human Services, 1990b). In urban areas the incidence of black infant mortality is remarkably high. For example, in Boston, the rate in 1987 for black infants was 20.1 deaths per 1,000 live births (Howe, 1989). Overall, the rate of infant mortality for black infants is more than twice the rate for white children (Committee on Ways and Means, 1992). There is extreme disparity in access to health care for the poor and for many urban residents who are disproportionately children of color.

The infant mortality rate in the United States is related to a lack of adequate prenatal care. Proper nutrition and early detection of problems can improve the success of a healthy birth. The lack of proper care during pregnancy doubles the probability of a woman giving birth to a low birth weight baby. Low birth weight, being born weighing less than 5.5 pounds, is the leading cause of infant death (Alan Guttmacher Institute, 1987). More than half of the approximate 40,000 infant deaths are due to low birth weight. Although progress in reducing the number of low birth weight babies was made in the 1970s, the 1980s witnessed a slight increase (Smythe, 1988).

Research demonstrates that adequate prenatal care could help reduce the rate of low birth weight babies and infant mortality (Grad, 1988). This is particularly true for young women, often reluctant to approach medical personnel, where the tendency to have low birth weight babies is greater. However, numerous barriers make it difficult for women to receive needed prenatal care. Programs are underfunded and geographically scattered, making it difficult to locate services. In spite of the documented and known value of early care, the proportion of women receiving no prenatal care rose each year during the 1980s (Children's Defense Fund, 1990b). Overall, one fourth of all mothers did not receive early prenatal care in 1988. Almost half of the women under 20 years of age lacked such care (U.S. Department of Health and Human Services, 1990b).

The lack of sufficient preventive health care services means increased costs in future care for sick infants and children. Children who do not receive adequate health care early in life are more likely to be disabled and to require costly special services throughout childhood and adolescence. The costs of caring for a low birth weight baby over a lifetime can reach $400,000. This contrasts greatly to the $400 needed for adequate prenatal care (National Commission to Prevent Infant Mortality, 1988a). This is a clear example where early prevention as opposed to a residual response is economically and socially beneficial.

Childhood Immunization

Great progress has been made in diminishing the spread of communicable diseases such as polio, mumps, rubella, DPT (diphtheria, pertussis, and tetanus), and measles. For example, the rates for measles was 245 cases per 100,000 total population in 1960, and dropped to 7.3 cases per 100,000 in 1989 (Simons, Finlay, & Yang, 1991). Immunization efforts peaked in the early 1980s and have decreased in recent years. In 1985, about 60% of children 1 to 4 years of age were immunized against all five of these childhood diseases (U.S. Department of Health and Human Services, 1990b). However, that leaves more than one third of young children not properly immunized. In poor neighborhoods, the rate of immunization is even lower, leaving impoverished children at greater risk of contracting and spreading preventable diseases (Children's Defense Fund, 1990d). On the positive side, most schools require full immunization upon entry, and the vast majority of children are immunized upon admission to elementary school. However, waiting until a child is 4 or 5 years of age is too late to prevent many childhood illnesses. Immunization is still important for young children to safeguard them from preventable diseases. It is probably one of the best ways to implement preventive health measures.

Nutrition

It is difficult to imagine that in a country as prosperous as the United States there is a problem with malnourished children. Unfortunately, millions of children in this country experience periods of hunger and poor nutrition. Hunger in America is difficult to assess. It does not take the form of starvation or famine as in other countries, but there are currently more people who are hungry in this nation than since the time of the Great Depression (Burghardt & Fabricant, 1987).

Malnutrition may affect as many as 500,000 children a year (Children's Defense Fund, 1989b). Hunger increases a child's susceptibility to illness, can lead to developmental delays, and makes concentration in school difficult. Most welfare families experience the stress of worrying about enough to eat as each month ends and their public assistance runs out. The results are long-standing deficits, physically and emotionally. Although there is enough food in this country, the problem rests with distributing it to those in need.

Health Issues Facing Today's Adolescents

Once children enter school, there is less of a focus on health care. There is a widespread tendency to think that after childhood, health does not become a central life issue until old age. This simply is not true. Adolescents face significant health concerns throughout their teenage years. Adolescents often find themselves in situations that are dangerous to their health. This is generally a consequence of their developmental stage and physical capability to act independently. Adolescents are more typically involved in dangerous activities such as alcohol and drug use, reckless driving, and promiscuous sexual behaviors than other age groups. These behaviors mean that adolescence must be considered as a unique period requiring specialized health care.

Teenage Pregnancy

Pregnancy is a major problem of adolescence. The United States has one of the highest teenage pregnancy rates in the Western world. More than one million teenagers become pregnant each year (Alan Guttmacher Institute, 1991). The rate of pregnancy among teenage women has been on the rise over the past 20 years. Since 1972, the rate has increased by approximately 12% (U.S. Department of Education, 1988). Although the pregnancy rate has increased, the number of live births has dropped appreciably, in large part due to the legalization and accessibility of abortions. Since the early 1970s the birth rate for 15- to 19-year-olds decreased by more than 18%, while the abortion rate more than doubled (U.S. Department of Education, 1988).

Each year, half a million teenagers give birth (Committee on Ways and Means, 1992). The consequences of those early pregnancies are frequently very costly to mother, child, and society. Low birth weight and infant deaths are greatest for young mothers. Pregnant teenagers are less likely to seek prenatal care and often wait well into a pregnancy before

telling anyone. As discussed previously, inadequate or nonexistent prenatal care leads to poor birth outcomes. Pregnant adolescents are more
prone to maternal mortality, anemia, pregnancy-related hypertension,
and maternal toxemia (Taborn, 1990). With a higher incidence of infant
mortality and maternal medical complications comes a higher cost in
health care. In many cases, children born prematurely and of low birth
weight have lifelong health problems and require specialized parenting
skills and economic resources.

There are a number of long-term consequences of teenage pregnancy.
Teenage girls who become pregnant are more likely to drop out of school
(Lewin, 1988). Without a high school degree, it is very difficult to have
the skills necessary to navigate through our modern society and to find
employment. The prospects for employment and/or marriage to an
economically stable partner for teenage mothers are minimal, placing
these young families at extreme economic risk. Research demonstrates
that first-time mothers who are teenagers are at greater risk to become
single mothers and have more children, and ultimately live in poverty
(Butler, 1992). Estimates place the cost of maintaining these young families at more than $16 billion a year in public expense (National Women's
Health Network, 1986). This does not include the lost earning potential
of the young mothers.

A summary of the research conducted by the Alan Guttmacher Institute (1991) reveals the severe consequences of teenage pregnancy:

- Greater likelihood of health complications at birth and throughout early
  childhood
- Socioeconomic disadvantage compared with women who delay childbirth
  until their twenties
- Less likelihood of graduating from high school
- Single parenthood and dependency on public assistance
- Children at greater risk of lower academic achievement and behavior
  problems
- Greater likelihood of a repeated cycle of teenage pregnancy for the next
  generation

Most teenagers are not prepared to assume the role of being a parent.
The demands and stress of raising a child are difficult under the best of
circumstances. The pressures of child rearing can lead to psychological

problems for adolescents thrust into the parental role. Adolescent mothers are more likely to abuse or neglect their children, responding to the pressures and frustrations of child rearing with anger and violence (Lockhart & Wodarski, 1990).

Pregnancy among teenage women is a reality. These young women are in need of prenatal care and ongoing services to improve the outcomes for them and their children. This is a social problem where an emphasis on early intervention and prevention can benefit both individuals and society greatly. Delaying social response until *after* the pregnancy only perpetuates the cycle of disadvantage, both for the young mothers and their children.

Substance Abuse

Another health concern for today's adolescents is the use of alcohol and drugs. Illegal substances frequently accompany high-risk behaviors among adolescents and are related to motor vehicle accidents, shootings, and suicides. For example, in 1987 almost half of all teenage deaths in motor vehicle accidents involved alcohol (National Highway Traffic Safety Administration, 1988).

The overall rate of drug and alcohol use by teenagers has declined slightly. From 1975 to 1986, the percentage of teenagers reporting the use of alcohol during the previous 30 days declined from 68% to 65%. So, too, did the rate of their reported use of any illicit drug, from 31% to 27%. However, drugs and alcohol continue to be a significant part of adolescence. By young adulthood, almost 60% of those 18 to 25 years of age had used illicit drugs (National Institute on Drug Abuse, 1989a). In 1989, 91% of seniors in high school reported having used alcohol, and a third reported that during the 2 weeks prior to the survey they had more than five drinks in a row (National Center for Education in Maternal and Child Health, 1990). The only notable increase of illicit drug use was in cocaine, which was used by 2% in 1975 and 6% in 1986 (U.S. Department of Education, 1988).

The increase in cocaine use may reflect the popularity of its cheaper and easier to use derivative, crack. A sizeable portion of crack users are young, unemployed school dropouts, who tend to be socially disorganized with minimal family support (U.S. General Accounting Office, 1991a). Smoking crack is a rapid and intense drug experience. Compared to cocaine, the relatively inexpensive cost, ease of use, and availability of crack are appealing to young people.

The long-term effects of crack are not well documented. Preliminary studies on infants exposed to crack reveal they have a greater range of medical problems and are more likely to continue to need long-term medical services (U.S. General Accounting Office, 1990a). The impact on the social service system as these children grow and the current effects of crack use on adolescents are unknown. However, the fact that crack is highly addictive, readily available, and increasing in rate of use suggests its strong potential to become an increasingly deadly force among adolescents.

Use of alcohol is still portrayed in the media as a positive, socially acceptable form of adult behavior. Characters on television and advertisements in magazines show alcohol as a key component of relaxation, comfort, wealth, sensuality, and joy. These images are persuasive, particularly to young people searching for their identities and ways to deal with the normal developmental difficulties of adolescence.

Research is not clear about the difference between use and abuse of drugs and alcohol. What seems to be evident is that substance abuse is part of a cycle of personal problems. Related to the abuse of alcohol and drugs are school dropout, delinquency, and sexual promiscuity. Some of the risk factors related to adolescent drug use include poor self-esteem, low academic achievement, depression, poor relations with parents, and extent of drug use by peers and adults (National Center for Education in Maternal and Child Health, 1991). Thus, substance abuse is often one way for a young person to cope with personal and social problems. Left untreated, early abuse of alcohol and drugs will lead to continued use and loss of opportunities for young people.

AIDS and Sexually Transmitted Diseases

The discovery of AIDS in the early 1980s and the subsequent public attention are a relatively new phenomenon. Until recently, AIDS was considered a disease of the gay community, with adult homosexual men representing the vast majority of people with AIDS in the United States. However, that has changed. The 1990s are witnessing a change in the composition of the AIDS population. Although representing a small portion of the total population of people with AIDS, adolescents are regarded as a group at risk of infection. Adolescents tend to engage in the high-risk behaviors of multiple sex partners, unprotected sexual contact, and drug use. These behaviors increase the likelihood of exposure to the human immunodeficiency virus (HIV) and other sexually transmitted diseases.

The prevalence of sexually transmitted diseases (STDs) is an important health concern for teenagers. It is estimated that each year 2.5 million adolescents are infected with STDs such as gonorrhea and syphilis (Select Committee on Children, Youth & Families, 1989d). This places young people as the age group with the highest reported rate and demonstrates the extensive practice of unprotected sexual activity (Johnson, 1988). Alcohol and drug use can impair judgment, lower inhibitions, and lead to more reckless behavior. Thus, substance abuse can contribute to the tendency of young people not to practice safer sex procedures.

By 1989, the cumulative number of AIDS cases among 13- to 19-year-olds was 461. Among 20- to 24-year-olds, however, the number was 5,090 (National Center for Education in Maternal and Child Health, 1990). Although the number of adolescent AIDS cases is small, the health concern is significant. The time between infection with the virus and the onset of AIDS spans an average of 8 years, and the majority of young adults with AIDS contracted the disease during their adolescence (Johnson, 1988). Without identification and prevention of the AIDS problem among adolescents now, the number of AIDS cases among young adults potentially may reach epidemic proportions.

Health Care Services

The unique health concerns surrounding the physical and emotional development of children and adolescents require services specially designed for their needs. Supportive health services can lower the incidence and severity of illnesses and improve the lives of the children served. Unfortunately, this country lacks a coordinated network of public health care. Services vary from community to community and are offered through federal, state, and local programs. The majority of services, however, are provided through nationally funded efforts. Although medical and health needs of children have grown, the majority of programs that do exist and have proven to be successful are inadequately funded and do not reach all those in need. The following are the major federally sponsored health care initiatives for children.

Medicaid

The largest public health care program for children is Medicaid. In 1965, the Social Security Act was expanded to include the Medicaid program (Title XIX). Medicaid provides medical services for low-income people by allocating federal matching dollars to states. States administer the program and medical services are made available through providers who are then reimbursed by the states.

From 1966 to 1986, expenditures for the Medicaid program ballooned from $1.5 to $45.8 billion (Cislowski, 1988). Even after accounting for inflation, the cost of medical care under Medicaid tripled in those 20 years. Three years later, in 1989, Medicaid expenditures rose to $57.9 billion. If current trends continue, expenses will reach more than $250 billion by the year 2000 (Social Security Administration, 1991).

Although billions of public dollars are spent for medical care, Medicaid represents only 25% of all public expenditures for health and medical care. Millions of poor children receive medical care through the program. However, the majority of expenditures were used for low-income elderly and disabled adults. Eligibility is restrictive for Medicaid. Although it is the only public health insurance program for poor children, 45% of the children living in poverty in 1989 were not covered by the program (Committee on Ways and Means, 1991). These children, without Medicaid, most likely received little or no health care at all.

Maternal and Child
Health Services Block Grants

While Medicaid covers general medical needs, the Maternal and Health Services Block Grant serves low-income mothers and children. This program is also a part of the Social Security Act. It provides health services designed to reduce the incidence of infant mortality and communicable diseases and improve the availability of prenatal and postpartum care.

Research through the Institute of Medicine (1988b) revealed that there is no direct maternity care system in this country for women who depend on public health care services. What services are available are fragmented, complicated, and difficult to access. Even though some clinics may offer services, pregnant women often do not know about them. The most common barriers to receiving prenatal care are a lack of money, transportation, and child care. Outreach and support services that complement a full range of care are needed in order to improve the prospects for healthy births and early medical care for children. Without fundamental changes in our health care delivery system, low-income women, teenagers, and uninsured women will not receive adequate prenatal care and the United States will continue to rank very high in the rate of infant mortality and complicated births.

WIC: Special Supplemental Food Program
for Women, Infants, and Children

Proper nutrition is key to maintaining the health and well-being of children. It is particularly important during pregnancy and in the early years of a child's life. The design of the WIC program is to address the early nutritional needs of infants and pregnant women. Low-income mothers, infants, and children up to 5 years of age are eligible to receive supplemental foods such as eggs and milk or vouchers to purchase them. As a condition for receiving federal funds, programs must be operated by agencies that have access to health care. Thus, the program also serves as a link to prenatal care services. In spite of proven success, the WIC program reaches only half of the eligible mothers and children because there are not enough resources allocated (Children's Defense Fund, 1989b).

School Breakfast and Lunch Programs

School meal programs are vital to the well-being of children in poverty and can help to prepare them better for school. Both the breakfast and lunch programs subsidize school meals for low-income children. Some policy makers argue that the government should not provide what children should get at home and the programs are duplicative (Jones, 1989). Without these services, however, many poor children would start their days without breakfast. Nutritional deficits interfere with learning and physical development. Current allotments of public assistance often leave welfare families without enough food as the month progresses. School meal programs guarantee that poor school children will be nutritionally fortified for the school day.

Mental Health Status of Children

A crucial part of children's overall health is their emotional and psychological well-being. Future life opportunities and productivity rest on how well a child adjusts to surroundings, learns to relate to others, and perceives him- or herself. Numerous variables impact the mental health of children. Some, such as poverty, violence, abuse, and neglect, are covered in more detail elsewhere in this book. This section will discuss the general mental health of children in America and the adequacy and availability of programs and services.

Mental health and illness are illusive terms. They cover a wide spectrum of behaviors and definitions, vary greatly, and depend on numerous changing conditions. Typical healthy emotions such as sadness or fear may last longer than expected or occur in inappropriate situations and be termed an emotional problem. This is especially true for children, who are constantly changing as part of their growth and development.

It is estimated that between 7.5 and 9.5 million children and adolescents in this country have problems that require mental health treatment (National Mental Health Association, 1989a). The effects of these problems are far-reaching. Millions of family members are a part of these troubled children's lives and frequently are also in need of mental health services. Schools and other social agencies see these children daily and are consequently affected by the incidence of mental health problems among children.

The types of mental and emotional problems plaguing children today cover a wide spectrum. They include temporary adjustment problems in response to a changing environment, to more serious diagnosable mental illness. The diagnosis of mental illness by professionals is based on the categories and symptoms outlined in the third edition of the American Psychiatric Association's *Diagnostic and Statistical Manual—Revised*, or the *DSM-III-R*. Some of the designated disorders include:

- Behavioral: attention deficit and conduct disorders
- Emotional: anxiety disorders, depression
- Intellectual: mental retardation
- Developmental: autism, dyslexia
- Physical: eating and sleep disorders

The *DSM-III-R* serves as a compendium of diagnoses, but it has limitations. Mental health conditions are fluid and ever-changing. Trying to categorize people's symptoms, particularly children's, can be impossible. Each child is different and his or her own life circumstances are unique. Although the *DSM-III-R* can serve as a reference, social service professionals need to regard each individual from an ecological perspective and view the child's mental health in relation to the child's surroundings.

A growing group of children in need are those identified as severely emotionally disturbed (SED). There is no common definition of SED. Generally, severe emotional disturbance describes "functional disabilities which are of significant severity and duration" and require a range of different services (Stroul & Friedman, 1986, p. iv). SED children tend to have multiple needs—mental health problems compounded by other problems such as physical disability, learning disorders, poverty, or family disturbances. They are identified as multi-need children.

Multi-need children and families present a challenge to the current mental health system. The dimensions of their problems cut across different developmental areas and service agencies. A child suffering from emotional disorders will most likely exhibit behavioral problems in school and social activities. Emotional problems left unrecognized or untreated will eventually manifest into larger problems with the child engaging in behaviors that involve other social service systems, such as the schools, health, or juvenile justice. Thus, the millions of children with mental and emotional problems present a significant social problem requiring national attention.

Mental Health Services

In spite of the overwhelming number of young people in need of help, the vast majority do not receive services. Between 70% and 80% of the children in need of mental and emotional support may not get adequate mental health treatment (Office of Technology Assessment, 1986). Experts in child mental health suggest that the best way to treat children with mental and emotional problems is through community-based services that focus on both the needs of the child and of the family (National Mental Health Association, 1989a). However, localities tend to be narrow in service provision and delivery. Collaboration and coordination between systems such as mental health, child protective services, public assistance, health, education, and juvenile justice are greatly needed:

> The range of mental health and other services needed by severely emotionally disturbed children and adolescents is frequently unavailable. Many children are institutionalized when less restrictive, community-based services would be more effective. . . . This has left children and youth with serious and complex problems to receive services in an uncoordinated and piecemeal fashion, if at all. (Stroul & Friedman, 1986, p. 2)

Recognition of the fragmentation of services for SED children has prompted the development of a new model for service delivery, the system of care model. A system of care is "a comprehensive spectrum of mental health and other necessary services which are organized into a coordinated network to meet the multiple and changing needs of severely emotionally disturbed children and adolescents" (Stroul & Friedman, 1986, p. 3). Although there is strong national support for creating comprehensive systems of care, such initiatives are difficult to enact. Four barriers impede the development of systems of care (Knitzer & Yelton, 1990):

1. a strong tendency to rely on residential services as the best available treatment,
2. doubts about the strengths of parents and thus the bias to remove children from their families,
3. a lack of common language and philosophy between systems serving children, and
4. inflexibility of guidelines for current funds.

The system of care approach relies on many traditional mental health services and simultaneously promotes the development of innovative community-based services that are family focused and more preventive in nature. A comprehensive system serving SED children should include both nonresidential services such as outpatient services, home-based services, day treatment, and crisis services, and residential services such as therapeutic foster care, residential centers, group homes, and psychiatric hospitals (Stroul & Goldman, 1990).

With a range of services available, there is a greater chance that children and families will receive more appropriate mental health treatment. The additional benefit is that SED children will be served in the least restrictive environment, with mental health professionals less dependent on out-of-home placement as the treatment of choice because it is the only choice. A wider spectrum of services can also be cost effective: 6 weeks of intensive in-home crisis services costs about $1,100; a year in a day treatment program typically costs $15,000 to $18,000; the average daily cost for treatment in a state hospital is $300 with an average stay of 4.2 months, totaling more than $38,000; and the typical cost for an average 15-month stay in a residential treatment facility costs more than $52,000 (National Mental Health Association, 1989a).

The child mental health service system needs to be improved. Millions of children receive inadequate treatment, and untold numbers are ignored. Currents services are limited and fragmented. Although children with mental and emotional problems cut across many systems, there is minimal collaboration and coordination. Adoption of a system of care approach would better serve children and families and could prove cost effective over time. In addition, mental health concerns of children include environmental factors and other social issues such as poverty, violence, and abuse and neglect. Improving the mental health of children thus requires improving the social and emotional conditions for all members of society.

Policy Issues
Related to Health Care for Children

Two issues dominate discussion of health care in America. One is the rising cost of care and the other is the availability of care. In 1960, national health expenditures totaled $27.1 billion, representing 5.3% of the gross national product. By 1989, expenditures rose to $604 billion, which was 11.6% of the GNP (Committee on Ways and Means, 1991). When held constant for inflation, the dollars represent an almost sixfold increase. This jump in health care expenditures is in part due to a greater number of recipients of medical care. However, in large part it is a result of spiraling costs for medical procedures and advances in expensive medical technology.

The most pressing health care policy issue concerning children today relates to the extent and availability of health insurance coverage. The majority of children are covered by public or private health insurance.

There is a growing number, however, who are not covered by either. In 1990, more than 8 million children under the age of 16 were not covered by any health insurance. This represented almost 14% of all children less than 16 years of age (U.S. Bureau of the Census, 1992a). Many more children move in and out of coverage. Approximately 35% of all children under 18 years of age spent at least one month without any health insurance between 1985 and 1987 (U.S. Bureau of the Census, 1990a). Millions of families are not poor enough to qualify for public coverage through Medicaid, but are not in positions to receive coverage through private insurance.

The most common barrier to gaining health care is due to a lack of sufficient finances. The consequence of being uninsured is inferior medical care. The uninsured person is less likely to see a physician, has shorter hospital stays, and has a greater reliance on emergency rooms for routine service (Congressional Research Service, 1988). Low-income children who are uninsured receive 40% less medical care than do low-income children who are insured (Rosenbaum, 1989).

Uninsured children are less likely to get preventive care and will press the public care system over time as they develop more serious illnesses requiring emergency treatment. The result will be less healthy children and higher medical costs over the long term. Consequently, the public is becoming more insistent that policy makers consider alternatives to the current system of health insurance.

Numerous national health insurance proposals are being discussed, with no consensus on what would be best. They include a variety of reforms. Some advocate for a total overhaul of the health care system and others prefer to make incremental changes to the current structure. Discussion is currently focused on who should pay for increased health insurance coverage—the public, individuals, or employers. There is general consensus that the current system must be changed, but it is too soon to project what those changes will be.

Summary

The physical and mental health of children in this country affects all of society. Children are the future providers and caretakers of the nation. If we do not safeguard their early health and well-being, we will be faced with spiraling costs and a growing population of troubled adults. Preventive efforts are needed to lessen future costs and consequences, and a large part of that responsibility rests with the makers of national policy.

Health care continues to be a major policy issue throughout the 1990s. The presidential election of 1992 witnessed health care as a pressing political issue. Although health care reform will not happen quickly, politicians, the public, and health care providers are all in agreement that the current structure is inadequate and needs to be reexamined. Often, this level of agreement is the catalyst for social policy change.

3

Children and the Public Schools

The importance of education cannot be overstated. Schools play a vital role in transmitting values and skills and in preparing young people to become productive, contributing members of society. Public schools are failing to accomplish these goals with a minority of children.

The resources needed to accomplish the many tasks expected of the public schools are often lacking. This chapter examines the funding issues, identifies children at risk for academic failure, and discusses the challenges faced by public schools.

Public education is subject to frequent criticism and is a topic in political campaigns. Americans seem to want their public schools to do a better job of educating young people. This, however, is where the consensus ends. Interest groups have not been able to agree on solutions to the problems. This chapter examines some of the challenges faced by public schools and focuses on children at risk for educational failure.

Financing Education

A well-functioning society requires educated citizens willing and able to participate in the democratic process, who possess skills that will enable them to be productive members of the workforce, and who can contribute to the welfare of their communities. The job of preparing young people for these tasks has fallen upon the public schools. Even though education has been viewed as essential for individual and societal success, education has remained a responsibility of state and local government. Local communities determine the characteristics of the educational experience and assume most of the costs of providing that education. Relatively little federal money is allocated for public education.

There are advantages and disadvantages to this system of financing. By relying on local government to finance education, control of the public schools remains at the local level. The schools reflect the values and ideology of the citizenry. The citizens, through the democratic process, decide who will work in the schools, what will be taught, and how much money will be spent to achieve educational goals. Community control of schools is ensured by community financing of schools.

However, this method of financing public education has created great disparity. There are more than 15,000 school districts and each spends a different amount of money to educate a student (U.S. General Accounting Office, 1989a). The amount of money a community spends to educate a student provides one measure of educational quality. These per pupil expenditures vary by state with some states spending more than twice the amount spent by other states. Even within states, the amount of money spent by local communities varies considerably. This variation is attributable to the major method of financing education, the property tax.

Problems With Financing With Property Tax

Relying on the property tax for financing perpetuates disparities. The property in wealthy communities is assessed at a high level, the tax rates are high, and the funds available for education can be considerable. Poor communities in which property values are low or declining simply cannot generate funds equivalent to those in wealthier communities. Poor communities cannot continue to raise tax rates without serious risks. If tax rates exceed the financial resources of residents, property may be abandoned, resulting in no tax revenue for the local government because the local government becomes the property owner.

Rural school districts as well as districts serving poor immigrant or minority groups are especially vulnerable to wealth-based disparities. This is troublesome because these youngsters may need additional services from the public schools least able to generate the funds to pay for these necessary services.

Financing mechanisms have been challenged in the courts and the results of the lawsuits have been inconsistent. A 1973 case, *San Antonio Unified School District v. Rodriguez*, was heard by the Supreme Court. The Court ruled that education was a state function and not a fundamental right. Fundamental rights are those outlined in the Constitution. States may use any number of methods to finance education, even if these methods perpetuate wealth-based disparities. Differences in funding levels can also be observed within states. In New York, the disparities are large. In 1987, Manhasset, a town on Long Island, spent $11,370 per pupil compared to $5,590 in New York City (Kozol, 1991).

Children at Risk for Educational Failure

One of the first groups to be recognized for special treatment at the federal level was handicapped children. These youngsters were at elevated risk for academic failure and some school districts did not address the needs of handicapped children, ostensibly due to meager resources. The federal government provides education funding to the states for specific categories of children. Although handicapped children were the first major group to be recognized, other groups have been added including minority children and children of immigrants.

Handicapped Children

The Title I program (now called Chapter I) was created by Congress in 1965 to help states educate severely handicapped children in state operated or supported institutions (Public Law 89-313, Elementary and Secondary Education Act). Ten years after Chapter I, Congress enacted a much larger program, Public Law 94-142, the Education of the Handicapped Act (EHA). These two major federal programs are similar and have been amended a number of times over the years. In school year 1988-1989, Congress appropriated $151 million for Chapter I and $1.4 billion for EHA (U.S. General Accounting Office, 1989e).

Chapter I provides an example of how some states can use the lack of clear regulation in order to obtain increased federal funds. Chapter I serves approximately 259,000 students with an average cost of $581 per student. EHA serves 4.2 million with an average cost of $331 per student. It is to a state's advantage to have students assigned to Chapter I programs instead of EHA programs. The EHA program divides the amount appropriated by the number of students enrolled in the program. The funding for Chapter I is more complicated and depends on what each state spends on educational services. In general, states receive about 75% more funds per student from Chapter I than from EHA (U.S. General Accounting Office, 1989e).

Chapter I was originally created to serve severely handicapped children. However, states were allowed to decide who to include in the program. Some states have included conditions not generally considered to be severe, such as speech impairment and learning disabilities. Four states, New York, Massachusetts, Illinois, and Pennsylvania, account for 47% of the children served by Chapter I even though they contain only 20% of the handicapped children in America. New York accounts for 17% of the children enrolled in Chapter I and received $29 million in federal funds. California has 9% of the nation's handicapped children yet it accounts for less than 1% of the Chapter I population and received only $1.2 million. Illinois accounts for 16% of Chapter I children, contains only 5.6% of the nation's handicapped children, and received $22.2 million (U.S. General Accounting Office, 1989e). The lack of definition has allowed states to interpret federal regulations creatively.

Both EHA and Chapter I require that children participating in the program have a written individualized education plan (IEP), which should be developed jointly by school officials and parents. The IEP identifies learning goals and a timetable for achieving the goals. The IEP contains a list of services to be provided by the school district, at no charge to the child or family, and can include a variety of services such as:

- medical and psychological services
- special equipment such as reading materials in braille
- physical, occupational, and language therapy
- transportation to school
- vocational education

Extracurricular activities may also be included in the IEP in an attempt to provide handicapped children with the same opportunities for healthy development available to nonhandicapped students. The IEP requires schools to educate handicapped children in the least restrictive environment and with nonhandicapped children (mainstreaming) whenever feasible. Parents can review the IEP but their approval is not required. The law contains instructions for appeal procedures in the event the parent disagrees with the plan.

Chapter I and EHA are attempts to ensure that handicapped school age children have access to a free and appropriate public education. In 1986, Congress amended the act to encourage states to offer services to children younger than 6 years of age (P.L. 99-457). Part H of the amendment established a discretionary program to provide services for children from birth through 3 years of age. The intent of P.L. 99-457 is to minimize the effects of developmental delays by intervening early in the lives of children at risk for such developmental challenges. States are required to establish an Interagency Coordinating Council to design the components of the early intervention programs.

Instead of an IEP, an individualized family service plan is developed. The family focus is an essential component of early intervention programs. Early intervention services include:

- family training
- counseling
- home visits
- medical, psychological, nutritional, and nursing services
- occupational and physical therapy
- diagnostic evaluations
- case management services

Eligibility for services is based on criteria that differ significantly from those used in IEPs. Handicapping conditions in older children, such as learning disabilities, emotional disturbance, and mild mental retardation, can be difficult to identify in infants and toddlers. Youngsters with developmental delays in one or more of the following areas are eligible: cognitive, physical, language, speech, psychosocial development, or self-help skills. In addition, youngsters with a diagnosed physical or mental condition that has a high probability of resulting in developmental delay are also eligible. Conditions such as fetal alcohol syndrome and Down's syndrome meet this criteria. States may also include individuals who are at risk of developmental delay if early intervention services are not provided.

Early intervention programs have much to offer young children and their families. Disadvantages present at birth can often be ameliorated and developmental outcomes improved through the provision of services to the child and the family (Gallagher & Ramey, 1987). There are a number of important issues concerning early intervention programs that have yet to be resolved. For example, methods for accurately estimating the number of infants at risk have not been developed. There is disagreement in how to measure and define risk. Labeling a very young child as "special" is controversial because there may be long-term negative consequences associated with the label. Large numbers of children and their families may need multiple services. Questions arise about how to finance these services.

Dropouts

There are a number of groups of young people vulnerable to substandard education and reduced chances for life success. Clearly, young people who "drop out" of school comprise a large number of the vulnerable. The national dropout rate is more than 25%. This number seems high and yet it disguises the significant differences in dropout rates for minority children and other vulnerable groups such as foster children. In some large urban areas, more than 50% of minority children drop out (Comer, 1988). Hispanic students now have the highest dropout rate of any group (U.S. General Accounting Office, 1991c). Less than 30% of adolescents in out-of-home placement either graduate from high school or earn a GED (Cook & Ansell, 1986). The picture is further complicated by a lack of agreement on how to define a dropout.

The federal government uses three definitions of *dropout* (U.S. General Accounting Office, 1991d). The event dropout rate measures the proportion of students who quit school each year and is easy for schools to calculate because they simply keep track of the number of students who do not attend school. This measure does not reflect students who enroll in another school district. The event dropout rate may be higher than the actual dropout rate. The status dropout rate measures the proportion of students who have not completed high school and who are not enrolled in any school. The cohort dropout rate reports the high school completion and dropout rates for one group of students followed across time. The event dropout rate has been declining since 1978. In 1989, approximately 12.6% of young people, ages 16-24, had not completed high school and were not enrolled in school.

The dropout rate varies by race. In recent years, the dropout rate has been increasingly markedly for Latinos while declining for Anglos and African Americans. In 1991, 8.9% of Anglos, 13.6% of African Americans, and 35.3% of Latinos dropped out of school ("Latino Dropout Rates Up," 1992). In addition, Latinos are less likely to be functioning at grade level. By age 17, one in six Latinos is 2 years behind and two in five are 1 year behind. Among 20- to 24-year-old Latinos, 37% have not received diplomas compared with 21% of African Americans and 14% of whites (Children's Defense Fund, 1990a).

The costs associated with dropping out are potentially high for both the individual and society. The changing nature of work, the loss of well-paying blue-collar jobs, and the move to a more technologically and service-oriented economy requires a literate and skilled workforce. Individuals without these skills are at a disadvantage. There are also costs to the society when individuals have difficulty obtaining employment. Low earnings and periods of unemployment result in a smaller tax base for government bodies and an increase in public assistance and social insurance payments. The social cost associated with the average dropout is estimated to be $200,000 (Catterall, 1987).

There are other measures that indicate that clusters of children are not well served by the public schools. A minority child is 2.3 times more likely than a white child to be labeled educable mentally retarded (EMR), and overall math and reading scores for African American children, at every age level, are lower than for white children (Black Child Advocate, 1989). African American children are three times as likely as white children to be placed in classes for the mentally retarded but only half as likely to be in classes for the gifted (Kozol, 1991, p. 119). There are a number of factors that contribute to the elevated risk for educational failure of minority children.

Ability Grouping in the Public Schools

Classification schemes are commonly used in school settings. A number of arguments are used to justify this practice. Children have different abilities and require special learning opportunities in order to develop these abilities. Grouping children with similar abilities enables schools to use their limited resources in the most efficient fashion. Ability grouping, one method of classifying, also known as tracking, has been a disservice to many students (Oakes & Lipton, 1990).

The validity of the assumptions that support tracking is, at best, questionable. The assumption that bright students are bored or are slowed in their learning if they are mixed with other students and that homogenous groups provide the best learning opportunities has not been supported by research (Grant, 1991). The assumption that low-ability students will suffer damage to their self-esteem if mixed with high-ability students has not been supported by research and there are some studies that suggest just the opposite occurs (Grant, 1991). Children learn very quickly which ability group they have been assigned to and where it ranks. Those in high-ability groups run the risk of developing an unrealistic sense of their abilities and those in low-ability groups are likely to be viewed as slow. The accompanying expectations of teachers combined with a self-fulling prophesy may help the student placed in the high-ability group, but can hurt the student placed in the low-ability group.

The Place of Testing

The methods used to place students in ability groups has been subject to scrutiny. Standardized tests have been the primary method for tracking. Much has been written about the gender, racial, and class bias that permeates standardized tests. Poor and minority students score lower on these tests than do nonpoor and white students. There is no credible evidence to support the notion that intelligence is related to class, ethnicity, gender, or race. Yet, the federal government reports that a disproportionate number of minority students are placed in lower ability classes and that at least 10% (about 1,770) of school districts group students according to ability in a discriminatory manner (U.S. General Accounting Office, 1991d).

There are other complicated issues associated with testing that raise questions about the utility of tests for tracking students. For example, there is a science to questionnaire construction. A quality test excludes questions that most people answer either correctly or incorrectly and includes only questions that just a few people answer correctly. This is the discriminating power of a test. Questions that many students answer correctly are not worthwhile for a test designer even though such questions could suggest that most students have the desired ability or aptitude. A quality test results in a range of scores from low to high. Questions arise about whether the items few students answer correctly really measure the dimension being tested and if these test results should be the basis for determining the educational future of young people.

Standardized tests may actually retard the academic performance of students. Considerable resources are devoted to testing, resources that could be used to increase educational materials or the number of teachers. Test materials are expensive and states can allocate millions of dollars for testing programs (Bierlein, 1993). In addition, teachers may prepare students for the tests rather than focus on the development of high-order skills (Bierlein, 1993; Darling-Hammond, 1991).

In an effort to address some of the major problems associated with standardized tests, scales for assessing adaptive behaviors have been developed. These instruments provide data on how a child functions in a number of settings such as in the family, community, with peers, as well as in the academic setting (Allen-Meares & Lane, 1983). The results of adaptive assessments are used to supplement the data obtained from conventional IQ tests.

Administration of Punishment

Another index of disadvantage, incidence of school administered punishment, indicates that minority students are again at an elevated risk for this negative event. African American students are more likely to be suspended and disciplined than are white students even though the incidence of self-reported misconduct is similar for the two groups (McCarthy & Hoge, 1987). The disparity in incidence rates has been explained by a number of related factors. McCarthy and Hoge (1987) suggest that the student's demeanor, academic performance, and recent punishment history all operate to increase the risk of punishment.

Beliefs about the effectiveness of physical or corporal punishment have not been supported by the research. The advantages are few. Corporal punishment may temporarily suppress the offending behavior. It fails, however, to teach a new behavior other than violence. It does not encourage the development of internal controls, a necessary skill for effective social functioning (Hyman, 1990). Many school districts use corporal punishment. There are some notable exceptions to this practice, such as New York City and Chicago, but the administration of physical punishment remains a pervasive practice. Statistics indicate, once again, that African American male children are most likely to be the recipients of this form of violence (Children's Defense Fund, 1985; Hyman, 1990).

Corporal punishment is a form of violence, and public schools should avoid assuming the role of perpetrator of violence. This is especially true for the youngster who may be a victim of violence in the home. These children are at risk for academic problems and low self-esteem (Tower, 1992). Further trauma at the hands of school personnel serves to exacerbate the pain in the lives of these children.

Addressing the Inequities

Disadvantages accumulate over time. In order to reduce the dropout rate and improve the academic performance as measured by standardized tests of poor and minority students, a number of programs have been developed. With guidelines and funding from the federal government, states have been encouraged to participate in these specialized programs. The most researched program is Head Start.

Head Start

Poverty received new attention in the 1960s. President Johnson declared a War on Poverty and placed emphasis on the prevention of poverty. Head Start was established in 1965 as a result of the Economic Opportunity Act of 1964. The intent was to prevent poverty by providing multiple services to low-income pre-school age children and their families. These children would then be able to profit from public school and grow up to become productive members of the society.

Head Start was a complex program providing multiple services. These services included:

- medical and dental care
- nutrition services
- parent education
- school readiness programs
- active parent involvement (parents either volunteer or are paid staff)
- social services (including home visits)

The model for Head Start was the Perry Preschool Program in Ypsilanti, Michigan. Using an experimental design, the Perry Preschool program examined the effects of providing quality early childhood programs for children from low-income families. Three- and 4-year-olds with low IQs were program participants. For 2 years these children received intensive services, including weekly home visits. The program participants are now young adults, and longitudinal studies have yielded some interesting findings about their productivity and contributions to their communities (Soobiah, 1990).

The criteria for determining the success of early intervention programs must include measures other than IQ scores. Programs such as the Perry Preschool Program and Head Start cannot present themselves as vehicles for increasing IQ points. The importance of selecting realistic outcome variables cannot be overemphasized. It is true that both the Perry Preschool Program and Head Start were able to improve the IQ scores of the children. However, these gains are short lived. Within 3 years of attending public schools, the increase in IQ points disappeared (Ziegler & Rescorla, 1985).

Children may have profited from this temporary gain in IQ points. The first 2 or 3 years of school are important and may establish a pattern that can persist. For example, teachers may have had elevated expectations for the child's performance, and teacher expectations play a significant role in how well a youngster performs. The child may have experienced more success in the first few years of school, thus increasing the child's self-confidence. Attending school then becomes a positive experience for the child.

Instead of focusing on only one easily measurable but unrealistic outcome, the Perry Program operationalized success more broadly. When compared with the control group, children who attended the program were:

1. less likely to have received special education,
2. more likely to graduate from high school,
3. more likely to be employed,
4. less likely to have been arrested,
5. less likely to receive public assistance, and
6. older at the birth of their first child (Committee for Economic Development, 1987).

These variables measure quality of life rather than IQ points. Thus, they are more realistic indicators of program success.

Head Start is one of the few social welfare programs to enjoy Congressional popularity. Attempts to reduce Head Start allocations by President Reagan in the early 1980s were unsuccessful. Head Start is federally funded and state administered. Programs exist in all 50 states. The Department of Health and Human Services provides more than 1.2 billion dollars to the states annually to serve more than 450,000 children aged 3 to 5 (U.S. General Accounting Office, 1989c). Only 18% of the 2.5 million children who are eligible participate in the program (Children's Defense Fund, 1988).

Here is yet another program that works but is underfunded. The costs associated with early intervention programs appear high until they are compared with the costs of failing to provide services. The financial costs associated, for example, with failing to complete high school—unemployment, incarceration, early childbearing, and public assistance—far exceed the cost of the Head Start program.

Troubled Children

Although Head Start is effective in preparing toddlers for school, there remains another underserved minority. Emotional disturbed preschool and school aged children are at great risk for neglect. Between 12% and 15% of America's children have mental or emotional problems and should be receiving treatment, and 70% to 80% are not receiving appropriate services (National Mental Health Association, 1989b).

The school can play an important role in the identification and treatment of emotionally troubled children. This can be a difficult task for the school to perform. Teachers may view troubled students as either disruptive or nondisruptive. The shy youngster who is internalizing her or his problems is not as likely to receive attention and subsequent referral for evaluation as is the aggressive child who is externalizing his or her behaviors.

The child who is disruptive may still not receive needed evaluation and referral because teachers have their own definitions of disturbance and view of what that particular child needs (Rickel, 1982). Schools respond to children who cause trouble by labeling and isolating them, which frequently serves to exacerbate problems.

School systems need to incorporate methods for screening young children so that appropriate remedial and mental health services can be provided. This requires schools to acknowledge that there is more to preparing children for adulthood than learning basic skills. Schools also need the resources (money and skilled staff) to provide these services.

Responses to Problems

There are multiple levels of response. At the level of the individual school, the school social worker has an important role to play. At the policy level, there are multiple programs to address the problems. There is no consensus, however, on which policies to implement.

Humanizing the public schools and helping them become sensitive to the needs of at-risk children is a task for school social workers. In addition to helping the individual child profit from education, school social workers focus on macro issues that effect large groups of children within the district. Creating, monitoring, and evaluating special education services for handicapped students is one area of practice for the school social worker. Involving parents in the educational process and fostering a partnership between parents and schools is another task for the school social worker. Advocacy efforts are important and the elimination of corporal punishment is a goal for many school social workers and their professional organization.

Former President Bush and his Secretaries of Education have suggested remedies for the ailing education system. In April 1991, the President called for national standardized tests for fourth, eighth, and twelfth graders. He did not address the issue of whether this meant that a national curriculum was needed. This is a controversial notion because the federal government has historically played a limited role in selecting classroom content.

Perhaps the most controversial political suggestion for improvement is "choice." This is an extension of free market ideology and treats education like any other commodity. There is an assumption that competition will reward good schools and punish bad schools (Bierlein, 1993).

There are variations on the choice theme. The basic idea is that parents can choose, with some restrictions, what school their child will attend. Schools receive funds based upon the number of students they enroll.

Therefore, schools will have an incentive to provide the kind of education parents want.

It will take time and much research in order to evaluate the effectiveness of choice. Variations on the theme of choice have been in existence for decades. Magnet and specialized schools were designed as methods for promoting voluntary desegregation. The schools offered an incentive to enroll, such as a focus on the sciences or the arts.

Choice may offer positive options for many students. However, educationally at-risk youngsters may not find choice to be much help. Schools are interested in attracting talented, motivated, bright students with few problems. These students are likely to experience academic success. In addition, in order to exercise choice, parents must understand the options, and there need to be alternatives. Families in which English is a second language or where parents did not experience success in school may have difficulty negotiating the choice process.

Questions also arise about transportation issues. Schools used to serve neighborhoods. Choice plans alter the neighborhood concept and could result in significant numbers of students transferring out of local schools. Children could spend considerable time in traveling.

Choice plans may also threaten the racial balance in some schools. Public schools have struggled and on occasion have resisted desegregation since the 1954 Brown decision. The Brown decision required public schools not to be segregated. After this decision, South Carolina attempted to repeal its public education law. Many years have passed since Brown, and yet desegregation has not been achieved. The courts continue to be involved with monitoring the public schools.

Summary

The school system represents many opportunities for youngsters to grow and develop into productive citizens who can care for themselves and contribute to their communities. The school is an important institution that can play a preventive role. For children environmentally at risk the school can be a calm, predictable, safe haven staffed with nurturing adults. This may be the only source of stability and care for some children. Teaching multiplication is but one task for the school and it cannot be accomplished when students are hungry, tired, or frightened.

The school system is failing to meet the needs of some children. For example, one million adolescents are not getting diplomas and another 700,000 are being graduated but are functionally illiterate (Committee for Economic Development, 1987). The mental health needs for a minority of children are not being recognized by the schools, and few children are receiving the early preparation essential for academic and life success. The school system has generally met the needs of middle-class students. However, race, class, gender, and ethnicity challenge the school system (Cardenas, 1990).

The solutions are complex and influenced by values, politics, and resources. Plans for change need to involve parents as well as school personnel. Issues to be addressed include funding, curricula, teacher preparation, and methods for evaluation.

PART II

The Residual Nature
of Child Welfare

The nature of our child welfare system is to provide services in response to the perceived failure of families to care for their children. This residual response is the focus of Part II. Chapter 4 presents the growing phenomenon of poverty among children. It examines the negative consequences associated with pervasive poverty and the social policy response. Chapters 5 and 6 look at the vulnerable groups of children historically served by our child welfare system. The residual nature of services for maltreated children is illustrated.

4

The Juvenilization of Poverty

Over the past decade, the economic well-being of children has deteriorated. Children are proportionately the largest group among the poor, with more than one out of five children officially living in poverty. The consequences of growing up in poverty are extensive and become the foundation for adult life.

The juvenilization of poverty, the growing trend for children to be living in poverty, is covered in this chapter. The programs and policies designed to address the needs of poor children are examined. The residual nature of social welfare programs for the poor and the consequences of this policy are discussed.

The United States is the most prosperous nation in the world. In spite of this well-being, each day millions of children do not have enough food to eat or clothing to wear, lack safe places to live, and do not receive the medical care they need. These youngsters are America's children of poverty. Because of economic deprivation, these children are not as healthy, as educated, nor as safe as the rest of the children in this nation. This is not startling news. A report issued by the bipartisan National Commission on Children (1991) concluded that America has failed many of its children: "If we measure success not just by how well most children do, but by how poorly some fare, America falls far short. The evidence of that failure is everywhere one cares to look" (p. 4). This chapter looks at the extent of poverty among children, the consequences of it, and the services and policies aimed at alleviating economic deprivation for children and their families.

The Context of Poverty

Children have suffered the devastation of poverty throughout the history of this nation. Historically, the impoverishment of children matched that of the nation as a whole. However, the 1980s witnessed a new phenomenon, the juvenilization of poverty (Segal, 1991; Wilson, 1985). With little public notice, the 1980s witnessed growth in the number of children living in poverty and the consequential establishment of children as the number one poverty group. This occurred in spite of 7 years of national economic expansion, one of the longest such periods. How can a nation as wealthy as the United States and as committed to children and families as it professes to be, have such a significant number of children living in poverty?

In order to understand the juvenilization of poverty, it is important to consider the social values and conditions that go into defining the concepts of wealth and poverty. There are two ways to measure poverty. One is an *absolute* measure, setting a specific dollar amount under which a person is considered poor. Such a measure could be arbitrary or based on research to determine what indeed is poverty. The result is a set poverty line, with those above considered nonpoor and those below identified as poor. The second way is to compare the levels of wealth in the country and establish a minimum level based on the current distribution of wealth. This would be a *relative* measure of poverty. Minimum standards would reflect what we expect people to have compared to the overall well-being of the nation. Although what is considered "poor" here would certainly not be considered poor in most Third World developing countries, within our nation, a determination of what is and is not poor can be made.

In this country poverty is determined through the use of an absolute measure referred to as the poverty line or index. This measure is used by the U.S. Bureau of the Census to determine statistically the number of people who are poor and serves as the basis for determining who is eligible for many Federal welfare programs. Table 4.1 lists the 1991 dollar amounts according to family size. For a family of four, earnings below $13,924 would place them within the official category of poverty.

The method for developing the poverty index was established in 1964 by Dr. Mollie Orshansky, an economist with the Social Security Administration (Orshansky, 1965). The definition is based on the annual estimated amount of money it would take to purchase a "minimally

TABLE 4.1 Federal Poverty 1991 Income Guidelines

Size of Family Unit	Poverty Guideline
1	$ 6,932
2	$ 8,865
3	$10,860
4	$13,924
5	$16,456
6	$18,587

SOURCE: U.S. Bureau of the Census (1992b).

adequate" basket of goods and services required for subsistence. It is important to understand the values used to determine the index. The amount allotted for food was based on the Department of Agriculture's "economy food plan," a menu designed for "temporary or emergency use when funds are low" (Orshansky, 1965, p. 6). Based on living standards during the 1950s, families spent one third of their income on food. The poverty line was thus determined to be three times the economy food plan.

Based on this construction, two serious flaws are inherent in the poverty index. First is the expectation that a family can adequately live on the amount needed for temporary or emergency provisions, especially over a period of many years. The second flaw is that today, the cost of food no longer represents one third of a typical family's budget. Although the measure is useful as an indicator of a consistent level of poverty over the past 25 years, it represents a very minimal, if not inadequate, amount of money for a family in today's economy. Nevertheless, it provides the only standard of measurement, and serves as a way to compare trends in poverty over time.

Values also play a part in defining who is poor and who is not. This country was founded on principles of self-reliance and families caring for their own. It also adheres to a value of compassion for those in need. These values form the basis of the dilemma behind poverty assistance policies. The principle of self-reliance contradicts the concept of government stepping in with resources and cash assistance when families are poor, yet compassion calls for caring for those in need. This contradiction serves as the basis behind discussions of welfare policy. When speaking of children, this contradiction is especially apparent. The well-being of children is professed to be a strongly held value in this country, yet millions of children are officially defined as poor and have been so for decades. These differing values are important to remember when reading the section on social services and policies for poor children and families.

Economic Conditions of Children

Poverty has existed throughout history, but the past 40 years have witnessed the achievement of a modern era of economic growth and prosperity. Following World War II the atmosphere of the nation was that anything was possible. Two-parent familial life was valued and family size grew, thus creating the baby boom generation. The American dream of a good job, a home in the suburbs, and opportunities for upward mobility abounded. Such was not the case for all Americans. During the 1960s, when the country was expanding, Michael Harrington published his book *The Other America* (1963) that for the first time identified poverty in modern America. Harrington wrote about the uneven distribution of wealth and uncovered the numerous concentrations of poverty. He brought attention to the millions of rural Americans cut off from the postwar growth who were struggling to survive. His work was instrumental in moving policy makers to enact the "War on Poverty."

From 1960 to 1964, the poverty rate for children averaged almost 25% (see Table 4.2). The mid-1960s through the 1970s witnessed a period when the establishment of programs to help poor families, and specifically poor children, was a national priority. As a result, the rate of child poverty dropped to average 15.7% during the 1970s. However, the progress toward alleviating poverty diminished by the 1980s. The child poverty rate averaged 20.5 % throughout the 1980s and reached 20.6% in 1990.

Program cutbacks coupled with poor economic conditions erased much of the progress of the War on Poverty. The 1980s witnessed the concept of "trickle down" economics, advocated by then President Reagan. It was supposed to bring greater prosperity to all Americans. The thinking behind this policy was that an increase in the wealth of those at the top would "trickle down" to those at the bottom and lift everyone. For children, the policy failed. The gap between the richest and poorest in this country became and still is greater than ever. The top 1% of the population, or 2.5 million people, have as much income as the

TABLE 4.2 Average Percentage of Children in Poverty

1960-1964	24.7
1965-1969	17.0
1970-1974	15.1
1975-1979	16.3
1980-1984	20.8
1985-1989	20.4
1990	20.6
1991	21.8

SOURCES: U.S. Bureau of the Census (1992b); Center on Budget & Policy Priorities (1991).

bottom 40%, or 100 million people (Center on Budget and Policy Priorities, 1990). Households in the top fifth of the population have seen their income grow over the 1980s whereas those in the middle and bottom fifth have seen theirs decline. Instead of trickling down, the increased income at the top has stayed with a very small minority and has not improved the rate of poverty.

The poverty statistics are even more disturbing when considered by race (see Table 4.3). In 1991, almost 46% of all black children lived in poverty. For Hispanic children, the rate was more than 40%. Thus, the likelihood that a black child will grow up in poverty is almost three times as great as for a white child. Although poverty is problematic for more than one out of five children, children of color are severely disadvantaged.

Young children are also extremely vulnerable to poverty. The proportion of children under six living in poverty has grown over the past 10 years. Through the 1970s, about 17% of children under 6 were in poverty, but by 1983 that jumped to 25% and has remained at 23% through the rest of the decade (National Center for Children in Poverty, 1990). The preschool group is the highest proportion of poor within any age group in the United States.

Any national disaster that affected more than 13 million people would create a tremendous amount of media attention and bring a major public response. Yet the growing trend toward the juvenilization of poverty, the high concentration of poverty among children, has not evoked national concern. Poverty is a social problem that does not draw social attention nor action, although its pervasiveness places it as a national tragedy. The challenge to those working with children and their families is to understand the extent of poverty among children and advocate for greater attention to this national problem.

TABLE 4.3 Children in Poverty by Race (by percent)

	Total	White	Black	Hispanic
1991	21.8	16.8	45.9	40.4
1990	20.6	15.9	44.8	38.4
1989	19.6	14.8	43.7	36.2
1988	19.5	14.5	43.5	37.6
1987	20.5	15.3	45.1	39.3
1986	20.5	16.1	43.1	37.7
1985	20.7	16.2	43.6	40.3
1980	18.3	13.9	42.3	33.2
1975	17.1	12.7	41.7	NA

SOURCES: U.S. Bureau of the Census (1992b); Center on Budget & Policy Priorities (1991).

The Economic Decline of Families

Discussion of childhood poverty necessarily includes a look at the families of these youngsters. Children are not poor alone. They are part of families who are subject to changing economic conditions that are not favorable to adults raising a family. Table 4.4 illustrates the extent of poverty among families with children.

The poverty rate for all families with children was 17.7% in 1991. For families of color, the disparity was even greater. More than 39% of all black families were in poverty and almost 34% of all Hispanic families. For families without children, poverty is not as prevalent a problem. For example, the poverty rate in 1987 was 4.6% for families without children, compared to 15.5% for families with children (U.S. Bureau of the Census, 1990b).

Since 1983, the United States has experienced more than 7 years of economic expansion. In spite of that growth, the poverty rate for children has remained higher than during the 1970s. This trend is linked directly to a number of factors. One factor is the "feminization of poverty" (Pearce, 1978). The feminization of poverty reflects the trend toward more women, particularly those who are single heads of households, living in poverty. The average income for female-headed families in 1988 was $16,077 compared with married couple families with $37,069 per year (U.S. Bureau of the Census, 1990b). Again, minority families fared worse. For black, female-headed households, the poverty rate was 54%, and for Hispanic families headed by a single woman the proportion in

TABLE 4.4 1991 Poverty Status of Families With Children Under 18 Years (by percent)

All families	17.7
Married couple families	8.3
Female-headed families	47.1
All white families	13.7
White married couple families	7.7
White female-headed families	39.6
All black families	39.2
Black married couple families	12.4
Black female-headed families	60.1
All Hispanic families	33.7
Hispanic married couple families	23.5
Hispanic female-headed families	60.1

SOURCE: U.S. Bureau of the Census (1992b).

poverty was almost 58%. Although the costs for raising a child are similar whether there are one or two adults contributing, the economic means of a single parent, particularly a woman, are significantly less than those of a married couple.

Families with young parents are also at an economic disadvantage. Between 1967 and 1986, the poverty rate of families with heads of households under 30 years of age jumped from 12.1% to 21.6% (Grant Foundation, 1988). Most young parents are in the workforce, but are underemployed or have low-paying jobs with few or no benefits. Since 1979, the income of people under the age of 25 who were heads of households dropped 20%, while the income for those 35 to 54 years of age rose 28% (Congressional Budget Office, 1988). Young parents are earning less than previous generations and are at greater risk of being in poverty.

Recent economic trends further eroded the economic security of families. From 1989 to 1991, during the most recent economic downturn, almost 2 million more children fell into poverty. For families with children, their median income fell by almost 5% (Children's Defense Fund, 1992). Even though the recession of 1990-1991 was termed "mild," it had significant impact on families with children.

Raising children is a major expense for families and places them in a more precarious economic position. Families with children are three times as likely to be poor compared to families without children. Families with only one parent or young parents are even more susceptible to poverty. These differences clearly demonstrate the need for economic support of children through the family.

The Consequences of Poverty

Child welfare workers see firsthand the devastation of poverty on children. Growing up without enough to eat, living in unsafe and inadequate homes, lacking proper clothing, studying in crowded classrooms, and not receiving health care are the negative consequences of poverty. Children who live in poverty from the time before they are born until they become adults are less likely to grow up to become productive adults. Their development is impaired and the long-term costs to them and to society are great. The relationship between poverty and impaired physical, social, and emotional development is well documented.

> The close association between poverty and risk holds for every component of risk—from premature birth to poor health and nutrition, from failure to develop warm, secure, trusting relationships early in life to child abuse, from family stress and chaos to failure to master school skills. Persistent and concentrated poverty virtually guarantee the presence of a vast collection of risk factors and their continuing destructive impact over time. (Schorr, 1988, pp. 29-30)

This relationship is not new and is understood by those who are responsible for providing human services, as evidenced by the 1985 policy statement of the National Council of State Human Service Administrators:

> Poverty in America often entails a host of other social problems that afflict poor children and their families disproportionately. Abuse and neglect, poor health and malnutrition, inadequate education and substandard housing, crime and delinquency—all these occur with greater frequency among the poor than among the rest of the population. (1985, p. 5)

It is important to consider these consequences and understand the impact of the dimensions of poverty for children.

Health Factors

Childhood is an important time of growth and development. The best way to ensure optimal development is through a healthy childhood. The early health of a child directly affects future health status as an adult. Simple childhood illnesses, left untreated, can lead to lifelong disabilities. The earache not properly medically treated can result in hearing loss, affecting a child for a lifetime.

Unfortunately, for millions of children, early health care is minimal or nonexistent. In 1986, 37 million people did not have any health insurance, public or private (Congressional Research Service, 1988). Among this group were 12 million children. Most lived in families where heads of households worked and were therefore not officially below the poverty line. Unfortunately the jobs did not provide health insurance coverage. This reflects a trend that is likely to continue—the level of health insurance protection is dropping, and federal and state health care programs have not kept pace with the growing need (Starr, 1986). The typical health care for uninsured children is emergency care due to exacerbated untreated medical need. Preventive care and early intervention are virtually nonexistent. Without health insurance coverage, millions of children with medical needs go untreated until the need becomes a crisis.

Recent studies point to the link between poor health and poverty. Poor children are more likely to suffer from numerous conditions: premature birth, low birth weight, infant mortality, severe illness, injuries, inadequate nutrition, and chronic illnesses (National Center for Children in Poverty, 1991). The reasons for this link lie in the hardships of living in poverty and barriers to preventive care. Inadequate nutrition and housing are the results of not having enough money to purchase a healthy diet and a safe place to live. When a family's food allowance runs low, the nutritional choice in preparing a meal is limited. Children need well-balanced, complete meals to develop fully. There is extensive scientific research demonstrating the positive aspects of a healthy diet and the negative consequences of poor nutrition. Yet for poor families, there is simply not enough money to guarantee a consistently healthy diet.

A child's health is also affected by the environment. Housing that is affordable to the poor is often run down, with inadequate insulation, plumbing, and heating. These conditions place poor children at greater risk of incidence and severity of illness. They live in neighborhoods where there is higher risk of injury. Poor neighborhoods have a greater proportion of abandoned buildings, vacant lots, inadequate municipal services, and increased violence. These environmental factors contribute to poor health.

Education

One of the most consistent indicators of future wealth and social success is one's level of educational achievement. For those children who receive a complete education and are well grounded in their academic skills, higher paying jobs and opportunities for advancement are possible. The contrary is also true. For poor children who attend schools that lack resources, are overcrowded and dangerous, and graduate fewer students with the skills necessary for competitive jobs, opportunities for economic advancement are less likely.

A recent study of poor children (Zill, 1991) found that children on welfare are twice as likely to fail in school. By the time they reached their teenage years, 36% of the welfare children repeated a grade compared with only 17% of the nonpoor teens. The repetition of a grade tends to be linked to dropping out of school. Students held back a grade are three times more likely to drop out of school compared with students not held back (Children's Defense Fund, 1990d). In today's economic environment, without a high school diploma it is very difficult to find a job, particularly one that pays well and includes health benefits.

The early educational disadvantage that poverty places on children is compounded as time goes on. Youth of high socioeconomic status are almost twice as likely as youth of low socioeconomic status to enroll in college and are three times as likely actually to graduate with a 4-year degree (Select Committee on Children, Youth & Families, 1989d). In 1989, the median income for households headed by someone with less than 4 years of high school education was $14,859, compared to $48,126 for households headed by a person with 4 years or more of college (U.S. Bureau of the Census, 1990b). The college graduate is likely to earn more than three times the income of the person who does not complete high school.

Poor children begin life at a disadvantage. They come from families and communities with fewer resources and therefore attend schools that are inferior in quality to those attended by children of greater economic means. They grow up with poor health care and nutrition and consequently are physically less prepared to excel in the rigors of academic studies. With less opportunity for educational achievement, they are tracked to fall behind in future employment and socioeconomic advancement, thus repeating the cycle of poverty.

The Culture of
Poverty and the Underclass

Particularly since the War on Poverty, there has been ongoing discussion about the pervasiveness of poverty and the extent to which it influences all parts of a person's life. There are two general perspectives: (a) that individuals are poor because of a set of beliefs and values they have inherited, and (b) that people are poor as part of structural deficits that are imbedded in a community.

The first concept suggests a "culture of poverty"—low income is not just a level of economic means but is a set of attitudes that include alienation, apathy, and indifference (DiNitto & Dye, 1987). This "culture" is passed on from generation to generation. It follows from this concept that lowering the rate of poverty requires reacculturating people to the lifestyle of those who are not poor. Those who agree that the culture of poverty is the cause of economic deprivation view cash assistance and in-kind resources as perpetuating dependence. Such efforts will not make a significance difference because the culture of poverty perspective views the individual as socialized to live poor.

The second theory describes a growing "underclass"—the increase in groups who are socially and economically isolated from the majority of society (Wilson, 1987). Recent research supports the second concept of a growing underclass of people who live in inner-city communities that have become economically isolated. No matter what people may hope to achieve, the reality is that economic opportunity is unattainable due to geographic location. The result is that few jobs are available and children do not see working role models.

These concepts differ in where the foundation of poverty lies. The culture of poverty concept suggests it rests with the individual, while the underclass concept suggests the economic structure socializes people to poverty. Although there are undoubtedly examples of people who fit both categories, it is becoming evident that the structures of poor communities are instrumental in socializing new generations to feel alienated and economically isolated.

Though children are born with their own unique attributes, the environment can be key in determining how they develop. The consequences of growing up in an impoverished community are very likely to include becoming acclimated to the surroundings and learning coping skills that are appropriately matched. If we continue to allow millions of children to be raised in communities that are socially and economically deficient, then we are guaranteeing the continuation of future generations of adults who are outside the mainstream of society and adapt to poverty as a way of life.

Social Services and Policies
for Poor Children and Families

Although poverty is not a new problem, the United States lacks an organized and consistent national response to economic need. The social services system in this country is a patchwork of programs and policies that evolved incrementally. As is true of most social policy in this country, services for children were created in response to specific crises, such as hunger or health care, that gained attention. To date, however, no overall strategy to serve children has been developed. Thus, although a number of programs directed toward poor children exist, there is not a coherent policy for alleviating poverty among children.

The most extensive efforts to serve children in need have historically taken place on the federal level. The federal government plays a significant role in proposing policies and providing the funds to mandate states and localities to provide services. Services for economically needy children and their families can be divided into two categories: direct cash assistance programs, which provide cash allotments; and in-kind benefits, which include health care, housing, and food. The following is an overview of the major programs that serve children in poverty.

Aid to Families With Dependent Children

Aid to Families with Dependent Children (AFDC) is the largest and most well-known cash assistance program for poor children. AFDC was first enacted as part of the Social Security Act of 1935. It began as a cash assistance program to aid poor children without fathers. The early designers viewed the assistance as a temporary program that would become unnecessary once the full social insurance system was in place. In 1935, 88% of families receiving aid were in need because of the death of a father (Burke, 1991). However, demographic and economic shifts changed the composition of the AFDC program. By 1989, only 2% of the children served by AFDC were needy as a result of the death of a father (U.S. Department of Health & Human Services, 1990b). The typical AFDC family has changed since the inception of the program in 1935. The majority of today's AFDC families are headed by single women with little or no support from the fathers of their children. In 1990, 92% of AFDC families reported no father present (Committee on Ways and Means, 1992).

As a result of the change in AFDC families, it is clear that AFDC is not a temporary program. AFDC has become the primary antipoverty program for poor children. In 1991, almost 12.4 million people received cash assistance payments through the AFDC program, totaling more than $20 billion. Of those recipients, two-thirds or 8.4 million were children (Committee on Ways and Means, 1992). The majority of these children live in single-parent households headed by women. They are children who would not qualify for social insurance benefits because they were never covered by a parent who had a sufficient work history to qualify.

The average size of an AFDC household is three people. Almost three fourths of the households consist of one or two children. Even though the inaccurate image of the large welfare family getting assistance forever persists today, the majority of AFDC cases are families receiving aid for less than 2 years. In 1990, the median months on AFDC was 23 months (Committee on Ways and Means, 1992). The AFDC program, historically and today, serves as the only financial safety net for poor women and children.

Both the federal and state governments fund the AFDC program. Although the costs are shared, states are responsible for total operation of the program under federal guidelines. The major policy struggle under AFDC has been to provide cash assistance without undermining a person's incentive to work. This policy goal has been coupled with the American ethic that people should work and the government should not provide dollars to those not willing to work. As a result of these concerns, benefits have historically remained low. In 1988, the average AFDC family of three received $374 a month, or about $128 per person (Social Security Administration, 1990). In almost all states, the maximum cash benefit allotted through AFDC is less than 75% of the poverty line (Center

TABLE 4.5 Average Percentage of Children in Poverty on AFDC

1965-1969	34.6
1970-1974	73.2
1975-1979	74.0
1980-1984	55.9
1985-1988	56.8

NOTE: Table 4.5 developed from author calculations based on data from the U.S. Bureau of the Census (1990b) and the Social Security Administration (1990).

on Budget and Policy Priorities, 1988). The real value of AFDC payments has declined over the years. Between 1970 and 1989, the maximum monthly payment decreased by 37%, leaving the purchasing power of AFDC families far below that of two decades ago (Levitan, 1990).

From 1965 to 1969, only 35% of children in poverty received AFDC (see Table 4.5). By the 1970s, that rate had doubled to almost 75%. During that period, child poverty declined by about 40%. It would seem that the antipoverty strategies of the War on Poverty succeeded in decreasing the impoverishment of children. In spite of this apparent link between AFDC and a reduction in child poverty, the program is not viewed as a valuable tool in fighting child poverty. Although the poverty rate increased during the 1980s, the portion of poor children served by AFDC declined. From 1980 to 1984, during a time of economic recession, only 56% of children in poverty received AFDC. The decrease in the AFDC program was a direct result of policy decisions made during the early 1980s. Work requirements, restrictions on eligibility, and tighter calculations of income all contributed to a 19% loss in expenditures and a decrease of more than 400,000 families from 1981 to 1984 (Kimmich, 1985). These declines in AFDC were in spite of growing poverty among children.

The effect of restricted eligibility and low benefits resulted in the provision of minimal cash assistance to poor families. The belief is that the adults will pursue employment instead of AFDC. However, the emphasis on work instead of welfare has not proven successful and is punitive toward women (Miller, 1989; Segal, 1989). Most welfare work programs or the jobs available to heads of poor households are low-paying jobs. The income from these jobs is not adequate to raise children, and the jobs do not provide needed benefits such as health insurance.

For millions of poor families with children, the AFDC program is the only source of economic support. Yet, the program provides only a minimum of assistance. Welfare families do not live a comfortable life. The monthly assistance usually is spent well before the next check arrives. Mothers are faced with children who, through television and movies, see a well-to-do nation and want the same. Welfare families make painful choices every day about what they can and cannot do, and are hard pressed to plan for the future. One welfare mother spoke about the difficulty in buying her children chocolate bars. They were the most reasonable treats she could afford to purchase for her children, yet she was uncomfortable using her food stamps to do so. She felt judged by those around her in the grocery store. Her choice was to feel like she was "cheating" the system or deny giving her children the treats other parents had no difficulty in providing. Although AFDC is the primary form of cash assistance for millions of poor children, it does not provide them with a level of economic support that promotes a positive and healthy life.

Child Support Enforcement

Because the majority of AFDC children have biological fathers who are living, attempts have been made to press the fathers to provide economic support. The intent is that families will be lifted out of poverty through the collection of delinquent child support. In 1975, the federal government passed legislation to establish minimal child support levels and to aid in the collection of delinquent payments. The Child Support Enforcement Program was created as part of the Social Security Act. The belief was that as a result of increased collections, the number of families on AFDC would decrease.

The success of the child support program is not clear. Although additional legislation was passed in 1984, the overall impact has been minimal. In 1984 and 1985, only 1% of AFDC families were successfully lifted out of poverty as a direct result of child support enforcement efforts (based on calculations from data reported in Subcommittee on Social Security & Family Policy, 1988). The reality is that most children on welfare have fathers who are not financially capable of supporting their children. Nevertheless, child support enforcement efforts are important. Although not an extremely effective policy for reducing the number of families already on AFDC, the legislation strengthens the ability of many woman to keep their children's fathers economically responsible and not add to the numbers receiving welfare.

Food Stamps

The Food Stamp program is a significant part of the services available to assist poor children. The Food Stamp program is administered by the Department of Agriculture and was originally created as a system for the distribution of surplus food. In 1964, the Food Stamp Act legislated the direction of the program to assist low-income households in obtaining a more nutritious diet. The program is part of the network of in-kind benefits. Instead of cash, the program allots coupons that can only be exchanged for food items.

Though the Food Stamp program is administered by the states, all funding is provided by the federal government. Almost 19 million people received food stamps at a value of about $11.7 billion in 1989 (Social Security Administration, 1990). The funds translate to about $52 worth of coupons per month for each recipient. The Department of Agriculture estimates that children make up more than half the recipients of Food Stamps (Congressional Research Service, 1987).

Like AFDC, food stamps provide the minimum for bare essentials. It is virtually impossible to provide a healthy diet for growing children on $52 per month. In fact, when the maximum state benefits of AFDC and Food Stamps are combined, in no state except Alaska does the total even lift a family of three *to* the poverty line (Center on Budget and Policy Priorities, 1988). The policy response to poor children is clear—cash assistance and food resources are provided, but only at minimal survival levels. Poor children and their families are urged to care for themselves, in spite of the obstacles to finding economically viable employment and support.

Medicaid

Although AFDC and food stamps do not combine to lift a family out of poverty, participation includes one of the most valuable programs available to poor children—Medicaid. The program was added to the Social Security Act in 1965. It provides federal and state dollars to fund medical assistance for low-income persons. Medicaid is the primary source of health care for poor families.

In spite of the key role Medicaid plays in providing medical care for poor children, today it does not cover all those in need. In 1976, Medicaid served 99% of the nation's poor children. By 1984 coverage had dropped, and only 75% of all poor children received Medicaid services (Edelman, 1987). While Medicaid is crucial to the health care of poor children, the majority of its services are provided for needy adults. In 1989, about 44% of Medicaid recipients were dependent children under the age of 21, and another 24% were the adults of AFDC households. Although poor children and their parents represented 68% of the Medicaid population, they accounted for only 25% of the expenditures for Medicaid (Committee on Ways and Means, 1991). The majority of funds were spent on the medical care of poor elderly and disabled adults.

Medicaid costs have increased dramatically since inception. Over the past 10 years, program costs have more than doubled to $54.5 billion in 1989 (Social Security Administration, 1990). In spite of this increase, it is important to remember that three out of four dollars spent are for poor elderly and disabled adults. Thus Medicaid provides much needed medical care, but the funds are directed more toward needy adults than children.

Other In-Kind Services

The Maternal and Child Health Services Block Grant provides health services for mothers and their young children. The program is designed to increase the availability of prenatal, delivery, and postpartum care to low-income mothers. The overall goal of the program is to reduce infant mortality and decrease the incidence of preventable diseases among children. Although the program has proven to be effective, funding is low and less than half of all states have enough resources to provide comprehensive prenatal services (Children's Defense Fund, 1989b).

Another program targeted for poor children is the Supplemental Food Program for Women, Infants, and Children, commonly referred to as the WIC program. The program provides supplemental foods to enhance the early nutrition of infants and young children. In spite of the valuable resources of the program, less than half the eligible population is served by WIC (Select Committee on Children, Youth & Families, 1989d).

The Head Start program has demonstrated positive results in helping poor children to improve in their educational achievement (Levitan, 1990). The program offers educational assistance to poor children that has helped many perform better in school than children not served by the program. In spite of the positive results, due to insufficient funding for the program fewer than one in four eligible children participates in Head Start programs (U.S. General Accounting Office, 1988).

Summary

The data on child poverty demonstrate a significant change in the economic well-being of America's young. Over the past decade, children have disproportionately become firmly entrenched among America's poor. We have witnessed the juvenilization of poverty, the increasing tendency for children to be among the impoverished. In spite of this increase, national policy and program responses have been inadequate.

The main programs that serve children in poverty cover all the basic needs. However, the extent of that coverage is far below the level needed for healthy development. Millions of children are malnourished, receive inadequate medical care, live in substandard housing, and are educationally disadvantaged. The result is that we are raising a generation that will move from a disadvantaged childhood to an equally disadvantaged adulthood. The costs of this neglect will be borne by all of society. More poor children today means a greater need in the future for remedial programs and economic assistance for those who cannot be employed because of a lack of education and opportunities. The need described in this chapter must be addressed by new approaches and social policy. Chapter 12 outlines a way to address the problems of today so that children can grow and develop to become healthy, productive adults.

5

Child Abuse and Neglect

The abuse and neglect of children is a central concern to social welfare professionals. Definitions and conceptualizations of abuse and neglect have changed over the years, but the phenomenon is not new. Tremendous progress has been made over the past 20 years in recognizing the extent and consequences of abuse and in creating protective legislation. However, the phenomenon of child abuse and neglect continues and requires national attention. This chapter provides an overview of the area and discusses the services and policies related to the care of abused children.

One of the most extensive and debilitating social concerns for child welfare workers is the abuse and neglect of children. From the time they are born until adolescence, children need the care and protection of adults in order to survive. This vulnerability places children at the mercy and control of adults at all times. In most instances, children are adequately cared for by those adults. In a growing number of cases, however, children are not cared for properly and suffer from maltreatment. This chapter discusses what is meant by child abuse and neglect, how to recognize it, the consequences children suffer, and the services and policies that regulate the care of children.

History of Child Abuse and Neglect

The meaning and social understanding of childhood has changed over time. Historically, children were regarded as economic assets for families. A child represented another pair of hands to do labor and promised economic security when parents aged. Rather than perceived as economically useful, children are now emotionally valued (Zelizer, 1985).

In addition to the role of children, what is considered acceptable treatment of a child has changed greatly over time. When children were valued and needed for their ability to work and contribute to the family's economic welfare, working a child 12 to 14 hours a day in dangerous factories was common practice. By the early 1900s, however, social reformers argued this was inhumane and abusive treatment of children and advocated for children's rights. In 1904 the National Child Labor Committee organized to put an end to child labor. Within 10 years, almost every state had enacted legislation restricting child labor (Bruno, 1957).

The most famous child abuse case was that of "Little Mary Ellen," which was brought to court in New York in 1874 (Watkins, 1990). Mary Ellen was found by neighbors to have been physically and emotionally abused by her foster mother. Because no official agency existed to protect the rights of children, the president of the New York Society for the Prevention of Cruelty to Animals was approached by the concerned neighbors. Although the exact role of the Society is unclear, the public attention of the severe abuse inflicted upon Mary Ellen prompted the organization of child protective efforts and the creation of the Society for the Prevention of Cruelty to Children in 1875 (Tower, 1989).

Most early efforts to protect children were carried out by private agencies. It was not until 1935, with passage of the Social Security Act, specifically Title V of that Act, that the federal government intervened. Today, child welfare services fall under Title IV of the Social Security Act. Under Title IV, the federal government provides funds to help states establish services to protect and care for needy dependent and neglected children (Committee on Ways and Means, 1989).

Current concerns for protecting children rose out of the "rediscovery" of child abuse and neglect by physicians in the 1960s (Kempe, Silverman, Steele, Droegmueller, & Silver, 1962). The battered child syndrome, as it was called, referred to the growing medical evidence of cases of physical abuse to children. Although child protective services have long been a part of social work (Anderson, 1989), the attention garnered by the medical profession in the 1960s brought the issue national concern and paved the way for today's policies and programs.

Definitions of Maltreatment

The belief in physical punishment is still considered by many adults as the best way to raise a child. This nation has adhered strongly to the concept of "spare the rod, spoil the child" and has sanctioned physical punishment as an appropriate tool of child rearing. Although there is agreement that extremes of physical restraint and maltreatment are unacceptable, there is much room for debate. Today, there is not one clear and agreed upon definition of child maltreatment.

There are numerous views on what exactly constitutes child maltreatment. It can be defined socially, legally, and even situationally. How child abuse and neglect are defined have significant relevance for understanding the incidence and consequences of maltreatment.

Under federal law, the Child Abuse Prevention, Adoption, and Family Services Act of 1988, P.L. 100-294, spells out the general legal definition of child maltreatment:

> The physical or mental injury, sexual abuse, or exploitation, negligent treatment, or maltreatment of a child by a person who is responsible for the child's welfare, under circumstances which indicate that the child's health or welfare is harmed or threatened thereby, as determined in accordance with regulations prescribed by the Secretary of the Department of Health and Human Services [Section 14 (4)].

Using the legislated definition, the Department of Health and Human Services developed more detailed descriptions of the types of child maltreatment to measure the extent of the problem. These expanded definitions were used in the Study of National Incidence and Prevalence of Child Abuse and Neglect (National Center on Child Abuse and Neglect, 1988). The detailed description of abuse refers to intentional injury that harms a child. This includes physical, emotional, and sexual abuse. Sexual abuse is usually separated in incidence reports and refers specifically to abuse or injury caused by sexual contact by a caretaking adult. Child neglect results from the failure of a caretaking adult to provide for a child's basic needs. This act of omission causes the child to suffer harm or injury. Neglect can be classified as physical, emotional, or both.

How child abuse and neglect are defined affects the way the problem is viewed and the measurement of the extent of maltreatment. There is no one standard definition for child abuse and neglect. Although there are general federal guidelines, each state has its own statutory definition and there is great variability between states.

In a study of state definitions, Rycraft (1990) discovered that the variability among terms may contribute to the number of cases reported and consequently the level of services received by a family. For example, 60% of the states include poverty-related neglect in their definitions of child maltreatment. These states had higher rates of reports and substantiation than those without poverty-related neglect as part of the standard definition. Families where neglect is substantiated will enter the Child Protective Services (CPS) system and thus receive services. If a state's definition does not include those families, then they will not enter the system. Although substantiation leads to service, it in no way is preventive. Families may receive needed services, but they are also labeled as abusing and this designation can follow the family through other systems and services.

Hutchison (1990) argues that the social service system drives the way child maltreatment is defined. Because our CPS system is residual and responds to cases after abuse is reported, a narrow definition is used. Thus the determination of maltreatment and the protection of families' rights have dictated the creation of concrete guidelines for CPS workers to follow. With a preventive policy approach, however, a broader definition of child maltreatment would be appropriate. This broader definition would allow for the provision of services for a wider spectrum of situations and families.

Implementing definitions of child abuse and neglect is full of subjectivity. Confirmations of reports will vary with the workers who actually do the investigations. The more narrow the definition and concrete the guidelines, however, the more likely there will be a lower rate of substantiated cases of abuse and neglect. At the same time, too broad a definition means many families will be investigated who are not abusive or neglectful. Over-investigating can waste precious Children's Protective Services' resources and cause families to undergo unnecessary stress. Under-investigation can leave vulnerable children unprotected and at risk of maltreatment. Thus, how child abuse and neglect are defined has significant implications for child welfare workers. At present, definitions tend to be vague, which allows for the assessment of each individual case.

Incidence of Child Maltreatment

It is difficult to assess definitively the incidence of child maltreatment. Statistics represent those cases that are actually reported. Not all cases of abuse and neglect come to the attention of professionals. The social norm of family privacy often keeps people from reporting abusive behaviors that occur within the family. Many cases go undetected because some abusive acts are difficult to observe by those outside the situation. Although the true incidence of child maltreatment cannot be precisely determined, statistics on the reporting of incidents are informative.

The most comprehensive surveys of the incidence rate of child maltreatment were conducted by the National Center on Child Abuse and Neglect (1988) in 1980 and again in 1986. A comparison of the findings reveals a significant increase in both the number of reports and of substantiated cases of abuse and neglect. The follow-up survey used both the 1980 definition of maltreatment and a revised expanded definition. Using the original, more narrow definition, the National Center found that the overall incidence rate of countable cases of maltreatment increased 65% from 1980 to 1986 (see Table 5.1).

In 1980, there were 652,000 reported incidents of maltreatment, compared to more than 1 million in 1986. With the revised definition, the number rose to 1.7 million cases reported, almost one and one-half times the 1980 reported incidence total.

The National Incidence Study found that among the countable cases of maltreatment documented in the 1988 report:

- The most frequent type of abuse was physical, with an incidence rate of 5.7 per 1,000 children.
- Females were abused at a higher rate, and were four times more likely to be sexually abused.
- The incidence of child abuse increased with age.
- Children living in poverty were more likely to be maltreated or injured.
- Race, ethnicity, and geographic residence were not related to the incidence of maltreatment.

The American Humane Association (AHA) [American Humane Association (AHA), 1986] also collects data on the incidence of child maltreatment. The AHA collects state data to develop a national profile of

TABLE 5.1 Reported Incidents of Maltreatment*

	Original Definitions		New Definition
	1980	*1986*	*1986*
Total abuse	336,600	580,400	675,000
Physical	199,100	311,200	358,300
Sexual	42,900	138,000	155,900
Psychological	132,700	174,400	211,100
Total neglect	315,400	498,000	1,003,600
Physical	103,600	182,100	571,600
Psychological	56,900	52,200	223,100
Educational	174,000	291,100	292,100
Total abuse and neglect	652,000	1,078,400	1,678,600

SOURCE: National Center on Child Abuse and Neglect, 1988.
    *Subcategories may overlap.

reported cases of child abuse and neglect. According to their records, from 1976 to 1986 the estimated number of incidents more than doubled to over 2 million cases. Maltreatment rates rose from 10.1 reported cases to 32.8 per 1,000 U.S. children. The majority of cases, 55%, involved instances of neglect. The most vulnerable group were preschoolers, those age 0 to 5. Children under 5 years of age accounted for 43% of the cases. Two thirds of the children were white, while 18% were black and 11% were Hispanic. The number of reported incidents continues to climb. In 1989, there were 2.4 million reported cases of abuse or neglect (Children's Defense Fund, 1991), and the National Committee for Prevention of Child Abuse estimates that there were more than 2.6 million reported incidents in 1991 (U.S. General Accounting Office, 1992).

The nature of child maltreatment, particularly sexual abuse, carries the potential and tendency for cases not to be reported. The secretive nature and the power of adults over children keep many cases from being disclosed to authorities. Retrospective research on adults who were abused as children suggests that numerous cases of child maltreatment are never officially recognized (Starr, Dubowitz, & Bush, 1990). This suggests that the actual prevalence of child maltreatment may be greater than the reported numbers.

Reported incidents, although on the rise, are not alone conclusive of increased child abuse and neglect. The increase in reports could be due to greater publicity and awareness. For the Urban Institute, Ards and

Harrell (1991) examined the incidence data and restated the need to consider biases in reporting. The increase could be the result of several factors, alone or in combination: (a) more children are abused, (b) the recognition and identification of maltreatment of children have improved, and (c) the system for reporting suspected cases has improved. A review of numerous studies suggests that definitive data are not available because of the variability of factors such as public awareness and better reporting systems (Pecora, Whittaker, & Maluccio, 1992). However, based on the trends of the past two decades, the 1990s will witness continued growth in the reported incidence of child maltreatment. That growth will be significant. The CPS system needs to prepare for more reported incidents and increased severity of cases. Child abuse and neglect continue to be primary social problems facing today's child welfare workers.

The Role of Child Welfare Workers

The format for involvement of CPS agencies generally follows a similar pattern from state to state. Local public agencies are responsible for receiving all reports of suspected abuse and neglect. These reports come from the general populace and those mandated to report. Mandated reporters are professionals who, in the course of their work, may discover child maltreatment. Mandated reporters are set at the state level and may include school personnel, physicians, police officers, and other social service professionals. Child welfare workers must then follow up on each report in a timely manner.

Usually, each report is first screened through an intake process to determine if there is a need to send out an investigator. The decision and investigation usually occur within 24 hours of the report. A case record is made and the findings are documented. In many cases, the CPS worker develops a case plan and intervention services are provided under the direction of the agency. If legal action is required to protect a child, evidence must be gathered by CPS to substantiate the abuse or neglect in a court of law. Such protective cases go before the courts and a legal determination is made whether the allegation is true or not. Following the court hearing, a disposition is made that delineates the proposed services or action. See Figure 5.1 for the procedures in the State of Ohio.

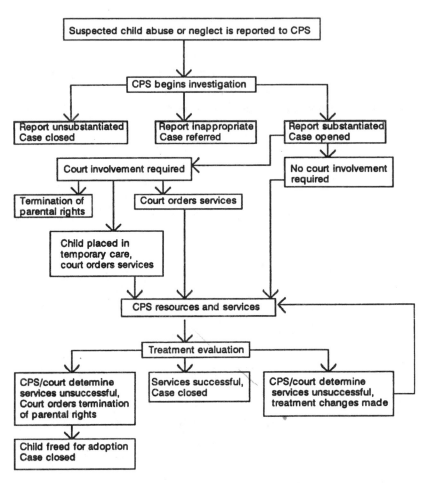

Figure 5.1. Processing Reported Cases of Abuse or Neglect
SOURCE: Adapted from the Ohio Department of Human Services (1988).

The responsibilities of CPS workers are numerous. The most pressing concern is the assessment of risk. Unfortunately, there is not agreement in the field about what exactly to look for and how to assess the risk of child abuse and neglect. Research suggests that CPS workers should consider multiple perspectives that include focusing on the caretaker and the environment, as well as the child, the family, and the interactions between them (McDonald & Marks, 1991). Assessing risk and determining the extent of state intervention require a number of skills that include:

- Interviewing adults, children, and other professionals
- Assessment of child and family needs
- Knowledge of treatment options
- Understanding of child development and the consequences of abuse and neglect
- Detection of the indicators of child maltreatment
- Ability to coordinate services
- Ongoing supervision and support of the child and family
- Understanding of the legal system
- Ability to follow bureaucratic procedures

Tasks must often be carried out over short periods of time and in hostile environments. The work of investigating child maltreatment, though considered necessary, is not highly regarded by society. Families are usually reluctant to have a child welfare worker investigate their private life, and even in cases where abuse has occurred, the children are often still closely aligned with the abusing adult. This creates a tense and stressful situation and can be extremely draining for CPS workers. Such pressures leave the CPS worker prone to burnout (Lewis, 1980). Due to the nature of child protection, it is important for workers to receive support, both professionally and personally, in order to remain effective on the job (Davis-Sacks, Jayrante, & Chess, 1985).

Much of the stress for CPS workers comes from the system within which they work. Recent research suggests that our nation's child welfare system is in disrepair due to a decline in resources and a shortage of qualified and trained personnel (Pecora, Briar, & Zlotnik, 1989). Only 28% of child welfare cases throughout this country are under the services of a professionally trained social worker (Lieberman, Hornby, & Russell, 1988). One child welfare worker reported to the authors that the CPS agency that hired her was so eager to place her on staff that they asked fewer questions than when she applied to work part time in a women's clothing store.

Almost three fourths of all child welfare cases are not handled by professionally trained social workers. Caseload size tends to be very high, ranging from 50 to 100 cases in many urban areas (U.S. House Subcommittee on Human Resources, 1989). This is in contrast to the Child Welfare League of America's recommended caseload standard of 17 cases per worker. The result is that CPS workers are having greater difficulty in carrying out timely investigations of abuse and neglect reports (Center for the Study of Social Policy, 1987).

The increase in child abuse and neglect cases, coupled with limited resources and personnel, are causes for concern for child welfare workers. Policies that are more supportive of CPS workers need to be developed. In addition, resources and programs must be expanded to deal effectively with the continuing problem of child maltreatment.

Indicators of Abuse and Neglect

The recognition of abuse and neglect is the necessary first step in dealing with the problem. The substantiation of abuse and neglect requires a working knowledge of the characteristics of maltreatment, normal child development, and an ability to gather evidence and put together a picture of what actually occurred between the child and an abusive or neglectful adult. Although identifiable characteristics can be listed, each case is unique. It is important to stress that any list of indicators represents a range of behaviors that possibly indicate the presence of child maltreatment. Cases must be investigated and thoroughly documented. The recognition of abuse and neglect ultimately rests with the knowledge, skills, and sensibilities of the CPS worker. Although not exhaustive, the following list outlines possible key indicators of child maltreatment (Gargiulo, 1990; National Center on Child Abuse and Neglect, 1980; Tower, 1989):

POSSIBLE INDICATORS OF PHYSICAL ABUSE

- Injuries such as bruises, burns, fractures, lacerations, and abrasions
- Head injuries
- Internal injuries determined through medical examination
- Passive behaviors
- Overly aggressive behaviors
- Fear of physical contact
- Acts frightened of parent or caregiver
- Verbal inhibition
- Regressive behaviors
- Absence of curiosity
- Reports of injury by parents or adults

POSSIBLE INDICATORS OF NEGLECT

- Abandonment
- Long periods without adult supervision
- Poor personal hygiene
- Inappropriate or inadequate clothing
- Lacking needed medical care
- Hunger, reports of frequent hunger
- Exhaustion, lethargy
- Poor academic performance, frequent school absences
- Delinquent behaviors

POSSIBLE INDICATORS OF SEXUAL ABUSE

- Injuries to genital, anal regions
- Torn, stained, or bloody undergarments
- Sexually transmitted diseases
- Swollen or red cervix, vulva, or perineum
- Early pregnancy

The presence of some or many of the above indicators may indicate the existence of child maltreatment. It is also necessary to consider the behaviors of the parents or caregiving adults and their interactions with the child. The following are some characteristics of maltreating adults:

CHARACTERISTICS OF ABUSIVE AND NEGLECTFUL ADULTS

- History of abuse or neglect as a child
- Use of excessively harsh discipline
- History of mental illness
- Lack of concern about the child
- Misuse of alcohol and/or drugs
- Chaotic home life
- Emotionally withholding, cold, rejecting
- Socially and/or geographically isolated

CHARACTERISTICS OF SEXUALLY ABUSIVE ADULTS

- History of sexual abuse as a child
- Protective or jealous of child

- Encourages child to engage in inappropriate sexual behaviors
- Experiencing marital difficulties
- Misuse of alcohol and/or drugs
- Socially and/or geographically isolated
- Frequent absence from the home

It is important to remember that listing indicators or characteristics alone does not indicate the presence of abuse or neglect. Investigation of the social environment and the behaviors of all those involved must be considered. Risk assessment must include: consideration of the age, personality, and development of the child; the psychological and social traits of the parents; the extent of the cooperation and capabilities of the parents; the behaviors of the perpetrator; the environment; and the potential for future harm (Tower, 1989).

Contributing Factors

There is a variety of theories that explain the causes of child maltreatment. The most plausible suggests that child maltreatment is the result of the interaction of a number of factors. However, the factors that contribute to abusive and neglectful behaviors are as varied as the number of cases and individuals affected. The psychological makeup and personality traits of the parents, the characteristics of the child, and environmental factors all interact and combine to result in occurrences of maltreatment (Biller & Solomon, 1986). The interaction of individual characteristics and environmental factors coalesce to produce an "ecology" of child maltreatment (Vondra, 1990). The ecological perspective takes into account forces both within and outside the family. It thus provides a comprehensive framework upon which to analyze the various factors that contribute to abusive and neglectful behaviors.

Child maltreatment can be found among all socioeconomic and cultural groups. Several studies have identified some significant contributing variables. Poverty, neighborhood dysfunction, substance abuse, mental health problems, and children with special needs are found in greater frequency in abusive families (U.S. Advisory Board on Child Abuse and Neglect, 1990). Other contributing variables include stressors such as unemployment, financial difficulties, isolation, and lack of social support (Videka-Sherman, 1991). Poverty, as discussed in the previous chapter, places tremendous stress on families and is found to a greater extent among young families and female-headed households. Poor families struggle to raise children with fewer resources and supports. Thus, they are more susceptible to the stress and effects of environmental contributors to abuse and neglect.

Social support is important to all families raising children. Isolation, lack of social support, and the subsequent belief that needed help is not available are significant contributors to the incidence of child abuse and neglect (Schorr, 1988). More women working, greater population mobility, and the erosion of a sense of community contribute to the decrease in informal supports. Without family and friends to turn to, the task of raising children is more difficult. The child welfare system becomes the only form of support for many families, and this system gets involved only when actual reports of maltreatment are made.

Consequences of Maltreatment

Human development builds on the experiences of childhood. Disciplines such as psychology, sociology, and anthropology have contributed research to attest to the power of childhood experience as a determinant of adult life. The relationship is true for both positive and negative experiences. Thus, in order to understand fully the impact of abuse and neglect it is important to consider the lasting effects of maltreatment on children.

Certainly many children are abused early in life and still mature to be stable and well-adjusted adults. However, maltreated children are more likely to experience negative outcomes as a result of abuse or neglect. The following is a general list of the consequences (American Academy of Child and Adolescent Psychiatry, 1990; Tower, 1989; Youngblade & Belsky, 1990):

- Poor self-image, low self-esteem
- Depression
- Suicidal thoughts and attempts
- Sleep and eating disorders
- Behavior extremes

- Delinquent and deviant behaviors
- Impulsiveness, inability to delay gratification
- Social withdrawal and avoidance
- Excessive anxiety
- Delayed cognitive, social, and emotional development
- Short attention span, inability to concentrate
- Frequent complaints of illness and physical discomfort
- Alcohol and/or drug abuse
- Sexual promiscuity
- Poor peer relationships
- Feelings of helplessness
- Lack of trust

The consequences of abuse and neglect are manifested in different ways when considered across age groups. Youngblade and Belsky (1990) provide an excellent review of what is known about the developmental effects of maltreatment on children. During infancy and toddlerhood, abused children tend to suffer insecure attachments to the primary caregiver, usually the mother. Such youngsters exhibit more aggressive behaviors; are avoidant of other children; less prosocial; and have difficulty showing concern, empathy, and sadness at distress in others. As maltreated children age, they exhibit generalized antisocial behaviors, have low self-esteem and poor self-concepts, are mistrustful and can be more dependent. They lack social skills and may externalize their feelings through aggressiveness and disobedience, or internalize through self-destructive and less social behaviors. By adolescence, the behaviors of childhood often are entrenched in a young person. Families of maltreated adolescents tend to be more enmeshed and chaotic. Abused adolescents exhibit more developmental delays. They are also more likely to mistreat their own offspring, having "successfully" learned the child-rearing techniques of their own parents.

Victims of sexual abuse are particularly susceptible to developing self-abusive and antisocial behaviors (Ralston, 1986). Many turn to drugs or alcohol or run away to escape an unbearable situation. Depression, low self-esteem, and self-hate are all too common. Sexual abuse, particularly incest, during childhood often leads a person to become promiscuous as a teenager or adult. The potential for sexual exploitation is increased. Studies of adults who were sexually abused as children found they were more vulnerable to stress, psychiatric and personality disorders, and severe depression (Bagley & Young, 1990).

Policies and Programs

The lasting effects of abuse and neglect are varied. Critical factors include the personality of the child, the duration and frequency of the maltreatment, and the degree of social and emotional supports available to the child while growing up. The continued existence of child abuse and neglect and the growth in the incidence have given rise to the development of intervention strategies and mandated policies to serve those in need.

Intervention Strategies

Successful intervention requires a comprehensive strategy. Four key elements are identified for effective intervention with victims of child maltreatment: a wide range of services providing different types of support, coordination of those services, a service plan that builds on the strengths of a family rather than focus on the weaknesses, and concurrent efforts for the prevention of abuse and neglect.

The identification, report, and assessment of child maltreatment are the beginning phases of intervention. These initial steps lead to the involvement of CPS workers. The next phase of intervention includes judicial involvement, protection, and treatment (Gemmill, 1990). Because of the dynamic nature and uniqueness of each case, interventions should be flexible and closely monitored. Although this is the ideal, the reality is often otherwise. As discussed previously, the resources and personnel available to work with victimized children and their families are inadequate and overtaxed. In spite of these barriers, there are a number of proven strategies and programs providing needed services.

There are three types of intervention. The first is to provide services to identified cases of abuse and neglect, the second is to provide preventive services to families most at risk for maltreatment, and the third is to provide supportive services to all families, regardless of level of risk. The identification of abuse and neglect stresses immediate protection and the cessation of maltreatment. Intervention for families at risk for maltreatment include strategies that provide social support, therapeutic services for the child and family, parenting skills training, and that minimize isolation. Taking a preventive approach targets all families and includes support services, parenting skills training, and school-based programs. Preventive intervention also stresses public education about child maltreatment and how to prevent it from occurring.

Community intervention strategies can reduce the incidence of abuse. Darmstadt (1990) found that parent education and home visitation services can enhance the relationship between parent and child, teach parenting skills, and provide social supports. These strategies help parents to cope better with the stresses of child rearing and can reduce the occurrence of child abuse. Other effective interventions include home-based services, peer support groups, lay counseling, and family and group therapy (Dubowitz, 1990). While the immediate concern is to protect the child, efforts to change the abusive situation must include the entire family system. Effective and successful services thus focus on family intervention.

The majority of services provided are targeted toward cases of already identified abuse and neglect. Though this approach is certainly important, without preventive efforts abuse and neglect will continue and the incidence will grow. The key components of successful prevention programs are early intervention in the family, service delivery through community centers or health care settings to minimize stigma, services that stress parent-child interaction, and parent education components (Videka-Sherman, 1991).

Programs and services that address the problem of child maltreatment are a significant part of the nation's child welfare system. The current state of child welfare is one of limited resources and growing needs. Emphasis is placed on crisis intervention and not prevention. In order to truly have an impact on the incidence of child abuse and neglect and improve the lives of millions of children, greater efforts must be directed toward the prevention of maltreatment. A large-scale preventive approach calls for an understanding of the current policies that legislate child welfare programs and services.

Child Protection Legislation

Direct federal involvement in child abuse and neglect occurred with the enactment of the Child Abuse Prevention and Treatment Act of 1974 (P.L. 93-247). Until that time, services were provided at state discretion and varied greatly. Most states placed child abuse services at low priority and reserved limited resources for investigation, treatment, and prevention (Society for Research in Child Development, 1984).

Passage of federal legislation in 1974 was the culmination of increased public and professional awareness. In large part, Congress was alerted to the problem of child maltreatment as a result of the previously discussed "rediscovery" of the battered child syndrome in the 1960s. In 1971 the Senate created the Subcommittee on Children and Youth, and the committee began to press for legislation aimed at preventing child maltreatment. In response to fiscal restraints and political pressures, the result was an incremental approach (Hoffman, 1978). The bill established a modest program of monetary support and technical assistance to states, and provided funds for research and demonstration programs.

As a result of the Child Abuse Prevention and Treatment Act the National Center on Child Abuse and Neglect (NCCAN) was created. NCCAN was designed to encourage research and data collection on child maltreatment and to serve as a national information clearinghouse. Currently, the Act provides state grants for programs to prevent and treat child abuse and neglect and family violence; for training and technical assistance; and to improve the investigation, handling, and prosecution of cases. States must meet certain criteria in order to qualify for federal funds. These criteria include the implementation of state laws regulating the reporting of child abuse and neglect, demonstrated procedures for training personnel and developing facilities to handle maltreatment cases, legal representation for victims, and the assurance of confidentiality.

Federal funding for activities under the Child Abuse Prevention and Treatment Act grew from $4.5 million in 1974 to $22.9 million in 1980. However, funds were cut 30% in the early 1980s as a result of Reagan administration policies focused on lessening federal involvement in domestic care. By 1989, funding had been restored to earlier levels with $25.4 million appropriated for services under the Act (Robinson, 1989).

Additional funds for the protection of children are provided through Titles IV-B and XX of the Social Security Act. Title IV-B, Child Welfare Services, authorizes state use of funds for serving children in need. Title XX provides for social services and can include the expenditure of funds on programs related to the prevention and treatment of child maltreatment. There are no requirements for states to report specific usage of the funds and programs are left to state discretion. The vast majority of Title

IV-B dollars are spent for foster care, while only 10%, or $270 million in 1989, of Title XX funds are spent for child welfare services (Robinson, 1989). Overall, federal support for the prevention and treatment of child abuse and neglect has not been overwhelming. The bulk of responsibility rests with states, where there is great variability and local discretion.

Summary

Unfortunately, the abuse and neglect of children in this country is not a new problem. Over the past 20 years, the adverse effects of child maltreatment have gained national recognition and response. All states have reporting laws and child protective services systems. Federal efforts and funds are earmarked for treatment and prevention, in addition to state services. However, federal efforts have focused predominantly on treatment rather than prevention of maltreatment according to analysis of current programs by the U.S. General Accounting Office (1992).

More children are reported to be abused and neglected each year. Although many current strategies seem to be effective, new policies and programs with an expanded scope are needed. Such an approach must include the prevention of abuse and neglect, as well as the treatment.

6

When the State Intervenes

Foster Care, Adoption, and Permanency Planning

The state assumes responsibility for the care of children when parents are judged unwilling or unable to provide care. Studies of the foster care system revealed that children could spend long periods of time in substitute care and experience multiple living arrangements. In an attempt to correct many of the problems in foster care, major federal legislation was enacted in 1980.

This chapter examines the foster care system and the characteristics of children most likely to be placed by the state. The effectiveness of the 1980 reform efforts are evaluated.

Foster care and adoption are the most well-recognized and traditional child welfare practices as well as the most researched services provided by social welfare organizations. These services employ large numbers of child welfare professionals and receive attention from media and politicians. This chapter examines the complex policy and practice issues related to these residual services.

Foster Care

Relatively few of the millions of children reported to public child welfare agencies are placed in foster care. States are now required to provide services to families in order to help the family remain together.

When these services fail or needed services are not provided, the child may be placed in foster care.

Incidence of Placement

Foster care is intended to be a temporary service for troubled families in which children receive substitute care while their parents receive services. A child welfare professional plans and coordinates these services with the ultimate goal of returning the child to the parents. If this cannot be accomplished in a specific period of time, generally 18 months, then another plan for providing stability to the child is implemented. Although this is the intent of foster care, it is not always achieved.

The numbers of children entering and leaving care over the years has fluctuated considerably. During the mid-1970s, the foster care population was estimated to be 500,000. It dropped in the early 1980s and began climbing again in the late 1980s. From 1986 to 1989, the foster care population increased 29% from 280,000 to 360,000 (Committee on Ways and Means, 1991). This is equivalent to approximately 4.8 children in foster care per 1,000 children. At the end of 1992, the foster care population was estimated to be 440,000, an increase in excess of 50% since 1986 (Pelton, 1993).

The exact number of children in care is unknown. In 1986, the federal government, through Public Law 99-509, sought to establish a national information system within 5 years. Due to funding problems, however, its implementation was delayed. Using other sources such as data from state and private welfare agencies it is possible to estimate the number of children in care although the estimates are subject to error.

Reliance upon foster care as a child welfare service varies substantially among the states. There are 10 states that account for 55% of all children in foster care (see Table 6.1) and two states (New York and California) account for one third of the national foster care population (Committee on Ways and Means, 1991).

Characteristics of Placement

Foster care was designed to be a temporary service. In some circumstances, children spend years in foster care. The length of time children spend in substitute care should depend on individual characteristics and needs of the children and their families. If this were accurate, then there

TABLE 6.1 Foster Care Population by State

	Fiscal Year	
State	*1986*	*1989*
California	47,327	66,763
Florida	6,802	7,544
Georgia	9,311	13,325
Illinois	14,472	19,276
Massachusetts	7,546	10,284
Michigan	8,566	11,303[a]
New Jersey	6,597	8,798
New York	27,504	52,198
Ohio	11,966	14,200
Pennsylvania	14,685	15,416

SOURCE: Committee on Ways and Means, 1991.
NOTE: a. Data is for FY 1988.

should be relatively little variability among the states. However, length of time in care seems to be influenced by geography. In 1986, the average length of stay in foster care was 9.3 months in Oregon, 12.7 months in South Carolina, 19.1 months in Georgia, and 24.1 months in Texas (U.S. General Accounting Office, 1991b).

Not only is foster care to be a time-limited service, it should involve a minimal number of placements. For some children, foster care can be a lengthy experience with multiple placements. For example, national data for 1985 indicate that:

1. 27% of the children had been in care more than 3 years
2. 15% had been in care for 5 or more years
3. 50% experienced at least two placements
4. 21% had three to five placements
5. 6% had six or more placements (U.S. General Accounting Office, 1989b)

Prior to the 1980s, very young children comprised a small percentage of the foster care population. School age children were most likely to enter foster care. This may have been a reflection of the reporting laws and the incidence of referrals from public schools. Of the children entering care in 1987, however, 34% were adolescents, 37% were 5 or younger, and children under the age of 1 accounted for 12% of the entering population (Committee on Ways and Means, 1991).

The age distribution of children in care varies by state although the reasons for these variations are unclear. In 1986, one third of the children entering care in New York City, Los Angeles, and Georgia were under the age of 3 while only 15% of the children entering care in Oregon fell into this age group (U.S. General Accounting Office, 1991b).

The two primary reasons children enter substitute care are neglect and abuse. More than 70% of the children in care in 1987 had been placed for their own protection (from abuse) or because their parents were absent or unable to provide adequate care. The remaining 30% had been placed due to behavior problems (delinquency or status offense) and other reasons (Committee on Ways and Means, 1991).

Foster care serves primarily poor children and their families. However, poverty should not be the basis for removing children from their parents' care. The First White House Conference on Children in 1909 issued a statement opposing the breaking up of families for reasons of poverty alone. The majority of children in foster care come from families supported by AFDC (Committee on Ways and Means, 1991). Poverty is, at the least, a contributing factor to child placement (Pelton, 1989). Half of the children in care in South Carolina entered because their parents could not provide food, clothing, shelter, or medical care (U.S. General Accounting Office, 1991b).

Minority Children

Minority children are at an elevated risk for placement and are likely to spend more time in care than are white children. Minority children comprise 46% of the foster care population (Committee on Ways and Means, 1991). In 1986, more than 40% of the children entering care in New York City, Georgia, and South Carolina were African American (U.S. General Accounting Office, 1991b). This pattern is reversed when examining the race of children leaving care. More than half (55.4%) of the children leaving care in 1987 were white, and 26.5% were African American (Committee on Ways and Means, 1991).

Native American children have been particularly vulnerable to out-of-home placement and adoption by non-Indians. The situation was so serious that federal legislation was enacted in an attempt to keep these children in their communities. The Indian Child Welfare Act of 1978 (Public Law 95-608) granted jurisdiction to tribal courts over most child custody cases.

The National Black Child Development Institute (NBCDI) surveyed more than 1,000 children during a 2½-year period in five cities in 1986. This survey also found significant differences by city. For example, children remained in care an average of 14 months in Seattle and 24 months in New York. Other major findings included:

- 65% of the children came from families supported by AFDC
- 49% of the children were 5 years old or younger
- the mean age of the mothers was 29 years
- 55% of the children were discharged to a parent
- the leading reason for placement was neglect
- children averaged 2.2 placements [National Black Child Development Institute (NBCDI), 1989]

The caretakers of these children faced multiple problems. Drug abuse was reported in 36% of the population, 30% had inadequate housing, 8% were homeless, and 41% suffered from mental illness (NBCDI, 1989).

The Neglected Foster Child

The state becomes the substitute caretaker for children after they have been removed from the custody of their parents. In too many instances the state has been a neglectful caretaker.

The process of removal from the home of parents can be a stressful experience for children. Not only do they leave their parents, they may also be separated from their siblings. Placement can mean a change of neighborhoods. This results in a loss of friends, neighbors, and school. Infants are sensitive to changes in caretakers and older children can find the experience traumatic. The children have already been subject to some type of maltreatment. They may be required to appear in courts (both criminal courts and family or juvenile courts). The children may be interviewed by law enforcement, school staff, caseworkers, attorneys, judges, counselors, medical personnel, and foster parents.

The Multiple Needs of Foster Children

Maltreated children can suffer from physical, academic, and emotional problems (Wodarski, Kurtz, Gaudin, & Howing, 1990). A survey of 149 children entering care in the Chicago area revealed that 20% had a cardiovascular problem, 12% an ophthalmologic disorder, 25% a dermatological abnormality, 20% a neuromuscular problem, and 24% a developmental delay (Hochstadt, Jaudes, Zimo, & Schacter, 1987). Maltreated children are overrepresented among children with learning problems (Frisch & Rhoads, 1982) and are more likely to be referred for special education services (Runyon & Gould, 1985).

Foster care represents an opportunity to assess and provide needed services to vulnerable children. Most children who enter care are victims of abuse or neglect. These events can interfere with growth and development. The maltreated child may be at an elevated risk of mental health problems, such as depression and aggression (Grey, 1984). In order to determine if a child needs services the child must be evaluated. Evaluation is not standard practice. The NBCDI study reported that:

1. 80% of children 5 years old and younger had no record of a psychological or developmental assessment,
2. 12% of the school age children were reported as "below average," or not functioning at grade level,
3. 59% of the case records of 6- to 12-year-olds and 44% of 13- to 18-year-olds lacked a mental health assessment, and
4. 5% of the records contained no information on the health status of the child.

Foster children seem to be at an elevated risk of academic problems (Gustavsson, 1991b). Less than 30% of adolescents in placement graduate from high school or earn a general equivalency diploma; and 30% of foster children are at grade level by the 12th grade compared to 70% of children living at home (Cook & Ansell, 1986).

New threats to the physical health of children, such as drug exposure and acquired immunodeficiency syndrome (AIDS), adds to the need to provide health care for foster children. More handicapped children are entering care although the reasons for this increase are unclear (U.S. General Accounting Office, 1991b).

Perhaps the saddest threat to the well-being of foster children can come from foster parents. Although the overwhelming majority of foster parents are dedicated, caring people, performing a difficult job with little remuneration or appreciation, there are some who abuse and even kill their foster children. Such abuse is a major source of stress for child welfare workers who remove children from parents because of neglect, especially poverty-related neglect, and then place the children in foster homes where the children should be safe.

Obtaining accurate statistics on the incidence of foster parent abuse can be a challenge. Most child abuse central registries run by the states have some data. Foster parents are the reported abusers in 0.5% of child abuse reports (Russell & Trainor, 1984). An Arizona study reported that 7% of the foster care population is abused by foster parents (Bolton, Laner, & Gai, 1981).

Liability for Harmful Foster Care

Child welfare agencies are generally not legally responsible when children are injured by their parents, even in instances in which the child welfare agency knew or should have known of the risk of such injury (*DeShaney v. Winnebago County Department of Social Services*, 1989). If the child is in foster care, however, the state may be held accountable.

Courts have held child welfare agencies responsible for the abuse and neglect of foster children. When children are removed from their parents, they become dependent upon the child welfare agency. This special relationship between foster children and the agency requires the agency to protect and serve the children. When agencies fail to do this, they risk violating federal law and may have to pay monetary damages to children hurt by the foster care system.

In *Taylor v. Ledbetter* (1989), a child suffered severe and permanent injuries as a result of beatings by the foster mother. The 11th Circuit Court of Appeals ruled that if the agency was grossly negligent or deliberately indifferent, liability could be imposed. In another Maryland case, *L. J. By and Through Darr v. Massinga*, 1989, the state settled out of court by establishing a trust fund for each of five children who were injured while in foster care. Each of the children suffered either physical, emotional, or sexual abuse; neglect; malnutrition; and bizarre punishments.

The Costs of Care

Foster care is an expensive system. However, obtaining exact information on the cost is difficult. This is due to the complex funding mechanism. There is no single federal foster care program. Each state also contributes funds to foster care. Foster care in the United States is estimated to cost more than 3.5 billion dollars a year (Besharov, 1984).

There are three primary sources of federal funds. In 1980, Congress created a new program, Title IV-E. Funds were provided to the states to maintain AFDC-eligible children in substitute care, pay for administration costs, and fund data collection efforts. In fiscal year 1990, $1.2 billion was authorized for Title IV-E.

Another title of the Social Security Act, IV-B, funds an array of child welfare services such as preventing placement of children and costs associated with reuniting placed children with their families. In 1990, $253 million was authorized. How much of this money went for foster care services is unknown. The federal contribution is 75%, states provide the remaining 25%.

The third source of funds is Title XX, the Social Services Block Grant. This program funds a number of social welfare services, such as institutional placements for children when needed, services to protect children from abuse and neglect, and preventing inappropriate placements. It is unknown what portion of Title XX funds are spent on foster care. For 1988, it is estimated that states spent $500 million or 20% of the $2.7 billion appropriated for general child welfare services, including foster care (U.S. General Accounting Office, 1989b).

Billions of dollars are being spent in the foster care system; however, the direct providers of care see very little money. Rates vary by state and by age of child. Generally, payment for adolescents exceeds payment for younger children. Payments may increase if the child has a serious medical or emotional problem. Most state board and care rates range between $200 to $300 per month (American Public Welfare Association, 1988).

Foster parents are poorly paid for the services they perform. In some states, the cost of keeping a dog in a kennel for a month exceeds the monthly foster care payment. Of the federal dollars spent on foster care, about half goes to maintaining a child (U.S. House of Representatives, 1990). The remainder is spent on administrative costs.

Although foster care is expensive, there are other types of substitute care that are more expensive. On average, states spend about $10 per day (for board and care) to maintain a child in foster care. A residential facility averages between $100 and $300 per day (U.S. House of Representatives, 1990).

Permanency Planning

The foster care system is expensive and represents a threat to the well-being of some children, even though it helps other children. Studies of children reared in foster care reveal that they generally do as well as their non-foster-home-reared cohort (Shostack & Quane, 1988). There are some children who are poorly served by foster care. The problems in foster care have been well documented for decades (Mass & Engler, 1954). Some foster children are denied permanent or secure homes. They experience multiple placements and are rarely placed for adoption. Children in placement are entitled to permanent, stable homes. In 1980, the federal government acted to reform the foster care system and provide children permanent homes.

Uncertainty in Foster Care

Prior to federal legislation in 1980, many children were adrift in the foster care system. If they were not reunited with their families within 18 months of entering the system, their chances of ever being reunited were greatly reduced (Mass & Engler, 1959). If they did not have visitation with their families regularly, their chances of returning home were significantly diminished. This continues to be the case today. Only half of the children who had regular visitation in 1986 were in care for more than one year, compared to 90% who received infrequent visits (U.S. General Accounting Office, 1991b).

The longer the children remained in care, the greater the likelihood of multiple placements (Fanshel & Shinn, 1978). The median length of stay in care was 31 months in 1977, and toddlers entering New York City's foster care system were spending an average of 7 years in foster care (Fanshel, 1979). In the mid-1970s, half a million children were in foster care, some without any plan for a permanent home. The foster care system of the 1970s was marked by serious problems. In the 1980s, intensive reform efforts began.

Billions of dollars were being spent to maintain large numbers of children, many of whom would be in care for protracted periods, moving from placement to placement, lost in a system that had no plan for providing them long-term, secure homes. This was the background to the federal attempt to reform the foster care system.

Public Law 96-272

Using money as the incentive, the federal government required states to improve their child welfare service delivery system or lose federal reimbursement. The Adoption Assistance and Child Welfare Act was signed into law on June 17, 1980. It required states to:

1. develop a statewide information system that would include information on the location, characteristics, and placement goals for each child,
2. conduct an inventory of children in care and determine if placement is necessary and appropriate,
3. develop a written case plan that includes services needed by the child, parents, and foster parents,
4. review the status of each child every 6 months and hold a dispositional hearing no later than 18 months after the original placement to determine a permanent plan, and
5. protect the due process right of children, parents, and foster parents.

There were other provisions in the law, such as requiring states to make reasonable efforts to prevent the removal of children (although *reasonable* was not defined). Children were to be placed in the least restrictive placement and in proximity to their parents. Nationally, fewer children are being placed in institutions although there are wide differences across states. There has been little improvement in meeting the goal of placement proximity and in some areas more than 40% of children are placed out of county (U.S. General Accounting Office, 1989b).

In addition to altering child welfare practices, the law also changed adoption practices. States were now authorized to provide adoption subsidies in order to encourage adoption. The subsidies are used to offset some of the costs associated with adoption and do not exceed foster care payment rates. Prior to this change, adoption meant an end to state support for children. The adoptive parents assumed total financial responsibility. Some states had adoption subsidy programs prior to the federal law in an attempt to encourage the adoption of special needs children. Older children, sibling groups, minority children, and children with medical, physical, emotional, and mental conditions are considered special needs.

The law removed some of the traditional barriers to adoption, such as a lack of money and lack of clear laws. Subsidies can make adoption more realistic. The costs associated with rearing a medically fragile child,

TABLE 6.2 Permanency Goals for Foster Children, 1987

Goal	Percentage
Reunification	53.7
Long-term foster care	15.9
Adoption	15.1
Guardianship	3.6
Other/unknown	11.7

SOURCE: Committee on Ways and Means, 1991.

for example, are exorbitant. The 18-month dispositional hearing requires the courts to impose a permanent plan for a child and adoption is one such plan. Historically, actions to free children from the custody of their parents occurred sporadically and could be lengthy. The law now encourages actions to free children for adoption more quickly.

Permanent Plans

In an attempt to prevent foster care drift and to give children a stable living arrangement, the law authorized four types of permanent plans and prioritized the plans. The first plan is return to the parent. If this cannot be achieved, then adoption must be considered. If adoption is not feasible, then guardianship or long-term foster care are evaluated.

Reunification is the goal for the majority of children in care (see Table 6.2). However, long-term foster care was the second most common permanency goal in 1987. This is in conflict with the law's preference for adoption. The NBCDI (1989) study reported similar results. Reunification with mother or another relative was the goal for 59% of the sample. Adoption was the goal for 17% of the children.

Requiring courts to order permanent plans for children does not guarantee stability. There has been considerable research on the permanence of permanent plans, and the results are cause for concern. A minority of children return to the foster care system after receiving a permanent plan. For some children in care, stability continues to be an elusive goal.

Although successful for the majority, reunification is an unstable experience for some children. Children are entering foster care, reunifying, and then entering foster care again. Of the children reunified with their families in 1986, 27% reentered foster care, although this varies by state (U.S. General Accounting Office, 1991b). Texas reported a 12% reentry rate and Illinois reported a 26% rate. Other studies report reentry rates of 27% to 32% (Block & Libowitz, 1983; Wald, Carlsmith, & Liederman, 1988). These rates are high and suggest that:

1. the problems in the family were of such a serious nature that reunification may have an inappropriate goal, or
2. the families were poorly prepared for the return of the child, or
3. aftercare services are needed.

A more stable type of permanent plan is adoption. Studies on disruption in adoption report widely differing rates. Disruption rates for older or troubled children are higher than for younger children. A California survey reported an 11% disruption rate (Barth & Berry, 1988). A New York study reported an 8.2% rate (Festinger, 1986). Other studies have indicated rates as high as 23% (Boyne, Denby, Kettenring, & Wheeler, 1984) to 31% (Fein, Davies, & Knight, 1979). The disruption rate for adoption is about one half the rate for reunification.

There are few studies on the stability of guardianship (Fein, Maluccio, Hamilton, & Ward, 1983). Guardianship can be viewed as a compromised adoption in which the child's ties to the parent do not have to be broken and the guardian assumes additional legal responsibility such as being able to consent to medical care. The guardian does not become the parent (as is the case in adoption) and the child has no right to inheritance.

Long-term foster care, the permanency goal for more than 15% of the children in care, is the least stable. Recidivism rates are high. As many as 50% of the long-term foster care placements disrupt (Fein et al., 1983; Stone & Stone, 1983). Although stability is difficult to achieve for some youngsters, the majority of children experience stability when returned to their families or adopted. Nevertheless, the foster care system can be improved to provide more stability.

Intensive Services

Foster care is a residual service and now must deal with increasing complex and difficult problems such as parental drug use and prenatal drug exposure. Rather than waiting until the child has been removed before providing services, the Adoption Assistance and Child Welfare Act required states to make reasonable efforts to keep families together. These efforts can be classified as intensive family preservation or home-based services. There are several models of such services.

For example, family preservation programs are characterized by prompt, highly intensive services usually delivered in the home for a brief period of time and are offered to families experiencing serious problems. The goals include protecting the children, strengthening the family bonds, increasing the family's skills, stabilizing the crisis, preventing the placement of the children, and helping the family to use formal and informal resources (Tracy, Haapala, Kinney, & Pecora, 1991).

Evaluations of intensive family services incorporate multiple measures of success. In a study of a matched group, families in the intensive group had a placement rate of 44% compared with an 85% rate for families receiving traditional services (Pecora, Fraser, & Haapala, 1990). Other variables such as children's school performance, family relationships, and emotional climate all improve with intensive services (National Resource Center on Family Based Services, 1988).

Home-based services can have a high per client cost. When compared to the cost of foster care or residential treatment, however, intensive services provided in the home are less expensive. For example, Homebuilders is one model of intensive family services and has a per client cost of $2,600. In the state of Washington, foster care costs about $370 a month. Over a 12-month period the cost of keeping a child in foster care would be $4,440. The per month cost of residential care averages more than $2,000 a month, and one month in an acute psychiatric hospital costs more than $11,000 (Kinney, Haapala, Booth, & Leavitt, 1991).

Changing Adoption Practices

Public Law 96-272 encouraged a new relationship between child protection and placement agencies and adoption agencies. Adoption is particularly vulnerable to environmental changes. A number of factors combined to reduce the supply of white healthy babies at the same time the demand for these children was increasing. The Adoption Assistance Act gave new life to many adoption agencies by providing a steady supply of children. Many of these children, however, were viewed as unadoptable in the past. A redefinition of this term has occurred making more children available for adoption and allowing adults to adopt who previously did not meet adoption agency standards.

The adoption subsidy, which in some states is not need based, allows adults with limited incomes to adopt. Foster parent adoptions are becoming more common. Adoption of older children and special needs children requires agencies to offer postplacement services in order to ensure the success of these adoptions. Adoption agencies now actively recruit minority adults, and single parent adoptions are no longer rare. Research indicates that special needs children fare well in their adoptive homes (Berry & Barth, 1989).

The demand for infants has not diminished, however, and new methods of meeting this need are developing. International adoption remains an option for some couples. Children from Asia, South America, and Romania are ideal candidates. Details on how the children are procured are sometimes vague. Questions can arise about the circumstances of parental consent to the adoption (Herrmann & Kasper, 1992).

Advances in medical technology, and infertility technology in particular, are presenting new challenges to the field of adoption. It is now possible for a child to have five parents: an egg donor, a sperm donor, a woman in whom the fertilized egg is implanted, and the couple who will rear the child. This technology is relatively new and the courts and legislatures will have to develop new definitions of *parent* as they try to balance the rights and needs of the various parties. There is a demand for children that exceeds the supply.

Summary

Children enter foster care when efforts to keep them with their families fail. The foster care system serves some children well, and studies of children reared in foster care reveal they do as well as their non-foster-home-reared cohort (Shostack & Quane, 1988). Nevertheless, the system is expensive, and it is harmful to some children. New challenges are taxing public child welfare as children and their families experience more frequent, intense, and intractable problems.

Research has consistently demonstrated the utility of services for both children and their families, yet services remain infrequent (NBCDI, 1989; U.S. General Accounting Office, 1989b). Such services minimize the need for placement and can stabilize permanent plans by reducing the frequency of disruption in reunification and adoption. Attempts to reform foster care and implement permanency planning have had limited success for some children. Permanence and stability remain elusive goals for some children.

PART III

New Threats to Children

Social, economic, and political changes of the 1980s contributed to a worsening of existing problems. The unwillingness of political leaders to respond adequately to the new threats to children has placed a substantial minority of children at risk. Concurrent with these new problems has been a shift from federal to local responsibility. The three chapters illustrate areas of increasing vulnerability within the context of the social, economic, and political changes of the past decade.

7

HIV and Chemical Exposure

In the 1980s, attention was focused on children at risk because of parental chemical use. Beliefs about the incidence and consequences of maternal drug use supported punitive policies such as criminal prosecution of pregnant drug-using women.

Acquired immune deficiency syndrome (AIDS) was first identified in the 1980s. The virus that causes it is acquired through contact with contaminated bodily fluids such as semen and blood. Intravenous drug use by pregnant women places both the woman and her unborn child at risk for this infection. In the early 1980s, a few dozen children were diagnosed with AIDS. By the end of the decade, thousands of children were diagnosed with AIDS.

This chapter examines the incidence and consequences of maternal drug use and critiques the policies developed to deal with this problem. The issues associated with AIDS in children and adolescents are explored, and the response of the child welfare system is analyzed. Alternative policies are outlined.

During the past decade, two serious threats to the physical and emotional well-being of children emerged. Chemical dependency and HIV (human immunodeficiency virus) infection are relatively new threats and adversely influence the health of children of all ages, from the fetus to the adolescent. Chemical abuse and HIV infection are preventable. Prevention is particularly important in HIV infection because options for effective treatment are limited. The costs of failing to prevent these problems are exceedingly high. Maternal chemical abuse can threaten the health of the fetus. The pregnant intravenous drug user places both herself and her fetus at risk for HIV infection. Transmission during the perinatal period is the primary method of HIV infection in infants.

This chapter examines the frequency and consequences of these threats, critiques the services available to assist children and their families as they cope with chemical use and HIV infection, and proposes policy and service strategies to help families affected by chemical use and HIV infection. The residual response to these two potentially devastating events has been inadequate. Services are frequently nonexistent or fragmentary and uncoordinated. Advocacy efforts must focus on designing and implementing comprehensive preventive policies and services.

Defining Chemical Use

The mental health literature of the past few decades reflects an evolution in thought about chemical use. The classic distinction between addiction (a physical/medical condition) and dependency (an emotional/ psychological condition) has not proved useful. Psychiatric nomenclature now uses the term *psychoactive substance use disorder* to describe a cluster of cognitive, behavioral, and physiologic symptoms that indicate a person has impaired control of a psychoactive substance and continues using the substance despite adverse consequences (American Psychiatric Association, 1987, p. 166).

There are a large number of substances that can be abused. Alcohol, marijuana, and cocaine are three of the substances discussed in this chapter. Nicotine is the most commonly used chemical by women and can pose a threat to the health of the developing fetus. There is evidence to suggest that nicotine use by pregnant women results in below normal birth weight babies (Office on Smoking and Health, 1988).

Opioids (heroin and methadone) are briefly reviewed. The intravenous use of heroin or other drugs places infants at double risk. Intravenous drug use is a major method of HIV transmission. Perinatal exposure to heroin has been associated with a number of short- and long-term negative consequences. The use of these drugs by pregnant women and adolescents, in particular, is cause for concern.

Incidence of Chemical Use

Data collected by the National Institute on Drug Abuse (NIDA) indicate that a significant number of Americans use mood altering substances. NIDA is the most frequently relied upon source for drug use statistics. NIDA regularly surveys a representative sample of households and high school seniors. NIDA also collects data from medical facilities of drug-related medical emergencies. Using these three sources of data, incidence of drug use is estimated. Caution should be used when relying on NIDA data. Groups with a high incidence of drug use, such as the homeless and people living in group settings (jails, prisons, college dormitories), are excluded from the household survey and young people not attending the 12th grade are excluded from the high school seniors survey.

Marijuana is the most commonly used illicit drug for all age and racial groups. NIDA (National Institute on Drug Abuse [NIDA], 1989b) estimates that 11.6 million Americans had used marijuana in the 30 days prior to the survey (termed *current usage*). Alcohol, a legal drug, continues to be the most commonly used mood altering drug with more than 100 million current users. Data from the high school seniors survey indicate that 70% of white seniors used alcohol at least once in the 30-day period prior to the survey while 41% of blacks had used alcohol in the same time frame (NIDA, 1989b). Cocaine and "crack," a smokable, inexpensive derivative of cocaine, have received much attention. Fifteen percent of the population has tried cocaine, and 5 million Americans reportedly use cocaine regularly (Abelson & Miller, 1985). Of the regular users, 40% (2 million) are estimated to be women of childbearing age.

Just how many infants are exposed prenatally to mood altering chemicals is unknown, and estimates of the number vary widely. The lack of data on the incidence of chemical exposure is a serious problem. In order to develop services it is necessary to have an estimate of the number of people needing the service and the characteristics of these potential service recipients.

Most of the incidence surveys are conducted at large hospitals in urban areas that serve primarily poor minority women. A survey at Boston City Hospital, for example, reported that 27% of the mothers using the prenatal clinic had used marijuana and 18% had used cocaine while pregnant (Zuckerman et al., 1989). A 17% incidence rate for cocaine by women using prenatal care services was reported at another urban hospital (Frank et al., 1988).

The highest figure given for substance use by pregnant women is the result of a survey of 36 hospitals (Chasnoff, 1989). Substances were defined as heroin, methadone, cocaine, PCP, amphetamines, and marijuana. The average rate of incidence was 11%. If this 11% applies to all births, then more than 375,000 children are exposed prenatally to illicit chemicals. There are questions about this study that make extrapolating to the entire country questionable. The sample size, 36 hospitals, is small. Most of the hospitals were located in urban areas. The broad definition of chemicals served to elevate incidence rate. These factors limit the usefulness of the study.

A 1990 (Chasnoff, Landress, & Barrett) study of one county in Florida reported an overall drug use rate of 14% for women using both public health clinics and private obstetrical offices. Drugs were defined as alcohol, opiates, cocaine, and marijuana. Incidence rates for black and white women and for women using public and private clinics were similar. Black women were more likely to test positive for cocaine than were white women (7.5% vs. 1.8%). White women were more likely to test positive for marijuana than were black women (14.4% vs. 6%). However, black women were 10 times more likely to be reported to state authorities for chemical use than were white women.

Although the actual incidence of chemical use by pregnant women is unknown, there is some empirical evidence as well as anecdotal evidence to suggest that tens of thousands of infants are exposed prenatally to mood altering chemicals. There are thousands of older children whose caretakers may be suffering from a chemical abuse problem. Child welfare agencies may not routinely record the presence nor the contribution of parental chemical abuse to family problems such as child abuse and neglect. Even without accurate statistics, a substantial number of children are at risk due to parental chemical abuse.

Effects of Prenatal Chemical Exposure

Conventional wisdom dictates that chemical use by a pregnant woman is harmful to her fetus. Giving a newborn alcohol or an illicit chemical, for example, would be interpreted as an act of child abuse. Child abuse and fetal harm are two separate issues and the evidence to support the notion that perinatal chemical exposure is harmful is incomplete.

Much of the research that examines the effects of prenatal chemical exposure is flawed. Sample sizes are frequently small. Samples are rarely representative of the larger population when they are selected from only one location such as a hospital serving poor inner-city residents. Research without a control or comparison group makes it difficult to generalize results. Even in studies that include a comparison group, it has been difficult to match participants on important variables such as current living conditions, history of trauma (particularly a history of physical and sexual abuse), strength of support network, general health, and level of stress.

Chemical dependency is a complex and difficult problem that adds additional burdens to research design. For example, the chemically dependent tend to use and abuse more than one substance. Along with the illicit chemicals, alcohol and tobacco are frequently used. Each of these licit chemicals can be harmful to a fetus, as evidenced by regulations requiring cigarette packages and alcohol containers to carry labels warning users about potential harm to the fetus. Polyabuse makes it difficult to attribute a negative fetal or maternal outcome to one substance. In spite of these limitations, there is evidence to suggest a correlation between maternal chemical use and harm to the fetus.

The chemical that has been studied extensively and has a well-documented negative effect on the fetus is alcohol. Fetal alcohol syndrome (FAS) was identified in the 1970s (Clarren & Smith, 1978; Jones & Smith, 1973). The features of infants born with FAS include:

1. growth deficiency
2. central nervous system impairment characterized by developmental delays, learning problems, memory impairment, and hyperactivity
3. distinctive facial features such as a small chin and thin upper lip
4. cardiac problems

Fetal alcohol effect (FAE) is a more common condition in which the infant suffers impairment but does not show all of the characteristics associated with FAS. FAE is estimated to occur at ten times the frequency of FAS (Rosengren, 1990). What remains unclear is the exact mechanism of harm or how alcohol does this damage to the fetus. More research is needed in order to understand the contribution of other variables such as genetic factors; nutritional status; mother's use of other chemicals; and how much alcohol, how often, and during which phase of pregnancy results in fetal harm (Halmesmaki & Ylikorkala, 1988). Alcohol consumption by pregnant women remains the leading preventable cause of developmental delay in children.

Opioids are one of the more thoroughly studied drug categories. Heroin, an illicit drug and methadone, a licit drug used to treat heroin users, have similar effects on the infant. NIDA estimates that there are about 500,000 heroin users. Perinatal exposure to opioids results in an increased risk of preterm birth, low birth weight, elevated risk of sudden infant death syndrome (SIDS), long-term impairment of visual-motor-perceptual skills, and a neonatal abstinence syndrome (Wilson, 1989). Between 68% and 94% of infants exposed prenatally to opioids experience the syndrome, which is characterized by irritability, hyperactivity, exaggerated reflexes, high pitched crying, increased muscle tone, tremors, sneezing, sweating, diarrhea, apnea, and restless sleep. These symptoms appear shortly after birth (usually within 72 hours) and continue for a couple of weeks. Less intense symptoms may continue for several months.

Most studies on the effects of perinatal exposure to marijuana report an elevated risk of growth retardation marked by low birth weight, small head circumference, and decreased length (Zuckerman et al., 1989). Other studies have associated sleep disturbances and neurobehavioral abnormalities to maternal marijuana use, but still other studies have failed to support these associations. (U.S. Department of Health and Human Services, 1990a).

Cocaine and crack have received much attention. These drugs seem to have an especially devastating impact in poor communities and have been linked to criminal acts as well as violent behavior. Cocaine effects the pregnant woman as well as her fetus. Cocaine is a vasoconstricting drug. After ingesting cocaine, there are increases in maternal blood pressure, heart rate, and respiration. There is a decrease in the amount of blood that passes through the placenta and contractions of the uterus are not uncommon (McGregor et al., 1987). These effects on the physical well-being of the pregnant woman indirectly influence the physical well-being of the fetus.

Cocaine affects the infant in a number of ways. The most commonly reported consequences concern fetal growth. Low birth weight, small head circumference, and decreased length are consistently reported (Cordero & Custard, 1990; McGregor et al., 1987). Some studies have reported other negative consequences of perinatal cocaine exposure, but the results have not been replicated. One study reported a 15% risk of SIDS among cocaine exposed infants, while the rate among the general infant population is 0.03% and 4% among methadone exposed infants (Lewis, Bennett, & Schmeder, 1989).

Other congenital abnormalities such as malformations of the genitourinary tract, strokes, and high blood pressure have been reported (Chasnoff & Griffith, 1989). Adults with chemical dependencies may experience a withdrawal syndrome when they stop using the drug. Researchers have identified a similar syndrome in some infants exposed prenatally to drugs; this is called the neonatal abstinence syndrome. There is evidence that suggests that a neonatal abstinence syndrome, similar to that experienced by opioid exposed infants, may exist for the cocaine exposed infant (Bingol et al., 1987). Long-term consequences are beginning to be reported as these youngsters enter school. Preliminary research suggests that these children are more likely to have poor organization skills, reading problems, impaired mathematical abilities, and difficulty interacting with other children (Van Dyke & Fox, 1990).

A critical examination of the incidence and effects of prenatal chemical exposure reveals there is still much to be learned. Inconsistent research findings make it difficult to predict with accuracy the consequences of using a specific drug. Recent studies suggest that many of the difficulties observed in infants exposed prenatally to illicit drugs attenuate with age (Chasnoff, Griffith, Freier, & Murray, 1992; Zuckerman & Frank, 1992). Maternal chemical use must be viewed from an ecological perspective in which drug use comprises one element in the complex life of the woman. Although it may be a primary threat to the well-being of the woman and her child, it is rarely the only threat. Living in a nonsupportive or hostile environment that is characterized by deprivation, lack of services, and violence also threatens the well-being of the mothers and children.

Child Welfare Agencies
and the Chemically Exposed Infant

The number of children entering foster care began to increase toward the end of the 1980s. In 1986, 280,000 children were in care. By 1989, the number had increased to 360,000, more than a 28% increase (Subcommittee on Human Resources, 1990). Upon closer examination, only a handful of states have experienced a significant increase in their foster care population. California and New York have a disproportionate share of children in care. One third of all foster children in the United States live in either of these two states. There are another eight states (Florida, Georgia, Illinois, Massachusetts, Michigan, New Jersey, Ohio, and Pennsylvania) that, along with New York and California, are responsible for more than half of the number of children in foster care (Subcommittee on Human Resources, 1990).

The factor that seems to account for this increase in the foster care population is parental drug use. Los Angeles county reported a 500% increase in the number of children placed because of parental drug use in a 6-year period, and in some counties drug exposed children compose two thirds of the foster care population (Select Committee on Children, Youth & Families, 1989a). The foster care population in some areas of the country is young. San Francisco county, for example, reports that children under the age of 3 compose more than half of the total number of children in placement (Westin, Ivins, Zuckerman, Jones, & Lopez, 1989).

The states with the largest increases in foster care population tend to be states with large urban areas experiencing drug problems. They are also states that have modified their child abuse reporting statutes to include parental drug use as a reportable offense. In addition to modifications in reporting requirements, some states have enacted legislation that criminalizes the drug using behavior of pregnant women (Gustavsson, 1991a). Failure to deal effectively with issues of chemical abuse and dependency among the adult population has resulted in increases in the foster care population. Chemical abuse can compromise the caretaking ability of parents.

Parental Chemical Use as Child Maltreatment

Courts have interpreted chemical use by pregnant women as evidence of neglect (*In re Baby X,* 1980; *In re Troy D.,* 1989). No other allegation is necessary. Although the intent of this policy is to protect a fetus, it could serve to endanger women and their unborn children. If women using public health facilities are subject to drug testing, criminal prosecution, and loss of their children if the drug test is positive, they may be reluctant to obtain prenatal care. Lack of prenatal care and home deliveries place both mother and child at an elevated risk of harm.

The policy also raises equity issues that are difficult to resolve. Any gender-specific policy, especially one based upon a temporary biological condition, must be carefully scrutinized. Pregnant women are subject to laws and policies as a result of their pregnancy. Using pregnancy as the basis for determining criminal behavior raises legal and ethical issues. Chemically using men are not subject to these laws, yet there is some evidence to suggest that there is an elevated risk of chromosome damage among these men (Shafer et al., 1990).

Parental chemical use is certainly a factor that merits attention. To assume, however, that every parent who uses a chemical is a neglectful, abusive, or unfit parent is to make an insupportable assumption. For example, one of the most commonly used and abused drugs is alcohol. There are more than 100 million users of alcohol. It would be inappropriate and impractical to remove all of the children of alcohol users. Parental drug use should be viewed as one factor requiring attention. The families referred to child welfare agencies with allegations of chemical use are families with multiple problems.

Child welfare has been slow to respond to the complexities of parental chemical use. This is due to a number of factors such as a lack of knowledge about effective interventions for chemically abusing women and a lack of treatment resources. The federal government requires states to set aside only 10% of drug treatment funds for women with chemical abuse problems (U.S. General Accounting Office, 1990a). Pregnant chemically abusing women are in an especially precarious position because there are relatively few treatment agencies willing to accept pregnant women. The lack of treatment is a major threat to the well-being of both the mother and the fetus. Child welfare agencies may find it useful to contract for drug treatment services for the pregnant woman. Collaborative efforts with medical and health facilities, mental health agencies, and drug treatment agencies can offer the most comprehensive services. The chemically abusing pregnant woman is likely to be experiencing multiple problems. To address just one issue is to offer incomplete services.

Chemically dependent women frequently bring issues to drug treatment programs, such as their history of abuse and neglect and concern about their children and parenting ability. These are issues that are alien in settings that have historically served male chemical abusers. Chemically dependent women are likely to suffer from depression, low self-esteem, anxiety, feelings of isolation, and detachment (U.S. Department of Health and Human Services, 1981). Therapy styles such as confrontation developed in male-oriented treatment settings may be counterproductive for women.

Child welfare agencies can provide assistance in program development to drug treatment agencies. An effective treatment program must include both drug and child welfare goals. Child welfare workers must develop a new set of skills in order to assist families experiencing drug problems. Child welfare workers need training on how to identify chemical dependency and how to offer effective referrals. In-service training for current workers and incorporation of drug content in child welfare courses at the university level can meet this educational need at modest cost.

The chemically abusing parent presents major challenges to the child welfare system. These parents are likely to be experiencing many problems and need a variety of services such as housing assistance, medical care, financial support, job training, respite care, counseling, drug treatment, and parent education. Failure to offer these services will prove costly in both financial and human terms. The medically fragile infants of some chemically abusing parents strain the health and social welfare systems. As these youngsters age, other systems such as mental health, education, and juvenile justice will have to provide services. Prevention and early identification can reduce these costs.

HIV Infection and Children

The threats presented by parental drug use are further compounded by HIV, first identified in the 1980s, which suppresses the immune system, compromising the ability of the body to fight off infection. This virus may be dormant for years. During this asymptomatic phase, the individual can unknowingly infect others with the virus. HIV infection can progress to acquired immune deficiency syndrome (AIDS) or AIDS-related complex (ARC) in which the body produces fewer and fewer white blood cells and individuals are subject to "opportunistic infections" that eventually cause death. Children with AIDS are challenging the health, child welfare, and educational systems.

A couple dozen children were diagnosed with AIDS in 1983. In 1986, the Centers for Disease Control (CDC) reported 240 pediatric AIDS cases. By the end of 1987, there were 703 pediatric AIDS cases (Centers for Disease Control [CDC], 1987). By the end of 1991, there were projected to be 5,000 children with AIDS and another 10,000 to 20,000 with ARC or HIV (Dokecki, Baumeister, & Kupstas, 1989). Although the majority of HIV-positive individuals will continue to be adults, children will account for an increasing percentage of new cases. Minority children are at an elevated risk of acquiring AIDS. African American and Latino children account for more than three fourths of the reported cases (Centers for Disease Control [CDC], 1988). This may be a reflection of the incidence of intravenous drug use among minorities.

Disease Progression and Manifestation

Most of the research on HIV, AIDS, and ARC has focused on adult men because this was the first group to be infected by the virus in the United States. Knowledge about pediatric AIDS is limited. Data suggest that progression to AIDS after acquiring HIV is accelerated in children. Twenty percent of adults with HIV progress to AIDS in 5 years, and 50% within 10 years. Drugs may help to slow the progress of the disease. Nevertheless, 20% of 34-year-olds who are HIV positive develop AIDS within 5 years and die within 7 years of the diagnosis (Ozawa, Auslander, & Slonim-Nevo, 1993). For children, 25% progress to AIDS in the first year, 45% in the second year, 60% by the third year, and 80% by the end of the fourth year (Chin, 1990).

The methods of infection for children and adults differ. Preadolescent children acquire HIV perinatally and through contaminated blood products. Adults and adolescents acquire HIV by sexual contact, intravenous drug use, and contaminated blood products. The mechanism of perinatal transmission is poorly understood. Rogers (1987) suggests infants are infected either prenatal (through the placenta), intrapartum (in the birth canal), or postpartum (breast feeding).

Because infants do not have a well-developed immune system, caution must be exercised when testing for HIV infection. Infants may test positive for antibodies to HIV. However, the mother may have passed her antibodies to the infant. The HIV testing should be repeated after the antibodies from the mother are no longer present, about 6 months after birth. Why some infants do not get HIV infection from their mothers is not known. Studies report mother-to-infant transmission rates of 25% to 65% (Chin, 1990; Thomas, 1984).

Young children with AIDS suffer from repeated bacterial infections. This is similar to the medical manifestation of AIDS in adults. However, the neurologic manifestations of AIDS in children are more pronounced than in adults (Bridge, 1988). Developmental delays, regression, and delays in achieving developmental milestones are common (Rogers, 1987).

Adolescents and HIV

The characteristics and issues associated with HIV and AIDS in adolescents are more complicated than those observed in children. Children become infected with HIV through contact with their mothers or through infected blood products. Adolescents acquire HIV in the same ways adults acquire the virus, through intravenous drug use, sex, and contaminated blood products. Half of male high school seniors and one third of female seniors have engaged in intercourse (Hassner, 1987), and condom use is sporadic among adolescents (Planned Parenthood, 1986). Although there is some data on the incidence of drug use among adolescents, there is very little information on the methods used by adolescents to consume drugs. Surveys of high school seniors indicate that more than half admit to using illicit drugs (Bachman, Johnston, & O'Malley, 1987). This number is an underestimate of incidence because the survey excludes young people who are not attending school, a group at increased risk for drug use.

Adolescents (ages 13-19) account for about 1% of the known cases of AIDS (CDC, 1988). This is a low number and somewhat misleading. The next age group, 20-29 years old, accounts for 21% of AIDS cases (CDC, 1988). Because an individual can be infected with HIV and be asymptomatic for 8 or more years, it is safe to assume that many of the 20- to 29-year-olds acquired the virus during adolescence. Blood tests of Job Corps applicants, ages 16 through 21, indicate that 3.3 per 1,000 have tested positive for antibodies to HIV, which is approximately twice the rate among military recruits (CDC, 1987). Minority adolescents are especially vulnerable to AIDS. The Centers for Disease Control (1988) report that more than half of all adolescents with AIDS are either black or Hispanic.

In spite of the risk for HIV infection among adolescents, there are relatively few prevention programs designed for this age group. Much of the program material that has been used to prevent the spread of HIV is not appropriate for adolescents because it was developed for the adult male homosexual. Developing prevention programs for children and adolescents has been difficult. There are unanswered questions, such as in what grade should HIV content be introduced, how should teachers be trained to address this material, what should be the content of the educational materials, and how will schools pay for these programs.

Education efforts must address the primary methods of transmission, which are sex and drugs. The adolescent male homosexual is at elevated risk. There is a general reluctance to acknowledge homosexuality in adolescents, contributing to the further marginalization of this population (Teague, 1992). In addition, male adolescent homosexuals may use sexual activity as a method for exploring their sexuality, thus increasing their health risks (Uribe & Harbeck, 1992). Effective prevention requires the use of explicit and clear educational materials that discuss complex topics such as drugs, methods of contraception, homosexuality, and types of sexual behaviors in developmentally appropriate ways. These topics are controversial, and schools are reluctant to engage in controversial activities (Lamers, 1988). Religious groups may object to the use of explicit materials, and adults can find the topics uncomfortable. In order to prevent the introduction of HIV into a large proportion of the adolescent population, where it will spread rapidly the way other sexually transmitted disease have spread, these barriers must be overcome. The morbidity and mortality of the next generation of Americans must not be jeopardized because adults are uncomfortable.

HIV and the Child Welfare System

Adolescent and child HIV infection present different challenges to the child welfare system. Children with HIV tend to have acquired the infection perinatally, suffer a quick progression to ARC or AIDS, have a parent who is also infected, and be in need of placement. Adolescents, on the other hand, do not present with this picture. They have acquired the infection primarily through drug use or sex, may be asymptomatic for years, and have parents who are not infected. Adolescents are more likely to have contact with social welfare agencies other than child welfare. Juvenile probation departments, jails, and shelters for runaways may be the first agency contact for the HIV-positive adolescent.

The infant with HIV infection can strain the child welfare system. These infants may have parents who are drug users and HIV positive. The parents are in a poor position and may be unable to care for themselves, much less their children. The infant may need substitute care. Child welfare agencies in some areas of the country are struggling to recruit foster homes appropriate for medically fragile children.

Foster homes may be an appropriate placement resource for the HIV-positive infant. However, special efforts must be directed toward the recruitment and training of foster parents. An education/training program for foster parents should include material on the nature of HIV infection, methods of transmission, disease progression, and precautions that can be used to minimize the risk of infection. In addition to the training, foster parents need support in order to care for a child whose chances of surviving childhood are compromised.

The adolescent presents a different set of challenges to the child welfare system. Because infants acquire HIV from their parents, they are likely to have parents who are seriously or terminally ill from the ravages of HIV infection. Adolescents are likely to have parents who are healthy. Therefore, in-home services designed to help the adolescent and the family cope with HIV are likely to be effective. These families may require multiple services, such as medical care, financial support, education about the disease, advocacy with school officials, respite care, and counseling.

A diagnosis of HIV infection invariably leads to questions about how the virus was acquired. Parents may not have been aware or may have been reluctant to acknowledge that their adolescent was using drugs or was sexually active. They now face the complicated issues of drugs, sex, and a potentially life-threatening illness. Counseling services for the adolescent and the family are essential. Advocacy efforts may be needed in order to provide the adolescent with education and medical services.

The most effective service is prevention. Child welfare agencies should play a major role in developing and implementing prevention programs, especially for adolescents. All health and sex education programs should include explicit information on HIV. In addition to group education programs, individual education efforts are necessary. Case workers should discuss these topics with the adolescents currently served by their agencies.

Summary

Social problems that at first glance seem far removed from children can quickly challenge the expertise and resources of child welfare agencies. Drug use by adults has become a threat to the well-being of a minority of children. A health problem, first thought to be a disease of homosexual men, is threatening the survival of infants and adolescents and is compromising the ability of some parents to care for their children.

Chemical use and HIV infection should be viewed through a social work lens. These two difficult problems do not occur in isolation. People with chemical abuse problems are also likely to live in environments that are nonsupportive. They may suffer from health problems, have no insurance, live in inadequate housing, and be tenuously connected to their communities. The service needs of the chemically abusing and HIV-infected are substantial. Incorporating an ecological perspective in service design and delivery will enable child welfare agencies to support both the development and coordination of multiple services. Child welfare has historically been a reactive service. The new threats to children outlined in this chapter require a proactive, preventive focus.

8

Homeless Youth

The social problem of homelessness is not new to our society. However, the dimensions and characteristics of those who are homeless changed during the 1980s. In recent years, more and more children and families found themselves living without a permanent residence. The effects of homelessness are particularly devastating for children. Although this problem has gained national attention, the numbers of homeless have not diminished.

It is important for those who work with children and families to consider the impact of homelessness and what the national response has been. This chapter examines homelessness among children and presents the policies and programs that address this problem.

Young people out on their own is not a new phenomenon in our society. "Street urchins" and "waifs" have been present throughout history, often glamorized in literature with characters such as Huckleberry Finn or Oliver Twist. The fact of children living on their own has been viewed as a consequence of earlier eras when times were harder, poorer, and families did not have social services to turn to. It is difficult to imagine such children today. However, the reality of the 1990s is that there are tens of thousands of homeless youth, some with their families and many others alone, living on their own. Although it is difficult to determine exactly how many youth are homeless, there is no doubt that significant numbers of young people have nowhere to go on any given night. Their existence presents an increasing need for new social services and human service workers who are prepared to deal with their unique concerns.

Definition of Homeless Youth

It is difficult to develop one inclusive definition of who homeless youth are. The official definition of *homelessness* is reflected in the only federal legislation singly concerned with the homeless, P.L. 100-77, the Stewart B. McKinney Homeless Assistance Act of 1987 (U.S. Congress, 1987). The legislation defines a homeless person as an individual who lacks a fixed, regular, and adequate nighttime residence or who primarily uses temporary shelters for nighttime residence. This definition includes families who lack a permanent place to live.

Although P.L. 100-77 seems very clear, it becomes complicated when describing adolescents who are on their own. Often, youngsters without adult supervision fall into the category of runaway. The difference between runaway and homeless youth has been outlined by the Administration for Children, Youth and Families of the Department of Health and Human Services. A homeless youth is defined as a person under 18 years of age who is without a place of shelter where he or she receives adult supervision and care. A runaway youth is defined as a person under 18 years of age who absents himself or herself from home or a place of legal residence without permission of parents or legal guardians (Horn, 1990).

It is very difficult to distinguish clearly between runaway and homeless youth. In fact, the terms are frequently used interchangeably. Both are on their own, possibly living on the streets or relying on shelters and social services for care. The distinction seems to be a matter of timing rather than a difference in population needs or characteristics (Segal, 1990). Studies on runaways (Ek & Steelman, 1988; Janus, McCormack, Burgess, & Hartman, 1987; Powers & Jaklitsch, 1989) suggest that running away is the culmination of a series of events. Youth in these studies were found to have left home several times, each time for a longer period. This process reveals that running away often develops into homelessness. Thus, running away and homelessness appear to be ends on a continuum, depending on the circumstances of each child and his or her family.

Because of the overlap, most shelters and services lump homeless and runaway youth together, not being able to make a clear distinction. Where there does seem to be a difference is between youth on their own and those who are homeless, but still with parents or guardians. Thus, two distinct groups of homeless youth do emerge; those who are with their families and those who are alone.

Demographics and
Characteristics of Homeless Youth

Individual Youth

There are an estimated 100,000 to 300,000 adolescents who are living on the streets with no supervision, nurturing, or regular assistance from a parent or adult on any given night (National Network of Runaway and Youth Services, 1989). Advocacy groups such as the National Coalition of the Homeless report the number of homeless children on any given night is greater, closer to 500,000 (Committee on Ways and Means, 1992). Over the course of a year there are between 1 and 1.3 million homeless and runaway youth, most of whom are between the ages of 12 and 17 and come from all geographic areas, economic backgrounds, and family circumstances (U.S. General Accounting Office, 1989a). Among youth using shelters, surveys have found that as many as 60% report being physically or sexually abused by parents or other family members (Barden, 1990). Many homeless youth flee abusive homes and may be considered runaway, but for their own safety have nowhere to go and are thus homeless.

Some homeless youth are forced out of their homes by parents who themselves cannot cope. These young people have been referred to as "throwaways" because the adults in their lives do not want them. Other youth were removed from their families years earlier, possibly for abuse, neglect, or abandonment, and have run through a number of foster homes or temporary placements.

A growing number of youth find themselves on the streets after they become separated from their families. Homeless families may turn to shelters for services and a place to stay. Often, shelters cannot accommodate families, or only allow small children to stay with their parents. Consequently, many homeless families must split up in order to find shelter. The result is that the older children often end up on their own. These young people have clearly not run away, rather they are homeless due to family homelessness and disintegration.

According to the National Network of Runaway and Youth Services, young people leave home for a number of reasons:

- Crisis in the family
- Poor family communication

- Unresolved problems, such as a history of abuse or sexual molestation
- Disintegration of the family structure through separation, divorce, poverty, and high mobility
- Abandonment, not having a home to return to

A survey of service providers to runaway and homeless youths revealed that the majority of young people served had multiple problems, most frequently school-related, absence of father, family economic need, and adult maltreatment (Bass, 1992). All of these circumstances, although sometimes beginning as a short episode of running away, can lead to homelessness for young people. Whatever the reasons, homeless youth are on their own and therefore extremely vulnerable to the dangers of the street and the consequences of living with uncertainty.

Homeless Families

The decade of the 1980s has created the highest rate of homelessness among families since the Great Depression (Children's Defense Fund, 1989a). The fastest growing group among the homeless are families and children. According to a national survey of urban centers conducted by the U.S. Conference of Mayors (1989):

- Families make up 34% of the homeless population.
- One out of every four homeless people is a child.
- In some cities, families make up more than one half the homeless population.
- In 62% of the cities, there are times when families must split up to find shelter.
- For homeless families, almost one in four requests for shelter go unmet.
- In the survey cities, two out of three have shelters that must turn away homeless families because of insufficient resources.

Historically, family economic security centered on the ability to own a home. Home ownership is no longer accessible for many families. In 1980, almost half of all young families owned homes, compared to 1991 when only one third of young families were homeowners (Children's Defense Fund, 1992). Families, particularly those headed by parents under 30, are the most vulnerable to homelessness today.

Providing a detailed description of homelessness among families is difficult because of the nature of homelessness. By definition, a homeless person is without a permanent place of residence. Typical research methods and census gathering rely on people having a permanent residence and therefore do not work well as ways to gather information about homeless people. Much research is descriptive and based on cases of homeless families using shelters. Though there are gaps in our knowledge, data reveal some characteristics that do help to provide a profile of homeless families.

Estimates for the total number of homeless persons in this country vary widely. According to advocates for the homeless, there are anywhere between 2 and 3 million people who are homeless in this country, with families comprising one third of the total (Children's Defense Fund, 1989a). Counts of the homeless tend to rely on data collected from shelters and other service providers. However, not all homeless families use shelters. Many live out of cars, traveling from one community to another. Homeless families are reluctant to come forward because of the fear that social service personnel will have to categorize the children as neglected for living in substandard conditions. If parents cannot adequately care for their children, there is a greater likelihood that the children can be removed and placed in foster care or other temporary placements. Consequently, homeless families tend to be invisible and less likely to use shelters.

Most homeless families are headed by women who are single, separated, or divorced; have run out of resources; and turn to shelters as a last resort. A study done in New York City looking at more than 5,000 homeless families (Molnar, 1988) found that 86% were headed by women with an average of two or three children per family, half of whom were younger than 5 years old. The women tended to be in their twenties and had completed some high school education. These findings mirror other studies that looked at homeless families (Bassuk, Rubin, & Lauriat, 1986; U.S. General Accounting Office, 1989a). Many homeless mothers are victims of family violence and have family histories of residential instability (Institute of Medicine, 1988a).

Further research indicates that one of the most pressing problems for homeless families is a lack of a support network (Bassuk & Rosenberg, 1988). Emergency shelters are far from ideal places to spend the night, particularly for children. Most families who find themselves turning to shelters have gone through all available personal resources and those they can draw on from family and friends. In the New York City study, the majority of families had used shared living arrangements before coming to emergency shelters and turned to the shelters after exhausting all their resources.

Unique Concerns of Homeless Youth

Life without a permanent place to call home, moving about, each day uncertain and potentially dangerous, are all realities for homeless youth. For those youngsters with their families, the strain and stress of being homeless adversely affect parenting and normal family development. For the young person on his or her own, the dangers are even greater and consequently the opportunity for healthy growth and development is virtually impossible. As social service providers, it is important for us to understand the particular concerns and needs of homeless youth in an effort to alleviate the negative consequences of being homeless.

Emotional Well-Being

It is not surprising that family instability, minimal supports, and shelter life in general are detrimental to the emotional development of children. Bassuk and Rubin (1987) in their study of homeless families in shelters found that almost half the children tested had at least one developmental delay. Many of the children experienced sleep problems, shyness, withdrawal, and aggression. More than half the children had scores indicating the need for psychiatric attention and displayed high levels of depression.

Homeless parents often report changes in the behavior of their children after living in a shelter (Bassuk & Gallagher, 1990). The children seem to regress, acting more infantile. Children in shelters may display eating and sleeping disorders, introverted and withdrawn behavior, even their ability to communicate can decrease. These behaviors reflect the tendency to return to earlier levels of development, an understandable response to the stress and emotional strain of being homeless.

Shelters are very difficult places in which to raise children. They tend to be in constant flux, with different people coming and going. Shelters are usually located in the least desirable parts of towns, making them dangerous both inside and outside. Privacy is impossible, leaving family interaction visible to all, thus placing additional strain on adults trying to parent their children.

Boxill and Beaty (1990) studied 40 female-headed families in a shelter in Atlanta. They found that living in a shelter and being without a home distorts the role of parent and child. Six themes emerged from their research:

1. Children demonstrate a strong need to be recognized as individuals;
2. Ambiguity and uncertainty are continually manifest for the children and are reflected in their behaviors;
3. There is conflict between needing greater attention and the situational demand for independence;
4. "Public mothering," all dimensions of family behavior are in sight of all other shelter residents;
5. There is disintegration of the mother or parent role; and
6. There is constant external control.

The day-to-day schedules of shelter life add additional strains on homeless children. Most shelters close for part of the day in order to encourage people to look for employment. For the parent with small children this creates a real problem because most homeless families cannot afford any day care. Length of stays in shelters vary. However, most shelters for families are temporary and short term, from 2 weeks to 30 days. Emergency shelters often limit people to no more than three consecutive days. For the homeless family, this means carrying all their belongings with them wherever they go. For children, that means few if any toys, books, or clothing.

Homelessness distorts the daily activities that make up normal family life. This distortion makes it very difficult for children to experience healthy emotional growth. Living without the stability of a permanent home interferes with the ability of children to master developmental tasks that are crucial to becoming productive and well-functioning adults.

For young people on their own without any family support, emotional health is also severely compromised. These young people experience all the same uncertainties and lack of privacy, but are also extremely vulnerable to exploitation and danger. Youth on the streets are frequently abused, victimized, assaulted, and sexually exploited. Those who work with these youth find that after 48 hours on the street, one out of three homeless young people is lured into prostitution, and if still on the street after 2 weeks, that jumps to 75% (Mohn, 1988).

Homeless youth lack life skills and means to support themselves. Often, the only alternative for survival is to sell themselves or drugs. Many need mental health care, particularly for depression or substance abuse. Contemplation of suicide and clinical depression are high among homeless youth (Hughes, 1990), reflecting the hopelessness and emotional stress of being alone and without a home.

Health Care Needs

Being homeless exposes a person to a greater number of factors that endanger health. Overall, homeless people have a wider range of illnesses and injuries than does the population as a whole (Institute of Medicine, 1988a). For young children, the lack of preventive health care or intervention for minor ailments such as sore throats or earaches can lead to significant illnesses if untreated. This is particularly true for homeless children.

Homeless children face many of the same illnesses and health care needs that children who have permanent places of residence do. However, the rates of occurrence are much higher for homeless children. The health problems most commonly seen among homeless children are upper respiratory infections, minor skin ailments, and ear disorders. Homeless children experience these problems two to four times more frequently than other children (Wright, 1990). Poor nutrition can contribute to poor health. Many family shelters lack cooking facilities, most shelters are closed for part of the day and thus do not provide three meals, and very few shelters can provide for the special nutritional needs of pregnant women, infants, and growing small children (Children's Defense Fund, 1990d).

Living in shelters or on the streets without resources guarantees that children will not receive sufficient and well-balanced meals, will not be out of the cold and inclement weather, and will be exposed to more diseases and potential for physical harm. This fact guarantees lower resistance and reoccurrence of common childhood illnesses.

Lack of access to medical facilities is a tremendous barrier to receiving proper health care. The instability, flux, and poverty of being homeless prevent many homeless families from seeking immediate medical attention for typical childhood illness. There are fewer community mental health centers, hospitals and medical centers are cutting back on the number of nonpaying patients they will see, and often the red tape and bureaucratic procedures put homeless families off. Even in shelters where there is medical care, often it is inadequate. One of the major shelters for families in New York City has one nurse for 500 families (Kozol, 1988). The result of substandard living conditions and insufficient health resources is the recurrence of illness and subsequent complications. Repeated respiratory infections and earaches can lead to permanent damage, leaving children scarred physically, cognitively, and emotionally for the rest of their lives.

For homeless youth on their own there are additional health concerns. Because many of these young people are involved in risky sexual activity and the use of drugs, they are exposed to increasing health risks. Some programs for homeless youth report that 7% and more of the young people tested who use their services are infected with the HIV virus, which causes AIDS (Hughes, 1990). This is significantly higher than the rate for adolescents overall. These young people lack the knowledge and resources to protect themselves properly from infection. Furthermore, the adults who exploit them are not interested in protecting these young people from exposure to AIDS or substance and alcohol abuse.

Most shelter services for homeless youth are short term, allowing stays of no more than 2 weeks. If a young person cannot be successfully linked with transitional or long-term care, the only alternative is to return to the street. Crisis intervention provided by shelters rarely includes comprehensive health care and cannot offer preventive health services. Thus, homeless youth receive most health care on an emergency basis and common treatable illnesses are more likely to go undetected until they become severe.

Education

Homelessness severely limits a child's ability to attend school regularly, complete homework assignments, and feel a part of the social dynamics of a classroom of students. The homeless child is less likely to be in one place for a stable period of time, making it difficult to stay in a school system over the course of a school year. In a study of families seen by Travelers Aid, 43% of the school-age children in these families were not attending school (Maza & Hall, 1988). Of those still attending school, almost a third were below grade level. Bassuk and Rubin

(1987) in their study found that more than half of the school-age children experienced severe depression and the majority reported having had suicidal thoughts.

The lack of privacy in shelters and the high level of commotion make doing homework very difficult. In addition, teachers report that homeless children are more likely to be teased by other children because of where they live, wearing the same or inappropriate clothes, and poor academic performance (Children's Defense Fund, 1988). This leads to an unfortunate cycle where homeless children feel conspicuous in school, are less interested in doing schoolwork, fall farther behind, and no longer want to attend (Gewirtzman & Fodor, 1987).

Often children who live in homeless shelters are not even registered for classes, particularly when families are transient. A number of additional barriers prevent homeless children from attending school regularly: lack of transportation, missing documentation such as birth certificates, and lack of a permanent address (Children's Defense Fund, 1990d). Poor nutrition and inability to get a good night's sleep hamper a child's ability to concentrate while in school, further compromising a child's academic achievement.

Homeless youth on their own are often absent from school and tend to have a history of problems while in school. A study (Bucy, 1987) of all youth entering shelters in New York City in 1984 found that 44% of the girls and 71% of the boys had at one time been suspended or expelled from school. Very few of them were attending school at all by the time they arrived at the shelter. Three quarters of the youth had experienced changes in their living arrangements over the previous 12 months, with 25% having moved four or more times. Problems in school and sporadic attendance may precipitate homelessness, and they certainly follow once a young person becomes homeless.

In order to help homeless children attend school regularly and perform up to their capabilities, school systems need to consider a number of principles (Moroz & Segal, 1990):

1. Create flexible criteria within the school system to enable children who move frequently or have no permanent address to receive educational services,
2. Protect the privacy of homeless students,
3. Provide educational services to families and homeless youth in temporary housing and shelters or transportation to near-by schools, and

4. Strengthen school and community awareness and educational programs about homelessness and the unique needs of homeless children.

Without adequate schooling that encourages cognitive and social development, homeless children are doomed to fall far behind other children. This guarantees a cycle of being on the outside and isolated, a status homeless children face daily because they do not have a permanent place to call home.

The Link Between
Homelessness and Poverty

Even though there is no one identifiable cause of homelessness, there are significant contributing factors. Some of these factors emanate from the characteristics and pressures within families, but many are directly related to outside variables that often are beyond the control of homeless people. Two key environmental trends seem to have contributed to the rise in homelessness, (a) the growth in poverty among children and young families, and (b) the decrease in the availability of affordable housing.

Poverty

As discussed in Chapter 4, the economic well-being of children in this country has deteriorated over the past 10 years. Hardest hit by structural economic changes have been young families and female-headed families. Both groups are disproportionately represented among the homeless with children. In 1988, the rate of poverty in families headed by persons under the age of 25 was nearly three times the rate for the population as a whole. For female-headed households headed by a woman under the age of 25, the poverty rate was almost seven times the overall rate (U.S. Bureau of the Census, 1989). The real median income for young families has declined dramatically since 1973 (Johnson, Sum, & Weill, 1988) and these families are becoming increasingly disadvantaged. The result is a generation of children growing up without adequate housing, nutrition, health care, and education. These families are most likely to find themselves among the homeless.

During the late 1970s and early 1980s the availability of well-paying, low-skilled and semi-skilled jobs declined, whereas part-time service jobs lacking benefits and paying low wages increased. Raising a family is very difficult on the salaries provided by today's entry-level and service jobs. At the same time, cash assistance programs designed to aid poor families have not kept pace with inflation and have actually fallen in terms of real buying power (Congressional Budget Office, 1988).

Although many families become homeless following internal crises such as abuse, divorce, or severe illness, many more become homeless due to outside events. Factories have closed down leaving workers without jobs, employment has shifted to service-related jobs with lower wages and no benefits, and government cash assistance programs provide less today than 15 years ago. The link between poverty and today's homelessness among families, particularly young and female-headed households, is indisputable.

The Lack of Affordable Housing

The most frequently cited problem among urban centers is the lack of sufficient affordable housing (U.S. Conference of Mayors, 1988). This shortage is closely linked to the increase in homelessness in this country. As available housing units at reasonable cost are displaced by urban renewal and more expensive housing, people with low incomes are forced to use more of their salary for housing.

Housing costs are usually considered affordable if they consume no more than 30% of household income. However, for families below the poverty line in 1985, five out of six poor renters and three out of four poor homeowners paid more than 30%. Although the cost of renting or owning a home has increased, the number of low-cost housing units has shrunk. Between 1978 and 1985, the number of housing units with a cost under 30% of household income for poor families declined by 20% (Leonard, Dolbeare, & Lazere, 1989).

While the private supply of affordable housing has declined due to urban development, public support has also decreased. From 1980 to 1988, federal funding for low-income housing declined by more than 80% (Children's Defense Fund, 1990d). The number of households aided by federal rental assistance fell by 74% over the 1980s (Leonard et al., 1989).

Thus, while family incomes declined, particularly among young families and those headed by single women, the supply of affordable housing also shrank. Consequently, poor families have had to spend a larger portion of their income for housing over the past decade. The result of these two national trends is that more families find themselves homeless or very near to becoming homeless.

Societal Response to Homelessness

Homelessness sparked public interest during the mid-1980s. In part this was due to the increased numbers and visibility of homeless people, as well as closer examination that revealed a "new" class of homeless: children and families. Concurrent with the increase in homelessness was an awareness that existing services were insufficient to meet the demand. Most services for the homeless were supported by private groups or through local community resources. By 1986 it was apparent to advocates for the homeless that federal legislation was needed to begin to deal with the growing problem.

In the summer of 1987, Congress passed the Stewart B. McKinney Homeless Assistance Act (P.L. 100-770). The McKinney Act outlines a comprehensive set of programs and benefits to serve the varied needs of homeless people. The Act includes provisions for:

- Emergency services for food and shelter grants
- Housing assistance for emergency shelters
- Health care and substance abuse services
- Community mental health services
- Education, job training, and community services
- Education for homeless children and youth
- Food assistance
- Veterans assistance

The services outlined by the bill are comprehensive and attempt to address the pressing needs of the homeless as well as encourage some preventive measures to slow the increase in homelessness. However, the legislative intent of the bill has been hampered by the extent of available funding. For the first 3 years of the McKinney Act, actual federal funding has not matched the level originally called for by Congress. In 1988 and 1989, only 51% and 61% respectively were appropriated to fund the programs under the McKinney Act (U.S. Budget, 1990).

There is no federal legislation that is solely concerned with homeless youth. The Juvenile Justice and Delinquency Prevention Act of 1974 includes Title III, which provides for runaway and homeless youth programs. In 1989, $26.9 million was spent on services for runaway and homeless youth, the same amount spent in real dollars in 1983 (based on author calculations from U.S. Budget, 1990). Those who work with homeless youth cite insufficient resources and feel the frustration of trying to meet an increased need without additional funding for services. "There is absolutely no doubt that the need for services for runaway and homeless youth continues to grow. With an estimated one to one and one-half million runaways, there are just not enough beds available" (Walker, 1988, p. 42).

With that many youth in need, the federal dollars committed to runaway and homeless youth average out to about 20 to 25 dollars per young person. That does not include those homeless children who are still with their parents or other adults. Even though the problem of homelessness among children has gained public notice, legislative support and services have not kept pace with the need.

Summary

The number of homeless youth is growing and the severity of the problems these youth face is increasing. There is a greater incidence of sexual exploitation and AIDS among homeless youth, children living in shelters are experiencing significant developmental delays and emotional stress, life on the streets and in shelters is injurious to children's health, poverty is on the rise for children and young families, and affordable housing is moving farther and farther out of the reach of many low-income families.

All these trends have occurred during a period of economic expansion. With the changing events of the 1990s and the economy slowing down, we must face the growing problem of homelessness among children. We need to develop a national youth policy that is supportive of services for homeless youth and their families. In the meantime, child welfare service providers must address the social, physical, emotional, and educational needs of homeless youth while advocating for greater national support.

In addition, services for homeless youth must be considered from an institutional approach rather than the traditional residual approach. How can structural barriers be removed so that families can acquire affordable housing, adequate employment that includes benefits such as health insurance, and intervention before family crisis results in dissolution? These issues must be addressed in order to stop the rise in homelessness among today's younger population.

9

Violence and Children

For many children, the surrounding world has become more violent and less secure. Growing up in an environment where violence can erupt unexpectedly, where the media portray detailed accounts, and where violence is an accepted social phenomenon is becoming a reality for many children. The effects of violence on children, though still requiring greater understanding, are beginning to be seen by those who work with children. This chapter presents the dimensions of violence in children's lives, from neighborhoods and families to the media. The social implications and the need for a professional response are discussed.

Today's child lives in a world that appears to be more violent than that of previous generations. More and more cases of young people as victims, as well as perpetrators, of violence are gaining national attention. Media stories of young people carrying firearms and witnessing murders are heard more frequently. Metal detectors at entranceways and armed security personnel are a reality in many junior and senior high schools. The reality of the 1990s is that violence has become a significant part of children's lives. Children witness violence through the media, within the neighborhoods where they live, as a part of their family, and in their daily educational experience. As a consequence of this growing social phenomenon, debate has increased about how children are affected by exposure to violence. This chapter explores those dimensions and the implications for social service providers.

Definition of Violence

Violence can be defined as physical force used to control, damage, or abuse. This definition is broad. It includes areas such as child abuse (Chapter 5) and domestic violence that focus closely on violence within the family. The definition also encompasses the dangers of growing up in unsafe communities and the escalation of criminal behaviors that often include violent acts. Although much research has focused on family violence, little is written on violence and children in relation to the larger society. With the increase in violence by and among young people, this phenomenon needs to be addressed.

Incidence

Are we witnessing an increase in violence among youth, or are such violent acts a topic that provokes public interest because it is unusual and not widespread? The answer to this question is complex and not easily answered. Greater public attention can lead to increased reporting of incidents or increased police action resulting in arrests, although the true number of violent acts may not have actually increased. Statistics gathered by law enforcement agencies reflect the rates of arrest for violent acts and not the true incidence. Many acts go unreported or incorrectly reported. Thus, although the true incidence may not be accurately reflected by statistics, the data do provide important information in understanding the issue of violence among youth.

Youth as Victims of Violence

Among the entire population in 1987, young people between 12 and 24 years of age had the highest victimization rate for crimes of violence and crimes of theft of any other age group (U.S. Department of Justice, 1989). Youngsters, particularly adolescents, were more likely to be beaten or robbed than any other age group. The most at risk are young men. Males within the 15 to 24 year age group are five times as likely to be homicide victims in this country than are male youths in Australia, Canada, France, Israel, Italy, Japan, Norway, Sweden, West Germany, and the United Kingdom (Bureau of the Census, 1991a).

Homicide is the second leading cause of death for 15- to 24-year-olds in the United States; and for black youths, homicide is the number one cause of death (Select Committee on Children, Youth & Families, 1989c). Young black men are more likely than any other group in the nation to be killed before they reach their mid-twenties. The homicide rate for black males 15 to 24 years of age is almost eight times that of white males 15 to 24 years old (Committee on Ways and Means, 1991). This suggests that for young black men, their lives and the activities they are involved in are dangerous and violent. Accessibility to guns appears to contribute to the high homicide rate. In 1986, 49% of the homicide victims under the age of 19 were killed by firearms (Select Committee on Children, Youth & Families, 1988b).

Youth as Perpetrators of Violence

More than 28% of all serious crimes in 1988 were committed by youth under 18 years of age (U.S. Bureau of the Census, 1991a, 1991b). This means that more than one out of four murders, rapes, and robberies, all categorized as serious crimes, were committed by juveniles. To compound the problem, the incidence of youth as perpetrators of serious crimes is on the rise. For example, in recent years the number and rate of homicides committed by children and adolescents increased (Ewing, 1990). Between 1983 and 1987, the number of youths under 18 years of age arrested for murder increased 22.2%, forcible rape arrests rose 14.6%, and aggravated assault arrests increased by 18.6% (Select Committee on Children, Youth & Families, 1989c). The number of juveniles in public correctional facilities is also on the rise. In 1987 an average of 53,000 youths were in public facilities on any given day. This represented a 10% increase over 1983 rates. More than half a million juveniles spent some time in a public correctional facility in 1987 (Committee on Ways and Means, 1992).

Violence is a part of many children's everyday life. In many inner-city communities, children are exposed to violence that could be compared to that of living within a war zone. For example, research in some communities reveals that one in four teenagers witnessed a murder, and almost three fourths knew someone who had been shot (Zinsmeister, 1990). Another survey found that almost 40% of a group of more than 500 elementary school children had seen a shooting and 34% had witnessed a stabbing (Children's Defense Fund, 1990d). The increase in random violence has also received public attention. The most vivid example occurred in 1989 when a group of youths raped and nearly killed a jogger in Central Park (Pitt, 1989). This incident introduced the nation to the term *wilding*, which describes the activity of youths gathering for the expressed purpose of randomly attacking for their own enjoyment.

These statistics and incidents suggest that the incidence of violence among youth has increased. Although earlier research in child welfare focused on abuse and neglect, the issue of violence has surpassed those boundaries in the 1990s. Young people are more frequently committing violent acts and becoming the victims of such behavior. The impact of this phenomenon on children and the larger society has yet to be fully explored. It is important to examine more closely violence as a part of today's child's life.

Violence and the Media

Why some people behave violently and others do not has been questioned and researched by social scientists from numerous disciplines. Sociologists, psychologists, criminologists, and anthropologists alike have tried to assess the determinants of violent behavior. Arguments made to support the causes of violence range along a continuum from violence as determined by heredity to violent behavior as a product of one's environment. However, research that considers differences in attitudes toward violence both between cultures and within cultures suggests that violence among youth is predominantly a learned behavior (Shamsie, 1985). This concept suggests that children learn violent behaviors from their surroundings. It is important for child welfare workers to examine the sources of this learned behavior. One of the most commonly cited sources, unique to the past 15 to 20 years, from which children learn about violent behavior is through the media.

Young people today spend more time watching television than they do in school. During their viewing time they will have seen approximately 180,000 murders, rapes, armed robberies, and assaults (Comstock & Strasburger, 1990). This does not include the countless numbers of movies seen in theaters and videotapes rented, both of which include extremely graphic depictions of violent behaviors. A great deal of research considers the issue of media influence on children. The rather comprehensive field of literature gives strong support to the perspective that being exposed to television violence increases subsequent aggressive and antisocial behaviors (Comstock & Strasburger, 1990). This body of research includes long-term studies of young children that found a significant relationship between watching violence on television and developing aggressive play patterns (Singer & Singer, 1981).

Bandura's classic study of children viewing adult aggressive responses to a punching doll demonstrated the transfer of aggressive behaviors (Bandura, 1973). Using three groups of children, one was exposed to a televised sequence of aggressive behavior, another group to a live display, and a third group was not exposed to any demonstration. Both groups that witnessed the adult aggressiveness were later observed to imitate the behaviors, while the third group did not. This and subsequent research suggest the tendency for children to master the social learning of violent behaviors.

The portrayal of violence on television and in movies also creates an unrealistic view of the consequences of such behavior. Rarely does the hero die, although wounded week after week. In testimony before a Congressional Hearing (Spivak, 1989, p. 29), a public health doctor reported his experience with a 19-year-old youth. The youth had been shot, and as he was being treated in the emergency room, he expressed his surprise that the wound hurt. He was surprised because no one ever got hurt on television.

Television is a reality of life for virtually all children in society. It cuts across economic and social lines and touches children of all backgrounds. The amount of viewing time has steadily grown over the years and watching television seems to be the most consistent activity for children. In addition, the impact on children's behaviors is well documented—the more violence children view, the more aggressive and antisocial they become. Although social workers must face the consequences of increased violent behavior by children and adolescents, attention must be given to the policies, or lack of policies, that govern what can be portrayed through media.

Community and Family Violence

Community Violence

For some children, violence surrounds them on a daily basis. Going to school or playing in the neighborhood for many children is not a positive childhood experience, but a traumatic and frightening prospect. Alex Kotlowitz (1991) describes in detail the life of two brothers living in a public housing complex in Chicago. He describes day-to-day life in the projects from a journalistic perspective. As the boys are celebrating a birthday, gunfire erupts and the children drop to the ground and crawl to safety. Three days later as the children are returning home from school, the scene is repeated. Guns are becoming a common part of many children's lives. Instances of gunfire and youth carrying submachine guns suggest a day in Beirut or Northern Ireland, not a city in the United States. In many urban areas, however, random gun violence appears to be more common.

Schools are witnessing more instances of violence. Urban public schools are reporting increases in criminal behaviors and violent outbreaks (National Institute of Justice, 1986). Violence in schools impacts negatively on children and teachers alike. Learning is hindered, attendance decreases, and anxiety and fear become overriding realities (Evans, 1988). Attending school is the primary activity for children and affords them the opportunity for becoming educated and socialized to participate fully in our society. When school atmospheres are altered by the reality of fear and danger, children in those settings are denied equal access to education. Coupled with living in violent neighborhoods, children turn to socially unacceptable ways to cope.

In New York City, the fastest growing arrest category for teenagers is gun possession (Pooley, 1991). Statistics like these suggest it is becoming more and more common for young people in large urban centers to carry guns and to use them. "For many teenagers, a gun isn't a tool but a symbol of power and prestige, a charged, mystical icon in the urban rite of passage from childhood to manhood" (Pooley, 1991, p. 24). Guns have become both a symbol of power and the way to settle disputes through controlling the activities of peers. The tragic result is that guns can ultimately put an early end to a young person's life.

Although random violence affects all neighborhoods, it is disproportionately found in poor urban communities. Poor inner-city communities lack the needed resources to deal with the traumatic aftermath of such incidents. In May 1988, a 30-year-old woman named Laurie Dann burst into a second grade classroom in an affluent suburb of Chicago and shot six children, killing one (Enstad & Ibata, 1988). The incident brought national attention and in response the community mobilized with crisis teams of psychologists and social workers. In addition, the incident received great attention from policy makers, including the governor. Two days later, a 9-year-old boy living in public housing was shot in the head

by random gunfire (Kotlowitz, 1991); that incident rece
local attention and no team of specialists or crisis interven
Most victims of violence are first served by health care pr
health care system, therefore, is of primary importance in a
violent acts in all communities. Health care workers thus . _ _ u to be
trained in victim assistance and proper referrals.

What are the lasting affects of growing up in neighborhoods with
increasing violence? This is a growing phenomenon of the late 1980s and
early 1990s; future research will need to investigate the lasting effects.
Based on what we do know about the consequences of abuse and neglect
and intrafamily violence, however, it follows that children are at great
developmental risk when confronted by violence in their neighborhood.
The impact of abuse can lead to poor self-image, lack of trust, aggressive
and disruptive behaviors, passivity, school failure, and serious alcohol
and drug use (American Academy of Child and Adolescent Psychiatry,
1990). It follows that the constant fear and reality of violence in a child's
day-to-day life can only contribute to negative personal and social
outcomes.

Violence Within the Family

The primary source of support and nurturing for children is the family.
Historically the societal expectation has been that adults, particularly
parents, will oversee the development of children. When that relationship breaks down, outside systems and professionals are summoned to
intercede. Unfortunately for some children, the family fails to provide a
protective and nurturing environment. The phenomenon of violence
within the family is a reality for many children today. Chapter 5 docu-
ments the increase in child abuse and neglect and the deleterious effects
of such victimization.

Aggression and frustration in families can escalate to extreme degrees
of violent behavior. More than one fourth of the murders committed in
this country are by one family member on another, and of those family
killings, one half involve one spouse killing the other (Shamsie, 1985).
In a study analyzing crime over a 3-day period in San Francisco, 39%
of all assaults, attempted murders, and completed murders were related to family violence (Select Committee on Children, Youth & Families, 1984). It is erroneous to assume that every family can provide a
healthy environment for all children. We need to consider the charac-

teristics of violence within the family and the potential effects it has on children.

It is estimated that each year more than 6 million children witness parental violence (Davis, 1988). For many children, this leads to posttraumatic stress disorders including developmental delays, conduct disorders, low self-esteem, and depression (Silvern & Kaersvang, 1989). In addition to being at greater risk of developing psychological and behavioral problems, children who witness spousal violence are themselves at a greater risk of being abused (Suh & Abel, 1990). Children who do not have warm and supportive family relationships are more likely to develop antisocial behaviors (Shamsie, 1985).

If much of behavior is indeed learned, then children who witness acts of violence are more likely to be violent themselves. There is significant research that suggests that children, as a strong defense against feeling anxious and helpless, identify with the violent parent (Green, 1984). Children adapt and learn how to behave in order to fit into their family. Violence as a norm becomes their primary frame of reference for all of their early life and continues to be so through adolescence. While the generational transmission of abusive and violent behaviors cannot be conclusively proven, research suggests that generational transmission of violence exists. Retrospective studies of aggressive behaviors by youth suggest that many who were abused or witnessed abuse as children repeated the violent behavior they experienced (Green, 1984).

Children learn through observation and modeling and are frequently taught that violence is an appropriate method for conflict resolution. If the media, neighborhoods, and the family rely on violence to alleviate distress and solve problems, then children will learn to use those same behaviors. Methods to resolve problems that discourage aggression emphasize cooperation, communication, and social support (Davis, 1988). Intervention that focuses on the entire family system and social environment is necessary when dealing with family violence. However, such efforts are extremely difficult to achieve in communities that suffer from poverty and lack of resources and are in social disarray. In a society that promotes violence in the media and where many families with severe dysfunction go undetected, environmental change is difficult. Violence has become a part of our modern life. It will only diminish as a result of active efforts that reward cooperation and support within communities and families.

Violence and Gangs

Often the existence of gangs is linked to violent behavior. Poor urban areas frequently have weak social controls and few opportunities for youth to engage in legitimate activities. Although most youth avoid involvement in gangs, research suggests that for those who do participate, gangs facilitate delinquency (Fagan, 1990). Greater involvement in delinquent behavior ultimately leads to breaking laws and using powerful resources, such as guns, to have the authority to do so. With an absence of legitimate social activities, gangs provide the opportunity for teenagers to acquire status, social support, protection, and economic success.

Violence as a way to control others is a part of criminal activity. Although it is not new for young people to be involved in delinquent behaviors, drug trade and the accompanying growth in youth gangs have contributed to an increase in the rate of violence among juveniles. Between 1984 and 1986, the number of juveniles arrested for violent crime rose by 9%, while previously declining 20% over the decade before (Select Committee on Children, Youth & Families, 1989d). The overall arrest rate for 13- to 17-year-olds increased almost 12% from 1970 to 1987 (Select Committee on Children, Youth & Families, 1989b). More than half the states in this country report serious problems with gangs (Knapp, 1988).

Drug trafficking presents an economic incentive for youth to get involved with gangs, criminal behavior, and ultimately violence. Although most youths avoid joining gangs, those who are involved in gang life are more likely to use and sell illegal drugs (Fagan, 1990). In one study examining illegal behavior among adolescents living in Washington, D.C., researchers found that youth selling drugs were also more frequently involved in aggressive criminal behaviors (Urban Institute, 1989). Youth selling drugs were five times more likely to carry a concealed weapon than were those youth not involved with drugs. Those selling drugs were four times more likely to have shot, stabbed, or killed someone compared with those not involved, as well as compared to those who use drugs but do not sell them.

Social and economic changes have altered the nature of youth gangs. Drugs have provided street gangs with the economic means to become potent organizations. For youths living in inner-city neighborhoods where employment opportunities are minimal, educational resources are inadequate, and forceful acts of violence are becoming more and more common, gangs offer an organized way to deal with the environment (Taylor, 1990).

Although the activities promoted by gangs are illegal and place members at great risk, they do provide socialization, protection, and a sense of belonging. This is in stark contrast to more affluent communities where there are numerous legal alternatives for young people to fill those needs. Thus it is important to recognize the social and economic factors that contribute to the existence of gangs and violence. Until those realities are addressed, young people living in socially and economically isolated neighborhoods will turn to the most available options for socialization and economic opportunities—street gangs. As a part of that involvement, more young people will be involved in criminal acts and violence.

Missing Children

The abduction of a child is often one of the most publicized occurrences of violence. Public perception often views abduction as a common violent act. Statistically, however, those cases are very few. Because of the nature of abductions, determining the incidence is very difficult. Estimates place the number within the range of 25,000 to 500,000 per year (U.S. Department of Justice, 1986). Only a small number of those are nonfamily abductions. Of those children abducted, most are taken by a relative, usually as part of a custody dispute.

Abduction cases fall within the larger legal definition of missing children. Included among those reported as missing are runaways, throwaways, family abductions, and nonfamily abductions (U.S. Department of Justice, 1987b). As discussed in Chapter 8, there are more than 1 million homeless and runaway youth each year. These young people account for the majority of cases of missing children.

Violence permeates all aspects of being a missing child. Life on the streets as a throwaway or runaway places a youth at great risk of personal injury and victimization. Abduction by a stranger is a terrifying experience for any child. Even family abductions are traumatic. All such cases involve individual and family disruption and often are characterized by anger and violent actions.

This nation lacks a consistent and organized system for reporting the incidence of missing children. In 1984, Congress passed the Missing Children's Assistance Act as part of the Juvenile Justice and Delinquency Prevention Act. As a result of that Act, the National Center for Missing and Exploited Children was established (Garrison, 1987). Although efforts have been made to provide information and assistance to localities in dealing with the growing numbers of missing children, a comprehensive system is still lacking. The definition of a missing child and the requirements that result in a police investigation vary from state to state. National incidence studies are still needed to determine the extent of the problem. Until public policies effectively coordinate the reporting and investigation of missing children, the issue will be handled on a case-by-case basis. Child welfare workers need to understand the impact of violence that affects all missing children beyond those few cases that receive public attention.

Violence and Self-Esteem

The issues of suicide and self-mutilation are typically concerns that fall under the discussion of mental health. The reasons for such violence perpetrated against oneself frequently involve underlying psychological problems such as low self-esteem and depression. With the growth in the availability of weapons and drugs, however, and the link between violence in the media and aggressive behavior, the question must be raised as to whether these phenomena have any impact on self-destructive behaviors.

Although definitive research is lacking, some trends are disturbing. From 1970 to 1986, the rate of suicide among 15- to 19-year-olds increased by 73%, and for 10- to 14-year-olds it more than doubled (U.S. Bureau of the Census, 1991b). These statistics raise the question of why suicide has become more prevalent among young people. While it certainly relates to mental health issues, the social learning of violent behaviors as a solution to disputes and frustrations, coupled with the growing availability of weapons, contribute to the incidence of suicide. Suicide is the third leading cause of death among 15- to 24-year-olds, with accidents first and homicide second (U.S. Bureau of the Census, 1991b). Cases of group suicides, though rare, have received public attention (Dobbs, 1987) and raise the concern of growing violent behavior by youths directed at themselves.

Little is known about self-mutilation. One study looking at the rate of intentional injuries among children and adolescents found that more than 11% were self-inflicted (Guyer, Lescohier, Gallagher, Hausman, & Azzara, 1989). The vast majority of cases were between 15 and 19 years old. Adolescent girls are twice as likely to commit self-inflicted injuries. Frequently, self-injurious behavior is a response to childhood sexual or physical abuse or other traumatic events (Wise, 1989). It is important to note that child welfare personnel need to become more aware of the concomitant growth in the exposure to violence, the availability of weapons and drugs, and the pressures that young people are faced with today. These phenomena suggest that we will see more acts of violence by youth directed at themselves.

Summary

Unfortunately, as a result of television and movies, violence has become an everyday reality for all children. For inner-city, disadvantaged youth, violence has also become a way of life. For many other children in this country, violence continues to be a daily reality of their home lives. Possibly as a result of the increased exposure to violence, young people are considering it an alternative to the difficulties of growing up and as a way out of the pressures of today's society.

For social workers, this means calling attention to the issue of violence perpetrated on children as well as the growth in violent behavior by children. Enough evidence exists to show that such young people will have great difficulty in breaking the cycle of violence unless there is adequate intervention. These issues will not go away and are increasing in extent and severity. Ways to prevent violence among youth must be considered and implemented, particularly for those children growing up in violent homes and neighborhoods.

Intervention strategies need to take a community-centered approach. This includes public education; school programs that teach youth how to resolve conflicts through mediation rather than through violence; and the coordination of the criminal justice, social service, health, mental health, and children's services systems. Violence is often a learned behavior; therefore communities must organize and take action to promote positive socialization.

PART IV

Linking Research and Practice

Research and investigative inquiry provide a foundation for re-evaluating the residual nature of the child welfare system. Policies and practices are best informed by knowledge, experience and fact. Part IV presents emerging research from different disciplines useful in developing proactive and preventive child welfare policies and services. Chapter 10 discusses recent research in the child development field that supports the notion that young children are active responsive learners. Therefore, early supportive efforts are essential to ensure the health and well-being of America's children. Chapters 11 and 12 provide a blueprint for preventive and proactive policies and programs for children.

10

Assessing Infants and Children

A Developmental Perspective

Knowledge about children, especially young children, has increased significantly in the past 20 years. Infants are now viewed as active learners engaged with their environments as they master developmental tasks.

This chapter reviews some of the important research about children and their abilities and needs. Methods for assessing young children are evaluated and the need for policies to support children are discussed.

The past 20 years have been marked by rapid changes in technology and knowledge. These changes have influenced the design and delivery of child welfare services. For example, changes in infertility technology have influenced adoption practice. It is now possible for an infant to have multiple parents. Adoptive parents can purchase the services of a woman to carry an embryo (which may be genetically unrelated to the adoptive parents) to term.

Rapid increases in knowledge have also influenced practice, and this can be observed in the information available about the capacities of children. This chapter focuses on the abilities and needs of young children and how policies can facilitate the healthy development of children.

Infants as Active Learners

We are only now becoming aware of just how complex infancy as a stage in human development is. Early psychoanalytic theory suggested that infants had needs related to their hypothesized inner states. The oral phase in development presented a limited view of the infant as self-centered and seeking gratification. Later psychoanalytic thought presented infants as more complex with a rich affective life and involved with their caretakers. The psychoanalytic school provided an important base for understanding infancy.

However, for the first half of the 20th century, infants were generally viewed as passive recipients of basic care. Their needs were classified as primarily survival. Survival was an important issue because infant mortality rates were high. For example, in 1940, the infant mortality rate in the United States was 47 deaths per 1,000 births. The rate for nonwhites was 73.8 deaths (Children's Defense Fund, 1986). Infant mortality rates have declined. In 1988, the infant mortality rate was 10 deaths per 1,000 births and for African American children, the rate was 18 deaths. There are 21 other countries that do a better job of keeping their infants alive (U.S. Department of Health and Human Services, 1990c).

While the infant mortality rate declines, the childhood disability rate increases. Technological advances make it possible for medically fragile infants to survive. However, this survival comes at a cost. About 4% of children are seriously disabled and if the categories used in special education (such as learning disabled, speech impaired, mentally retarded) were included the percentage would increase to 10 (Rosenbaum, 1989). The special needs of these children require supportive and remedial services.

Research suggests that infants are not passive. Infants are actively engaged with their environments as they master developmental tasks. Infants have abilities, talents, and dispositions that are rapidly changing. For example, a newborn infant can distinguish his or her mother's voice. The infant learns quickly that the environment is a source of meeting needs. Environments that are unsafe, hostile, inconsistent, or non-nurturing can compromise healthy development.

Assessment Tools

In order to determine how an infant or child is developing, various techniques to measure constructs such as cognitive abilities and emotional well-being have been developed. These tools, when used as screening devices, can be used to identify youngsters at risk of problems. Early identification that results in the provision of appropriate services can compensate for biological or environmental deficits. There are dozens of screening tools.

Assessment of infants can begin very early, as early as 26 weeks gestational age, and as technology advances, assessment may begin at conception (Als, 1984). As efforts to uncover the composition of genes and where certain traits are located on the genes are successful, screening for biological anomalies could begin prior to conception. A tissue sample from a prospective parent can be analyzed. This analysis can tell the parent if he or she carries a gene that has been linked to a specific anomaly.

There are interesting and difficult ethical questions associated with this technology. For example, there are questions about the role of this information and how it can influence decisions about reproduction. Knowledge that potential parents have a defective gene that may result in a life-threatening condition in any biological child may cause the parent to not reproduce. Or, some parents may decide to reproduce regardless of the health consequences for their offspring. Questions may arise about the appropriateness of producing seriously medically compromised children.

Infants can be assessed in different areas. One of the first areas explored was the neurological. The best known instrument in this area is the Neonatal Behavioral Assessment Scale (NBSA) developed by Brazelton (1984). The NBSA tests reflexes and behaviors and is frequently used on premature infants. There are other screening devices used to assess the central nervous system and motor development. These tools are used by clinicians in medical settings and generally require training in order to be used appropriately.

One of the oldest screening tools for mental and motor development is the Bayley Scales of Infant Development (Bayley, 1933). The instrument is easy to understand. It provides age parameters for the accomplishment of specific tasks, such as turning over or walking. Scores indicate if an infant is functioning at age level. It can be used to evaluate the progress of high-risk infants. The scales are not difficult to administer and can be used with 2-year-olds.

Perhaps the best known developmental screening tool is the Denver Developmental Screening Test (Frankenburg, Fandal, Sciarillo, &

Burgess, 1981). The Denver is a brief, easy to administer test that can identify infants at risk for developmental delay. The Denver is also used with older children, up to the age of 6. The Denver, as well as other assessment tools, was not designed to be sensitive to issues or race and class. This cultural bias limits the applicability of the tests.

The newest area for exploration is infant temperament and caretaker/ infant interaction. The Home Observation for Measurement of the Environment for Infants and Toddlers (HOME) was developed in the late 1970s and identifies infants at risk of developmental delay (Caldwell & Bradley, 1978). It is administered in the home and, with some practice, is relatively easy to administer.

These and other techniques make it possible to assess motor and mental development of the infant. Prior to the development of these techniques, the Intelligence Test administered to the older child was the primary tool for identifying children at risk. It also labeled children and assumed intelligence was a static and unidimensional concept. Although intellectual ability is important, it is but one measure of this ambiguous notion of intelligence. Intelligence is a multidimensional concept and includes variables such as problem-solving skills, adaptive abilities, and creativity.

Cognitive abilities are one indicator of intelligence and can be compromised by biological core deficits and psychological and emotional difficulties. The first few years of life help to prepare the child for the more formal learning that occurs in school. Children who have not learned to concentrate, control their impulses, follow direction, or who lack self-esteem are unprepared for formal education and can find the classroom an unsettling place.

Children in Difficult Situations

Much of the research used to develop theoretical constructs and screening and testing tools has used middle-class children, living in supportive environments, with nurturing caretakers as subjects. Unfortunately, there are children who begin life with compromised health and live in difficult circumstances. Yet many of these children grow up to become happy and successful adults while children who are reared in seemingly ideal circumstances can grow up to become unhappy and unsuccessful adults. Identifying the elements that enable children to thrive in spite of adversity is important for policy development.

The Competent Child

The developmental construct that describes how well infants and children are able to adapt to the demands of their environments and maximize the resources available (both personal and environmental) to achieve positive outcomes is competence (Waters & Sroufe, 1983). The duality in this definition is consistent with the social work concept of person and environment. Competent children possess personal strengths, adaptability, and resources that enable them to use assets in the environment. The ability to use personal talents to get needed resources from the environment results in positive outcomes for these children.

Competence is a developmental construct and the dimensions of competence change with the phases in the life cycle. Competence in each phase has unique and age-specific characteristics. It is possible to describe a competent infant, toddler, school-age child, adolescent, and adult. Each phase presents challenges as well as opportunities to expand upon already established competencies and develop new ones. For example, the quality of peer interaction for infants is limited by the developmental phase of infancy in which other tasks take precedence. For the school age child, however, competence as evidenced by effective peer interaction becomes more salient.

Attachment and the Infant

An effective attachment relationship forms a basic building block of competence. Attachment both protects the infant and allows the infant to grow (Cicchetti, Cummings, Greenberg, & Marvin, 1990). Infancy is marked by two major needs that can conflict. Infants need to feel safe. Safety is often operationalized for the infant as closeness to caretakers. Infants also want to explore their environment. This requires the infant temporarily to leave the safety of the caretaker.

Attachment behaviors are protective in that they allow the infant to meet both of these needs. Attachment offers the infant a protective and responsive relationship with caretakers. The infant is then able to leave the safety of the caretakers and explore the environment.

The quality of the attachment relationship has been subject to examination. A secure attachment relationship has much to offer the infant. The caretaker that is warm, responsive, available (both physically and emotionally), and consistent offers the infant and toddler a secure base. The youngster is then free to explore the environment, secure in the knowledge that her or his needs will be met. When upset or unsure about experiences in the environment, the toddler can return to the secure base provided by the responsive caretaker and be comforted before returning to explore the environment (Davidson, 1991).

There are other types of attachment relationships. Some caretakers are neither emotionally available nor warm. Characteristics of the infant also influence the quality of the attachment relationship. An infant may have medical problems or a temperament that can interfere with attachment. Infants that are hard to comfort, do not smile, and do not like being held can be more difficult to parent. In these circumstances, an insecure attachment relationship can prevail. There are three categories of insecure attachment: insecure-avoidant, insecure-resistant, and insecure-disorganized/disoriented (Main & Solomon, 1986).

Infants of caretakers who are rejecting and unavailable to their infants are described as insecure-avoidant. These infants avoid the caretaker and do not engage in in-depth environmental exploration. Infants of caretakers who are not rejecting but are inconsistently available or interfering are described as insecure-resistant. These infants are passive, unsure about contact with the caretaker, angry, and resistant. The infant in the insecure-disorganized pattern tends to live in a family experiencing high stress and one in which maltreatment may be present. These youngsters behave in inconsistent ways and lack an integrated way of interacting with their environments.

The quality of the attachment relationship can be indicative of later developmental outcomes. The securely attached youngster is likely to be a competent child—resilient, able to interact with peers, and skilled at obtaining resources from the environment (Sroufe, 1979; Strayhorn, 1988). The insecurely attached child is at risk of later behavioral and developmental problems (Fagot & Kavanagh, 1990).

Barriers to Effective Attachment

If effectiveness of attachment in infancy is predictive of competencies in later developmental stages, then barriers to effective attachment need to be minimized. There are children growing up in stressful environments with impaired caretakers. Some of the factors associated with negative developmental outcomes are:

1. parental psychiatric illnesses including thought, mood, and personality disorders,
2. parental chemical abuse,
3. family disharmony, especially parental conflict and spouse abuse,
4. poverty,
5. overcrowding, and
6. out-of-home placement of the child.

These children are at an elevated risk of negative outcomes.

Caretaker characteristics have been studied in depth and have been consistently associated with developmental outcomes. Psychiatrically disturbed caretakers constitute one major risk group. Children whose parents suffer from alcoholism, antisocial personality disorders, schizophrenia, and depression are at risk of emotional, social, and cognitive difficulties (Gershon et al., 1985; Goodwin, 1985; Weissman et al., 1984.)

Of particular concern is the depressed mother. Children of these mothers are at an elevated risk of depression (Strober et al., 1988). Insecure attachments have also been associated with depressed mothers (Radke-Yarrow, 1991). Mothers who are unhappy, agitated, and hopeless are likely to respond inconsistently to their children and be emotionally less available. The incidence of child abuse may also be influenced by maternal depression (Hawton, Roberts, & Goodwin, 1985). There is limited evidence to suggest that the cognitive abilities of children may be negatively influenced by maternal depression (Cogill, Caplar., Alexandra, Robeson, & Kumar, 1986; Houck, Booth, & Barnard, 1991).

Family discord has been associated with psychiatric risks to children, especially the development of personality disorders. Conduct disorders have been consistently associated with marital disharmony (Offord & Boyle, 1986). Children from families in which spouse abuse has occurred are at an elevated risk of behavioral disturbances (Wolfe, Jaffe, Zak, & Wilson, 1986).

Very young children are sensitive to and aware of family conflict. Toddlers can become upset when around angry adults and show an increase in aggressive behaviors with peers after observing an angry verbal exchange between adults (Cummings, Lanott, & Zahn-Waxler, 1985).

Environmental stress takes a toll on children. Studies on the effects of stress on children suggest that overcrowding, poverty, parental conflict, and maternal depression negatively effect children's cognitive and emotional functioning (Shaw & Emery, 1988). Often these stressors occur in combination and may increase the risk of negative child outcomes.

Separation from parents and placement in foster or institutional care has been associated with depression and other psychiatric problems. However, it is unclear whether the separation plays the major role or if it is the parental disharmony and multiple stressors that frequently accompany the separation.

Surviving Distressed Environments

Child and parent characteristics can increase the risk of negative developmental outcomes for children. However, not all children growing up in distressed circumstances experience developmental problems. Although some associations are strong (such as the association between maternal depression and negative child outcomes) these are not causal associations. Learning what factors mitigate against negative outcomes is essential for the development of prevention and intervention programs.

Identifying the Competent Child

The competent child is able to thrive in difficult circumstances by using both inner abilities and environmental resources. The question then becomes, What are the characteristics of these children and how can we encourage the development of competent children?

Identifying the factors that can protect children in difficult situations is complicated. Some children may possess intrapsychic abilities due to genetic factors that make them less vulnerable biologically and emotionally to negative events. Temperament may also play a role. Infants who are irritable, difficult to soothe, and give the caretaker little positive feedback may be at risk of poor developmental outcomes. An alternative explanation focuses on environmental qualities and social skills. For example, there is research to support the role of social support in mitigating against negative outcomes (Crockenberg, 1981).

Other factors have been associated with resiliency in children. These factors include:

1. a positive relationship with a healthy, caring adult,
2. positive relationships with peers,
3. self-esteem, and
4. social skills (Rutter, 1985).

A positive relationship with a caring, healthy adult can be a protective factor. Positive relationships with peers also can serve as a buttress for the child. Good relationships provide positive feedback. Feedback from an impaired caretaker can be negative or distorted. Positive relationships also enhance self-esteem. Being liked and cared for are important building blocks in a positive self-image.

There is considerable overlap among these protective factors. An array of problem-solving skills that can be employed in any number of circumstances also helps the older child to cope effectively in a distressed environment. The effectiveness of the coping serves to increase self-esteem and reinforces the view that life presents challenges, not threats.

Implications for Interventions

There are a number of directions for policy makers as well as clinicians to pursue in order to help ensure optimal developmental outcomes for at-risk children. Intervening early or preventing problems not only reduces distress but is also cost effective.

The federal government has recognized the importance of infancy and early intervention. In 1986, the Education of the Handicapped Act (Public Law 94-142) was amended to provide services to handicapped infants and their families. Public Law 99-457 extended the services of P.L. 94-142 to the preschool-age child. Part H of the Act created a discretionary program for states to offer multiple services to infants and toddlers from birth to 3 who are at risk of developmental delay. The legislation requires the involvement of the family.

Social workers are part of the multidisciplinary team that serves these families; they provide many of the services, such as home visits, parent training, screening, and case management. However, social workers need a foundation in order to work with this special population. Part of the foundation includes knowledge of normal and atypical infant development, ethnic or cultural sensitivity, familiarity with disabilities, and methods of assessment. This information is not consistently offered in schools of social work (Bishop, Rounds, & Weil, 1993).

Practices and Policies to Support Children

Human service providers need to recognize that infants and young children are subject to emotional distress and cognitive impairment due to genetic and environmental factors. Many of these factors have been identified. The more factors present in the child's life, the greater the likelihood of negative outcomes.

There are factors that place infants at an elevated risk of negative developmental outcomes. Some of the identified risk factors include:

1. marital/family discord,
2. medically compromised children,
3. caretakers lacking social supports, and
4. separation of the infant from the caretakers.

These factors can influence both practice and policy. On the practice level, clinicians can incorporate into their work with adults the knowledge that conflict between adults is perceived and reacted to by very young children. Caretakers may believe that their young children are not aware of conflicts. The clinician can correct this misconception. Human service professionals who have contact with young children need to be vigilant for the presence of family conflict. Failure to address the conflict can interfere with attaining treatment goals.

The children of battered women may require treatment services. This has been a neglected population that is occasionally served by two different delivery systems. Shelters for battered women and child welfare agencies may both be involved in domestic violence situations, yet coordination of their activities can be difficult to achieve. The agencies may be based on two different organizational models. They frequently define different family members as their primary clients, resulting in separating the interests of children and their mothers. The separation impedes effective service delivery to both groups.

The caretakers of medically compromised children require additional services and supports. The child that is difficult to parent provides few rewards for the caretaker. Caretakers need support that can be provided by informal networks, professionals, and groups.

On the policy level, programs to enhance parent-child attachment and activities to reduce the incidence of medically fragile infants are cost effective. The attachment relationship is an important first step in developing competence, and programs to educate parents on methods of nurturing attachment may improve developmental outcomes. Low birth weight is a major threat to development and is a result of preterm birth. One method for reducing low birth weight babies is to provide early prenatal care.

In addition to the provision of prenatal care, infants and toddlers can profit from day-care and Head Start programs. High-quality and affordable day care is in limited supply. Child care has been viewed as a responsibility of parents. The voluntary sector and local governments have also played a role. Day care has become a political issue as more parents struggle to make child-care arrangements.

However, there has been little federal involvement in day care. The two political parties approach day care from different perspectives. Republicans favor using the tax system to help some families pay for care. Democrats favor direct actions to increase the supply of care. While the politicians debate, children wait.

Community-Based Services

Parenting is a difficult and stressful job. For parents without social supports, the task can seem overwhelming. Because the early period of development is critical to later success, providing resources to assist and support parents of young children is desirable.

Supportive services for parents can be provided by voluntary health and social welfare agencies. These services can be preventive and have an educational focus. These fundamental services include:

1. programs to encourage parent-child attachment
2. information on child development
3. activities for parent and child that encourage healthy development
4. on-site child care so parents can participate in activities such as discussions on limit setting, discipline, health, and nutrition

5. referrals to community resources
6. support groups and social activities

More specialized services may be needed by at-risk families. For example, families in which parental chemical dependency is an issue may need services such as:

1. crisis nursery
2. mental health and drug counseling
3. detoxification programs
4. education and job training
5. assistance in dealing with the criminal justice system
6. assistance with transportation and housing

For the older, school-age child the school provides an excellent setting for identifying and intervening with high-risk families. The school is a community institution and plays a major role in the life of the child. This role may expand in the future as policy makers debate using the public schools to provide care for preschool-age children. Techniques and tools for early screening for emotional and cognitive problems are available for the school-age child.

Child Welfare Services

Child welfare agencies can play an important role in the lives of infants and toddlers. This will require the agencies to allocate resources to train their workers and provide information on the needs and abilities of young children. By identifying at-risk families and offering appropriate referrals, child welfare workers can intervene early and help promote healthy development.

Child welfare workers are one of the few professional groups who make home calls and have the opportunity to observe youngsters in this most important setting. Home visits are an excellent—and in many instances the only—method for reaching difficult, suspicious, and isolated parents. Child welfare agencies have not historically defined their mission as early identification of at-risk families. The child welfare agency can act as a source of information about community services.

The historical child welfare service of foster care is needed to protect children but should be used parsimoniously, especially with young children. Separation and the events that lead up to it are sources of stress for children and can challenge and overwhelm their coping skills. Multiple placements or placement in less than adequate foster homes serves to further compromise these vulnerable children. Child welfare workers are in a frustrating position. Returning children to parents with poor skills or to unsafe homes is damaging. Keeping children in foster care where they may experience multiple placements and inadequate or harmful homes is also damaging. The solution may lie in implementing all components of permanency planning (see Chapter 6).

Insuring the Well-Being of Families

The United States lacks a policy to support families. Even basic supports such as child care, nutrition, housing, and health care are unavailable to many families. Employment can be considered a child welfare service because unemployment or underemployment results in no medical insurance as well as a lack of money. Parents cannot care for children without the ability to purchase needed goods and services.

In addition to health care and housing, income support is a pressing need for children. Chronic poverty and the deprivations associated with it compromise the healthy development of children. The only federal support for families is the residual AFDC program. Child allowance or family support programs available in other countries view each child as an essential resource and one that the state should help to support.

The income tax system has been used to provide limited assistance to parents. The Earned Income Tax Credit is designed to help working families. For the 1990 tax year, the maximum credit available to a parent with at least one child and who earned less than $20,264 was $953.

Another method of income support is a family allowance program. These programs are based, in part, on the belief that the state has an investment in children. The children represent the future of the country. There are a number of methods for administering such programs, but most include dispensing a minimal amount of money regardless of the income level of the parents. The money paid to wealthy families can be recaptured through the tax system by making the allowance taxable. Although the dollar amounts paid would not provide for a luxurious lifestyle, they would provide evidence that the state has an investment in children.

Summary

Expansion of the knowledge base in child development has provided insights on the special needs and abilities of infants and toddlers. By meeting the needs of this age group, optimal developmental outcomes can be achieved, and the children will be ready to meet the challenges of later developmental stages.

There are threats to the well-being of these children. The threats can be minimized by providing supports to the youngsters and their caretakers. Characteristics of the children as well as environmental factors increase the risk of negative outcomes for children. Family disharmony and maternal depression are particularly troublesome threats and require interventions at both the practice and policy levels.

Community-based family service programs can help to meet the developmental needs of families of infants and toddlers by providing supportive services such as education and training. Families at elevated risk require additional remedial services such as counseling and respite care. There has not been a national commitment to support families and reduce some of the known risks, such as lack of prenatal care, inadequate housing, and chronic deprivation. These policies and practices would help to foster healthy development in young children.

11

A Research Agenda
for the Future

Research is the basis for effective and efficient policy. In order to
target services it is necessary to know which children are at risk of
negative outcomes, what services are needed, and when these services should be offered. Problems in research design as well as
limited funding have contributed to a lack of rigorous research on
children.

This chapter discusses the limitations of research designs and the
lack of funding for research. Areas needing exploration are outlined,
and ethical issues in research on children are identified.

Issues that affect children have been the subject of researchers for years.
The published studies about specific topics such as education or foster
care are extensive. However, a closer examination of this research reveals
that there are limitations to both the quality and quantity of the data.
This chapter examines some of the gaps in research and knowledge
about children. The role of research in developing policies and services
for children and their families is explored.

Knowledge Gaps

Research could provide answers to fundamental questions such as
which children will experience difficulties and when these difficulties
will appear. Knowing which children should be targeted for prevention

and intervention efforts could make the delivery of these services more efficient and effective. Services can be directed at the most propitious time to children known to be at risk. Unfortunately, research has not been able to answer these questions adequately.

There are factors that place children at risk of negative outcomes. Research has identified some of these factors. For example, chronic prenatal exposure to alcohol increases the risk of fetal alcohol syndrome. Research has identified a relationship between a specific agent, alcohol, and a negative outcome, fetal alcohol syndrome. There is less information on other specific agents and the role they play in negative outcomes such as mental illness or learning disabilities. It is difficult for research designs to identify both the role and the contribution of any single agent to a negative outcome.

Problematic Research Designs

Correlations are not causality. Specific agents can be associated with negative outcomes. For example, growing up in a hostile, violent environment with inadequate and inconsistent caretakers increases the risk of negative developmental outcomes such as school failure, poor relationships with others, or delinquency. There may be an association between the environment and delinquency. However, there is no research to support the idea that these environmental agents cause delinquency. There are young people who are reared in difficult circumstances and become productive members of their communities.

One problem in trying to establish causal models relates to the complexities inherent in human beings as well as limitations in research and statistical methods. Retrospective studies, which are common designs in research on both adults and children, present special challenges in establishing causal relationships. Generally, retrospective studies examine an identified population, gather information on the history and characteristics of the population, and offer suggestions about possible relationships among factors.

Retrospective studies have been used with delinquents and alcohol dependent adolescents. These studies may indicate that the adolescents were reared in single parent homes in which the caretaker drank alcohol. There are adolescents reared in similar circumstances who do not have delinquency or alcohol dependency problems. In addition, there may be other factors, not identified by the research, that may account for observed differences. Perhaps the delinquent adolescents were also victims of physical abuse at an early age or placed great value on peer relationships. If the research design did not include questions about these factors, then their contribution to the delinquency would be unknown.

There are factors such as sample size, number of samples, and level of measurement that also influence the research process. Although sample sizes vary, small samples of fewer than 100 children are not uncommon. Comparison or control groups serve to strengthen research findings. For example, in order to identify the effects of prenatal illicit drug exposure on the infant, a two-group design would be helpful. In one group, the infants are exposed to the drugs. The second group is similar to the first group except there is no drug exposure. Because of the complex and multidetermined nature of many problems, finding a comparison group that is similar to the study group is difficult.

The level of data gathered (nominal, ordinal, interval, or ratio) influences which statistics can be used to analyze the data. Some of the stronger statistical models (such as analysis of variance or path analysis) that address the relative contributions of specific factors to an outcome require interval- or ratio-level data and large sample sizes.

It is difficult to take the findings of a research project and apply them to an individual child. Research findings usually describe characteristics of a group. For example, studies of adult women arrested for prostitution reveal that many report histories of sexual abuse. This is a retrospective group study. Although this may be an important finding it must be used with caution. It is not possible to say that any individual child who has been molested will engage in prostitution.

Retrospective group studies can yield ridiculous results. For example, a survey of inmates on death rows across the country could suggest that many were not graduated from high school, drank alcohol, and grew up in single parent homes. This is not the same as saying these factors caused the inmates to commit capital offenses. It is probably true that most of the inmates drank milk, ate bread, and played softball. No one would suggest that these are risk factors associated with criminality. It is inappropriate to try to use data from retrospective studies to make predictions.

The inferences that are drawn from retrospective studies can be harmful if applied to individuals. Research indicates that many of the parents who have abused their children were reared in homes where they had been subject to abuse. Maltreatment has been linked with other negative events such as drug use (Fitz, Galantes, Lifshutz, & Egelko, 1993), delinquency (Lewis, Mallouh, & Webb, 1989; Sandberg, 1989) and affective disorders (Stein, Golding, Siegel, Burnam, & Sorenson, 1988). There are also non-abusive parents who as children were exposed to abuse. By labeling and assuming that correlation is causality, young adults who were reared in difficult circumstances may needlessly doubt their parenting abilities. Some may actually be fearful of assuming the role of parent because they might repeat the dysfunctional behaviors of their parents. Research to support the notion of intergeneration transmission of maltreatment is weak (Star, MacLean, & Keating, 1991).

An additional problem concerns the people who participate in retrospective studies. The groups frequently studied have a special status (such as mental patients, inmates, clients at a counseling agency) and may not be representative of the larger population, making it more difficult to draw valid comparisons.

There is no definitive explanation for dysfunctional behavior. Some children reared in violent homes become abusive parents while others do not. It is difficult to explain why some youngsters reared in non-abusive families become abusive parents. Research has been able, however, to identify a cluster of variables that are frequently associated with negative outcomes. These variables can be considered risk factors. The presence of a risk factor or set of factors does not necessarily mean that the negative event will occur. It should, however, alert concerned adults to the possibility.

Research on Risk Factors

Factors associated with particular negative events are unknown. For example, it is not known what causes adolescent drug use, other than drugs. If the adolescent has no contact with drugs then there is no likelihood of the adolescent abusing drugs. This is not a helpful causal statement because it suggests that drugs cause abuse. One could also argue that contact with children causes child abuse because adults who do not have contact with children do not abuse children. These statements cannot be used to guide the development of prevention or intervention programs.

There are no single factors or even sets of factors clearly associated with particular negative outcomes (such as dropping out of school, drug abuse, delinquency, child abuse, or developing a psychiatric disorder).

What research has been suggesting is that there is a cluster of factors that increase the risk of negative outcomes.

The research on the correlates of drug use by adolescents contributed to the development of multiple risk models. No individual characteristic or environmental circumstance was consistently related to drug use; therefore, a multiple risk model was developed. The multiple risk model has much to offer the child welfare field since it incorporates an ecological perspective that includes individual characteristics (including biological traits) as well as environmental conditions and the interactions between the individual and the environment.

The 1986 Anti Drug Abuse Act (Public Law 99-570) established categories of young people to be considered at risk for drug use. The categories include youth:

- with a chemically abusing parent
- with a history of physical, sexual, or psychological abuse
- who have dropped out of school
- who are pregnant
- who are economically disadvantaged
- who have committed a violent or delinquent act
- with a history of mental health problems
- who have attempted suicide
- who have experienced long-term physical pain due to an injury
- who have experienced chronic failure in school

Using the material from the drug abuse field and including other known risk factors, it is possible to identify variables that should alert concerned adults, schools, social welfare agencies, and communities. The factors can be grouped into individual and social categories. As is illustrated in Table 11.1, research has identified many risk factors. No single factor or set of factors is causative of negative outcomes. However, some of these factors are likely to occur together, increasing the risks.

Mental Health Research

Millions of children suffer from emotional problems. Estimates vary, but approximately 12% to 15% or 7.5 to 9.5 million children have mental health problems serious enough to require professional treatment (Office

TABLE 11.1 Risk Factors

Individual Factors
Biological
a. prenatal exposure to noxious agents
b. preterm birth
c. chronic illness
d. difficult temperament
e. parent with a psychiatric disorder and/or chemical abuse problem

Personality
a. mental health problems, especially difficulty with anger, controlling impulses, and depression
b. criminal behavior, precocious sexual activity
c. school problems, especially grade retention

Interpersonal
a. tenuous or hostile relationships with caretakers
b. exposure to parental discord
c. history of victimization, especially violent physical or sexual abuse
d. poor relationships with peers

Social Factors
a. hostile, unsafe environments
b. economic deprivation
c. poor schools
d. lack of opportunity to participate in community life

---

of Technology Assessment, 1986). With so many children in need it is disheartening to learn that only 20% to 30% receive treatment.

Children have received little attention from the mental health industry. A review of the most widely used publication for diagnosing mental disorders reveals that children have been invisible. The *Diagnostic and Statistical Manual (DSM)* was first published in 1952 (American Psychiatric Association). It contained only two categories devoted to children. The second edition of the DSM added six more categories (American Psychiatric Association, 1968). The third edition, as well as the revised third edition, of the *DSM* recognized many more disorders (American Psychiatric Association, 1980, 1987).

Although this increased recognition is positive, it has not been without controversy (Garmetzy, 1979). Applying psychiatric labels to children should be performed with caution. The *DSM-III-R* lists delays in reading and math as categories of mental disorders. Development is not linear and children acquire cognitive skills within a broad time frame. A delay in learning to read is now defined as a mental disorder. *Mental disorder* implies a more serious, negative condition than does the word *delay*. It is questionable whether a learning disability such as dyslexia should be included in a book devoted to psychiatric problems (Gustavsson, in press).

In order to research the emotional problems of children, a system for classifying childhood disturbance is helpful. However, the system must be both valid and reliable. The validity and reliability of the DSM has been questioned. There do not appear to be clearly understandable differences among some disorders. For example, one study reported the children who met the criteria for oppositional disorder also met the criteria for conduct disorder and attention deficit disorder (Costello, Edelbrock, Dulcan, Kalas, & Kloric, 1984).

Depression in children can be a difficult diagnostic category. One study has reported that children meeting the criteria for depressive disorders also met the criteria for attention deficit disorder, anorexia nervosa, and conduct disorder (Carlson & Cantwell, 1980). These are important disorders and the inability to distinguish clearly among disorders threatens the validity of the *DSM*.

There are serious questions about the reliability of the *DSM*. There are various methods for determining reliability. One method involves looking at how often people observing the same behavior agree in their assessment of that behavior. If the observers agreed all the time, the reliability would be 100%. In statistics, this is referred to as a kappa of 1.00. Kappas of less than .60 (60%) usually indicate poor reliability. One study reported kappas for child disorders of .52 and .55, indicating low reliability (Rutter & Shaffer, 1980).

The primary method for classifying the mental health problems of children suffers from validity and reliability problems. Nevertheless, it at least recognizes that children can suffer from emotional problems.

Funding Research

The federal government is by far the primary funder of research on the emotional problems of children. There is no single federal agency or program dedicated to research on children. This makes it difficult to learn how much money is allocated to children's research. A number of federal agencies provide services for children and within each of these programs a portion of the budget is spent on child mental health research.

TABLE 11.2 Federal Funds for Research on Child Mental Health

Year	ADAMHA	NICHD	Total	(Total in Constant Dollars)
1983	39,873	38,118	77,991	(77,993)
1984	43,510	43,513	87,023	(81,712)
1985	52,215	50,198	102,413	(90,997)
1986	55,327	52,876	108,203	(91,947)
1987	57,180	58,062	115,242	(92,297)

SOURCE: Eisenberg, 1989.

The two largest federal agencies to fund child mental health research are the Alcohol, Drug Abuse, and Mental Health Administration (ADAMHA) and the National Institute on Child Health and Development (NICHD). Funding for research on mental health, and particularly child mental health, has had a low priority when compared to funds allocated for research on biomedical issues. This is disturbing because many more Americans are affected by mental health issues than any other disease.

As Table 11.2 illustrates, there is meager support for child mental health research. This creates a cycle that can slow the development of knowledge. Research is expensive. Researchers interested in children's issues are unable to get funding and therefore pursue research interests in other areas instead. When funds are allocated to an area, researchers redirect their interests to where the funds are. More could be learned about child mental health if children became a priority.

New Arenas for Research

Based on prior research, it is possible to develop a specific agenda for future research. For example, much effort has been devoted to identifying risk factors. However, knowing these risk factors creates new questions. This is typical of research in that for every question answered, new questions emerge.

The Role of Risk Factors

While identifying risk factors is important, it raises fundamental questions about how these risk factors interact, at what stage in development a risk factor is most salient, and which factors are associated with a particular negative outcome such as delinquency, depression, or drug abuse.

Knowledge of risk factors can inform prevention efforts; this is one of the primary purposes of risk factor research. Knowing what factors precede the development of a problem can enable practitioners to design early intervention programs that can prevent the problem. There are costs associated with prevention and although the costs are considerably less than the costs of treatment (see Chapter 12), they are a factor. Prevention efforts are of little value to those not at risk. Public health-oriented prevention models frequently target large groups, such as all school children or the general public, using limited resources inefficiently.

Two recent examples of this group approach have been used with drugs and AIDS. Television commercials, also known as public service announcements, are designed to alert the viewer to the dangers of drugs. In the late 1980s the Surgeon General mailed a pamphlet to every address explaining how to prevent AIDS infection. There is a debate within the public health field about the efficacy of such broad-based efforts because many television viewers are at low risk for drug abuse and many of the households receiving the AIDS pamphlet are at low risk for contracting the virus. At the same time individuals at high risk for drug abuse or contracting and transmitting the virus were not reached by the television commercials or the pamphlet.

In addition to debates on how to target prevention programs, questions arise about the usefulness of knowing the risk factors. Knowledge of risk does not necessarily mean knowing how to prevent the development of the risk. For example, low self-esteem is associated with a variety of negative outcomes such as depression, delinquency, and school failure. There is little doubt that low self-esteem is harmful, yet there is little consensus on the most effective way to prevent the development of low self-esteem, in what developmental stage the interventions should be applied, and which individual children or groups of children should receive the interventions.

Not only are there questions about how to prevent problems, there are questions about the effectiveness of interventions. There are many types of interventions applied to children suffering from emotional problems. These interventions include medication, play therapy, family therapy, cognitive therapy, behavior modification, group therapy, social skills training, peer counseling, and residential treatment.

Which of these interventions is most effective and with which types of problems and children can only be determined through research. Outcome studies are rare, especially when compared with outcome studies on adults. Mental health professionals have an obligation to intervene in the lives of children in a responsible manner. They cannot meet this obligation if they do not know what interventions are effective and under what circumstances.

It is important not to ignore the other side of risk factor research. Identifying factors that increase the vulnerability of children to negative outcomes can yield important information necessary for developing policies and practices. Knowledge of the factors that help to protect children from negative outcomes is equally important.

Identifying protective factors can provide valuable information for policy makers and service providers. Reducing the long list of negative factors will require extensive effort and resources. While the political groups debate the program, children suffer. Knowledge of protective factors can be used by communities to structure inexpensive programs. For example, support networks, positive role models, and close relationships with caring adults have all been identified as protective factors (Rutter, 1984; Werner, 1986; Werner & Smith, 1982).

Children and the Courts

Understanding children's emotional and cognitive capacities is more than an academic exercise. This can be illustrated in the field of criminal justice. As children enter courtrooms more frequently to testify against their abusers, judges and juries must determine the validity of children's testimony. Research has a vital role to play because it can identify the conditions children need in order to be able to recall and convey past events.

Evaluating children's testimony requires an understanding of developmental stages. The ability of children to perceive and accurately relate experiences is influenced by cognitive and emotional factors. As children grow, their abilities expand. Rapid fluctuations in abilities characterize development, making it difficult to establish rigid age ranges for particular abilities.

Research suggests that young children, under the age of 9, need help to recall past events and have difficulty attributing motivations to events (Nurcombe, 1986). The research on children's suggestibility is inconclusive. There are studies that suggest that adults can influence how young children recall events (King & Yullie, 1987). There is other research that suggests the opposite (Jones & McGraw, 1987). Anatomically correct dolls were initially regarded as a reliable tool for interviewing young, developmentally challenged, or nonverbal children. Research suggests that the dolls may not be a valid technique (Terr, 1988).

In order to evaluate the usefulness of anatomically correct dolls on the degree of children's suggestibility, more studies are needed. These studies can lead to techniques for interviewing children that courts can find acceptable. Justice for children will remain elusive until valid and reliable methods for enabling children to testify are developed.

Caution in Research

There is consensus that more research on children is needed. However, the research can pose threats to children. Caution needs to be exercised to avoid labeling children. Identifying which characteristics heighten the risk of a negative outcome can create a self-fulfilling prophecy. As parents and especially teachers become aware that factors are associated with problems, they may look for and inadvertently create those problems.

Children are open to the messages communicated by significant adults. The major source of information used in building self-esteem comes from the very adults who may be anticipating negative outcomes. As these adults communicate both verbally and nonverbally that the child has or will develop problems, the child may then meet the expectations of these adults and develop the problem.

The transitory nature of childhood makes prediction even more difficult. Childhood is characterized by nonlinear development and rapid changes. Many behaviors of children that can upset adults (such as fighting with peers, pica, and specific fears) are transitory and normal. Sibling rivalry, which can disturb parents, is common and not predictive of a lifelong pattern of conflict.

There are, however, other behaviors that are predictive of later adjustment problems. These behaviors are not transitory and require early interventions in order to help the child achieve his or her potential. Mental retardation, psychotic disorders, and antisocial behaviors tend to be long-lasting (Gelfand, Jensen, & Drew, 1982). Early intervention can help children with these disorders.

Research on children presents special ethical considerations. For example, young children cannot give informed consent. This places additional burdens on researchers. Older children, with cognitive and verbal skills, should be involved in the consent process. Although most states establish the arbitrary age of 18 as the demarkation between child status and adult status, studies indicate that from age 10 or 11, children understand abstractions and are beginning to form measured judgments.

Research on children should be subject to strict scrutiny. Any possible negative consequences of the research should be anticipated and plans for addressing the consequences need to be included in the project. Experimental designs that have much to offer the researcher interested in identifying causal relationships are fraught with ethical problems. For example, should children be exposed to a noxious event in order to see how they respond? What about children in a control group? Should these children be denied something beneficial, such as mental health treatment, in studies designed to assess the effectiveness of a new treatment?

Summary

Research is often overlooked as a child welfare activity. Yet policies and practices, in order to be appropriate and effective, should be based on empirical research. Through research, factors that can threaten the well-being of children as well as factors that can enhance well-being can be identified.

There is much that is unknown about children. The needs and abilities of children have been of low priority among researchers and funders. Research involving adults and medical issues receives higher priority. This is shortsighted because failure to ensure the healthy development of children results in increased costs when they grow up to become troubled adults.

Children's mental health is particularly overlooked. This is unfortunate since a significant minority of children experience mental health problems. Many of the interventions used with adults suffering from emotional problems cannot be applied to children. Research is needed in order to establish effective treatments.

Children present special challenges for researchers. The transitory nature of childhood makes prediction risky. Problems experienced by a young person one day may be gone the next day. Without rigorous designs, children could be placed at increased risk of being labeled. The vulnerability of children places added demands for ethical research practices. There are difficulties associated with research on children but none are insurmountable.

12

Preventive Policies and Programs in Child Welfare

The previous chapters in this book outlined the social problems affecting children and the deficiencies in the programs and policies designed to address these inadequacies. The state of children in the 1990s is in great need of a concerted social response. Professionals and child welfare advocates know many programs and approaches that work. The 1990s represents the decade when child welfare must become a national priority if we are to turn back the numerous negative trends facing today's children. This chapter stresses the need for a preventive policy approach to serving the social needs of children and outlines an agenda for action.

The previous chapters outlined the multiple concerns of children and families in this nation. Although we are a country of great wealth and freedoms, millions of children are closed out of opportunities for healthy growth and development. Due to race, status, geographic location, physical ability, or other notable differences, millions of children are outside the mainstream of society. The levels of inadequate care and neglect of children are severe nationwide. Millions of children live in poverty, hundreds of thousands are in foster care and other forms of temporary care, millions have no health insurance and do not receive basic medical care, and—for many children—runaway shelters and the streets are all they know as home.

The results of this national neglect of children are delayed development and a permanent loss of contributions from too many of our nation's future adults. This chapter covers the consequences and costs of national neglect, what social service workers can and should do, and concludes with a policy agenda to change the current status of our nation's children.

The Value of
Preventive Social Welfare Policies

Although it is impossible to prevent all social and human mishaps, much more can be done to protect people from social breakdown. The concept of prevention is rarely found in social welfare policy planning. Even though researchers have demonstrated the cost effectiveness of early service intervention, we as a country have been reluctant to embrace a preventive strategy in meeting the needs of children and families.

Although we know the value of early intervention efforts, the vast majority of social welfare services are residual—developed and implemented after a problem is identified (Wilensky & Lebeaux, 1958). The reasons for this approach are varied and lie in our social values and economic system. This nation was founded on principles of self-help and ability. When there is breakdown, the family is the first line of support. Only when those efforts fail are we willing to turn to state intervention for support. While this philosophy is not inherently flawed, the reality of our social structure makes it a problematic approach.

If we respond to social need only when there is an identified problem, there is never any attention given to the underlying cause. For example, we know that poor education and poverty are linked. Education can lead to better employment, and a good job can provide adequate income for a family. Yet, we continue to give grudging public assistance without seriously considering how to educate people nationally, regardless of where they live, the color of their skin, their gender, or family background.

For self-reliance and family support to work effectively, people must start with open access to ample opportunities and resources. It is impossible for an impoverished family to give children the same chances as a family of economic means. Barriers to opportunity such as racism, sexism, and limited knowledge of availability inhibit access to opportunity. Social welfare policy needs to focus on opening opportunities for healthy development, safe environments, education, employment, and growth rather than only directing resources to the breakdowns in society.

The dominance of a residual approach to social welfare over a preventive response demonstrates the dilemma between choosing short-term gain over long-term benefits. Preventive social policy calls for services designed to serve all, regardless of whether there is an identified need. Thus, there will be times when a person who does not need the services will receive them anyway. For example, if prenatal care were available to all women, there undoubtedly would be some women who would have delivered healthy babies even if they did not receive care. Those who argue against preventive services cite the waste of resources as reason to provide residual services, often referred to as targeted services. Thus, if only those who have identified needs receive services, resources would be distributed in an efficient manner.

The Consequences of Current Policy

Although, over the short term, residual policies may seem effective, preventive resources are needed to stem the continued growth of social problems. For example, over the past 50 years the response of policy makers in dealing with the problem of poverty has been residual. Policy makers focused on benefit levels and eligibility for existing cash assistance programs rather than on ways to lift people permanently out of poverty. Little attention was given to finding ways to prevent people from falling into poverty. Most social concerns gain public attention only after they become a problem. As homelessness was recognized as a social problem, initial public response centered on finding emergency shelters and food. Only after the problem was recognized to be more complex and more beds in shelters did not decrease the number of homeless persons, did providing decent affordable housing become a major social issue. It was not, and still is not, a national social goal, although as a nation we should be concerned with every citizen having a safe and affordable place to live.

Because prenatal care is not guaranteed, most low-income women receive little or no care. As discussed in Chapter 2, inadequate prenatal care often leads to the birth of underweight babies. Such infants tend to be born prematurely and require costly health care throughout their lives. The cost of prenatal care is about $600, but intensive care costs for a premature baby are $1,000 a day (Children's Defense Fund, 1989b).

Although we know the value of early health care for pregnant women, it is not a national priority.

The passage of major child welfare legislation in 1980 was a response to the realization that thousands of children were languishing in foster care without the prospect of ever having a permanent home. Little attention, however, was given to the need for support services to families *before* there is disruption and state intervention. Such policy changes, although significant efforts, attempt to "fix" the symptom rather than change the root cause of the problem. The end result is that we are caught in a perpetual cycle of responding to social breakdowns rather than creating supportive services that prevent breakdowns from occurring in the first place.

The Costs of Neglect

The development of human resources is vital for our national well-being. Students from poor families are more likely to drop out of school. For each class of high school dropouts, the nation loses $240 billion in unearned wages and unpaid taxes over their lifetimes (Butler, 1988). This does not include the public expense for remedial education, welfare, health, and social services.

The average annual cost to hold a young person at a juvenile detention center is $43,000 (Camp & Camp, 1987). For the same amount of money, preventive services could be provided to a child for his or her entire childhood (see Table 12.1).

Preventive services are beneficial in the long term. Most social problems that go untreated become very costly over time. Losses in childhood, such as in physical and emotional development, education, and socialization, become firmly entrenched by adulthood. The personal and social costs then become great. Social problems that are prevented from occurring save significant costs over time. Table 12.2 outlines some of the savings that can be realized by providing services *before* there is a problem rather than after the fact.

The overall benefit to society of caring for our children today is a healthy and productive workforce for tomorrow. The United States is developing a "human resource deficit" (Hewlett, 1991). The difference in the jobs to be filled and the abilities of those available to fill them is

TABLE 12.1 Costs of Essential Preventive Services

Program	Annual Cost ($)		Years of Investment	Total ($)
Medicaid	500	×	18	9,000
Head Start	2,500	×	3	7,500
Educational assistance	600	×	12	7,200
Summer jobs	800	×	4	3,200
Public college	4,000	×	4	16,000
Total				42,900

SOURCE: Children's Defense Fund (1988), p. xxxii.

growing. While caring for disadvantaged and neglected children is a worthy cause in itself, national survival will depend on it.

A complete social service system must provide for those social needs and mishaps that cannot be prevented, while simultaneously working to prevent social concerns from becoming problematic and dysfunctional. Social policy can strengthen families. Social institutions such as schools, community agencies, and religious organizations, as well as the government, can provide much needed support to families. Such a system must stress the cost effectiveness of preventive approaches as well as the social responsibility of giving all children chances to succeed.

TABLE 12.2 Cost of Services Versus Benefits of Prevention

	Cost vs. Benefits
Prenatal Care	$1 investment in care saves $3.38 in the cost of caring for low birth weight babies
Medical care	$1 spent on comprehensive prenatal care saves $2 in first-year care
Family planning	$1 spent on health, education, and family planning services saves $2 through preventing unintended pregnancies
Childhood immunization	$1 investment saves $10 in later medical costs
Pre-school education	$1 spent on pre-school education can save $6 in later social costs
Welfare hotels	$800-$1,000 a month in rent for a family compared to $3,000 in a temporary welfare hotel

SOURCES: Children's Defense Fund (1992); House Select Committee on Children, Youth & Families (1988a, 1990).

The State of Current Services
for Children and Families

The number of programs that exist to serve children and families in need appears comprehensive. There are medical care programs, school intervention services, nutrition and food programs, employment training, and housing assistance. In spite of the array of existing programs, children are poorly served.

Table 12.3 lists the major federal programs that provide services for children and families in need.

In fiscal year 1992, the federal government spent about $100 billion in cash assistance and in-kind services for disadvantaged children and their families. This outlay represented approximately 7% of the total national budget. Another $10-$15 billion is spent annually for services to all children, mostly in the form of tax credits (Committee on Ways and Means, 1991). In the same year that 7% of the budget went to aid needy children and their families, the federal government spent almost $290 billion for national defense and almost $300 billion for interest owed on the national debt. These two expenditures alone accounted for more than a third of the dollars spent by the federal government in 1992.

The elderly represent another group provided with national support. Although the population of children is more than double that of people over 65 years of age, and the number of poor children is three and a half times greater than the number of poor elderly persons, federal spending for the elderly accounts for about 28% of the national budget (Committee on Ways and Means, 1991; Social Security Administration, 1990). Over the past few decades, policy support for older persons increased while children's services garnered less support. This trend is problematic. Social service advocates are witnessing a tug of war between children's needs and those of older Americans. This split is counterproductive and positions groups both worthy of national support in adversarial roles. Today's elderly need today's children to guarantee a productive tomorrow.

Children's services, although covering an array of needs, have never been a national budget priority. Where a nation chooses to spend its money is important. It is shortsighted not to view spending on children as an investment in the future. The citizens of the United States have accepted the need to develop military strength and capabilities for the future as demonstrated by programs such as "Star Wars." Care for the

TABLE 12.3 Major Federal Programs to Aid Children and Families in Need

	FY 1992 Funding	
Cash Assistance		
Aid to Families with Dependent Children	$14.8	B
Social Security—Dependents' Benefits	$9.2	B
Child Support Enforcement	$668	M
Medical Services		
Medicaid—Children	$17	B
Maternal and Child Health Services	$650	M
Food and Nutrition		
Food Stamps	$21.8	B
WIC	$2.5	B
Other Child Nutrition	$6.1	B
Housing		
Lower Income Housing Assistance	$7.8	B
Education		
Head Start	$2.2	B
Compensatory Education—Chapter 1	$6.2	B
Education for Handicapped Children	$2.2	B
Employment		
Job Corps	$926	M
Summer Youth Employment and Training	$1.2	B
Social Services		
Social Services Block Grant—Title XX	$2.7	B
Child Welfare Services	$274	M
Foster Care and Adoption Assistance	$2.5	B
Child Abuse Grants	$39	M
Runaway Youth Program	$36	M
Juvenile Justice	$69	M
TOTAL	$99	B

SOURCE: Office of Management and Budget (1993).

elderly has improved over the years and accounts for 28% of the national budget. Unfortunately, we are negligent in preparing for the future through investment in children. This approach cannot continue. Our economic situation is worsening. The recession of the early 1990s is not loosening its grip. Social service programs cut back during the previous decade do not have excess dollars to return. And, as this book has demonstrated, the problems and needs of children are worsening and require more national attention. The social policy agenda must change, and the care of children must become a national priority.

Early Intervention

The majority of public programs for children are residual in nature, but there is a growing awareness of the value of providing services early in a child's life. Existing early intervention programs help young children develop educationally and socially. They provide learning experiences that help prepare children for school and develop better social skills, particularly for children from disadvantaged backgrounds.

Early intervention efforts provide a proven record upon which to develop broader preventive policies. Studies (Berrueta-Clement, Schweinhart, Barnett, Epstein, & Weikart, 1984; Lally, Mangione, & Honig, 1987; Schweinhart, 1989) have demonstrated that early childhood intervention efforts can have positive long-term effects. Research indicates that—particularly for at-risk children—early intervention programs can improve school performance, decrease the incidence of later juvenile delinquent acts, lower dropout rates, and decrease welfare dependence. Although children and their families benefit, early intervention efforts offer a cost-effective social policy approach. Positive outcomes beneficial to society include decreasing the future need for remedial education, juvenile delinquency services, and welfare costs.

The issue is not a lack of knowledge, but of will. Lisbeth Schorr's (1988) research outlines programs with proven results and the "evidence that crucial outcomes among high-risk children can be changed by systematic intervention early in the life cycle" (p. 292). Over the 25 years since its inception, the Head Start program has demonstrated positive results working with disadvantaged children, yet it has never received full support. Although by 1988 almost 500,000 children participated in Head Start programs, less than 17% of children from eligible low-income families are enrolled (Riddle, 1989). Advocates have been lobbying for increased funding so that more eligible children can be served.

Other services that employ an early intervention approach include home visiting and respite care. Home visiting programs are designed to provide services such as health care or social support to families within their homes. Evaluations of home visiting programs with an emphasis on early intervention demonstrate improvement in the health and well-being of participant families (U.S. General Accounting Office, 1990b). Programs have proven to be cost effective by providing services early, thereby decreasing the need for more costly services later.

Respite care provides child care on a temporary basis for families. Services are targeted for families with children who may be at risk of abuse and neglect due to stress. These children include those who live with disabilities, mental illness, chronic illness, or terminal illness. Respite care provides a break for parents of special needs children and as such serves the entire family and acts as a social support. Although little research is available, those involved in the provision and use of respite care cite it as very successful (U.S. General Accounting Office, 1990c).

The knowledge and skills for developing early intervention efforts exist. The long- and short-term benefits are clear and well documented. The task at hand is to develop broader support for early intervention efforts and promote a preventive social policy agenda for children. The key to achieving that goal rests with professionals who understand the needs of at-risk children and have the expertise to develop, implement, and evaluate successful preventive programs.

The Role of
Human Service Professionals

For those who work with children and families, it is not enough to have strong clinical practice skills. Child welfare practitioners must understand the social welfare system, programs, and policies that govern the services provided for children and families in need. Today's practitioner faces limited resources, barriers to service delivery and access, and ineffective systems. Often child welfare practitioners work with people who feel overwhelmed and powerless or are discouraged and angry with the social service system due to previous negative encounters. The residual approach fosters frustration and stigma because it is directed toward families that are identified as dysfunctional. All too often, child welfare services are developed in response to symptoms rather than causes. The current state of our child welfare system presents a challenge to today's practitioners.

Of great importance is the child welfare practitioners' ability to understand the system through the eyes of those with whom they work. Children who grow up as recipients of child welfare services have the system as their frame of reference. Their outlook on life, response to authority, and life expectations are all colored by their experiences. Greater emphasis on prevention and social support would help to alleviate the negative image of child welfare services. Preventive services can be more universal and not have the stigma of dysfunction attached. With a preventive social service approach, the causes of problems—not their symptoms—become central. Child welfare practitioners need to develop a proactive approach to policy making and program development in order to advocate for more preventive services.

Key steps to take in promoting a preventive approach to child welfare practice include:

- Understanding the child welfare system and being knowledgeable about the work you do
- Developing empathy for the children and families who are served by the child welfare system
- Educating the public about the needs of at-risk children and the cost of national neglect
- Collaborating with other professionals to develop a coalition to advocate for children
- Developing community-based services that help to empower families and support them in their home environments
- Becoming actively involved with local and national elected officials to advocate for children and changes in the current child welfare system
- Becoming committed to evaluation and research to aid in making decisions about resource allocation and to find better ways to care for children

Individual child welfare workers alone cannot change the current system. The above points need to be carried out in the context of larger organization. Denny, Pokela, Jackson, and Matava (1989) found that to be effective in influencing child welfare policy, organizations need to coalesce and develop organized strategies to have an impact on policy making and elected officials. The way to achieve this is through educating legislators on specific policy issues as well as influencing their values toward children and families. Human service professionals are well trained in interview techniques, person-to-person interactions, and understanding the dynamics of human behavior. These skills should be applied to influencing policy makers. Personal contact between elected officials and child welfare practitioners needs to become a priority for organizations serving children and families.

Policies Sensitive to Children and Families in Need

One of the goals of this book is to present the current state of children in the United States. Unfortunately, the quality of life and well-being of millions of children are far below what a wealthy nation such as ours can provide. This situation is gaining recognition from all parts of the political spectrum. In June 1991 the National Commission on Children released the results of 2 years of research on the status of children and families in the United States. The Commission, established by Public Law 100-203, consists of members appointed by the president and Congress. It is a bipartisan group representing a broad array of political beliefs. The Commission's report clearly outlines the need to improve the current system of care for children:

> At every age, among all races and income groups, and in communities nationwide, many children are in jeopardy. They grow up in families whose lives are in turmoil. . . . The harshness of these children's lives and their tenuous hold on tomorrow cannot be countenanced by a wealthy nation, a caring people, or a prudent society. America's future depends on these children, too. If we measure success not just by how well most children do, but by how poorly some fare, America falls far short. (National Commission on Children, 1991, pp. 3-4)

A year later, yet another national task force recognized the need to take a broader approach to caring for children because our "current programs are typically fragmented and uncoordinated" (Task Force on Youth Development and Community Programs, 1992, p. 12). There is no shortage of information on the shortcomings and inadequacies of child welfare services in this country. In addition, there is tremendous collective knowledge on what works and what benefits children in need. The challenge now is to develop the collective will to make changes and institute policies that are proactive and benefit children.

With the knowledge of what works and what does not work along with insight into the state of children in society today, an agenda for action can be developed. Such an agenda must provide for the immediate needs of millions of children as well as work to prevent the continued decline in the well-being of America's children. Although most current services are residual, there are ways to incorporate a more preventive philosophy into the existing structure (Segal & Gustavsson, 1990). While services must respond to immediate need and provide emergency care, progress can be made in countering the cause of the problem and working toward prevention of continued need. This approach involves response to the emergency, stabilization of the child and family, and a final goal of independence from the social service system. Thus the focus of child welfare practitioners progresses from response to emergency situations to aiding families to become self-supporting.

An Action Agenda

What follows is a set of recommendations to improve the lives of children, help families become self-supporting, and in the process improve the prospects for a positive national future.

1. SUPPORT AND EXPAND
EXISTING PROGRAMS THAT WORK

Programs that stress early intervention and are proven to have positive outcomes should be provided with sufficient resources and expanded to reach more children and families in need. Programs such as Head Start, WIC, childhood immunization, and well-baby clinics are current programs that must receive full public support.

2. FOCUS ON PREVENTIVE SERVICES DESIGNED
FOR LONG-TERM IMPROVEMENTS

The concept of prevention must be incorporated into current services. All new efforts must strive toward serving all children and families in order to stem the growth in social problems and ensure healthy opportunities for all children regardless of their social or economic background.

3. DEVELOP AND ENHANCE SERVICES THAT SUPPORT PARENTS IN CARING FOR THEIR OWN CHILDREN

Programs such as respite care, in-home services, and parent training assist families in staying together and help parents to develop better skills to care for their own children. These services need to be developed as a social support based in local communities.

4. DEVELOP SERVICES THAT SUPPORT ALL FAMILIES

Numerous social policies need to be enacted that provide support to all families. These policies include family leave legislation to allow parents to take time off from employment to care for a family member and still have their job when they return. Other "family friendly" policies needed in the workplace are flex-time and on-site day care to respond to the growing number of working parents. In addition, the supply of affordable and quality day care is well below the need and requires a commitment to greater resources.

5. EMPHASIZE COMPREHENSIVE SERVICE DELIVERY

Services need to be delivered from a system-of-care approach. Communities, to be in a better position to serve the multiple needs of children and families today, need to provide a wide array of services with a focus on the entire family. Comprehensive services include collaboration of all systems involved in the provision of child welfare services. Outreach and in-home care are key in reaching families who are not already served and in providing preventive services.

6. EMPOWER FAMILIES

Emphasis must be placed on tapping into the strengths of families. Service providers can be instrumental in urging families to become their own advocates and support. Training and knowledge can prepare parents to be the first line for service delivery for their children. Appropriate professional supports and respite care can create a system where parents are partners in providing services for their children.

7. ADVOCATE

The most important action for child welfare practitioners on the national level is educating the public and policy makers about the needs of children. Individuals and organizations must take an active role in politics and place children's issues on the agenda of all elected officials. Use of media and lobbying efforts are important skills for child welfare professionals to develop.

Summary

Children do not vote, do not contribute to election campaigns, and do not make policy decisions. The development and implementation of social policy for children rests with adults. Professionals who provide services for children must take an active role in influencing the state of programs and policies in this country. For too long, children's services have been fragmented and respond only once there is an identified problem. For the United States to be in a position to grow and prosper in the coming decades, its children must be healthy, educated, and socially developed.

Prevention of social problems through early intervention is key to improving the overall well-being of children. Preventive services have proven to be cost effective. Advocates for children must draw public attention to the importance of alleviating poverty; providing health care for all children; creating educational opportunities and training for meaningful employment; and protecting children from abuse, neglect, and violence. Child welfare practitioners must know their craft well to be effective service providers. However, the 1990s demand more than excellent practitioners. For children to be best served, child welfare professionals must become proactive and advocate for policies and programs sensitive to the needs of children and families.

References

Abelson, H., & Miller, J. (1985). A decade of trends in cocaine use in the household population. *National Institute on Drug Abuse Research Monograph, 61*, 35-49.

Alan Guttmacher Institute. (1987). *Blessed events and the bottom line: Financing maternity care in the United States.* New York: Author.

Alan Guttmacher Institute. (1991). *Facts in brief—Teenage sexual and reproductive behavior in the United States.* New York: Author.

Allen-Meares, P., & Lane, B. (1983). Assessing the adaptive behaviors of children and youths. *Social Work, 28*(4), 297-301.

Als, H. (1984). Newborn behavioral assessment. In W. Burns & J. Lavigne (Eds.), *Progress in pediatric psychology* (pp. 1-46). New York: Grune & Stratton.

American Academy of Child and Adolescent Psychiatry. (1990). Child abuse—The hidden bruises. *Facts for Families,* No. 5 (1/90).

American Humane Association. (1986). *Highlights of official child neglect and abuse reporting 1986.* Denver, CO: Author.

American Psychiatric Association. (1987). *Diagnostic and statistical manual of mental disorders* (3rd ed., rev.). Washington, DC: Author. (Original work published 1952; 2nd ed., 1968; 3rd ed., 1980)

American Public Welfare Association. (1988). *Foster care basic maintenance rates.* Washington, DC: Author.

Anderson, P. G. (1989). The origin, emergence, and professional recognition of child protection. *Social Service Review, 63*, 222-244.

Ards, S., & Harrell, A. (1991). *Reporting of child maltreatment: A secondary analysis of the national surveys of child abuse and neglect.* Washington, DC: Urban Institute.

Bachman, J., Johnston, L., & O'Malley, P. (1987). *Monitoring the future: Questionnaire responses from the nation's high school seniors: 1986.* Ann Arbor: University of Michigan, Institute for Social Research.

Bagley, C. R., & Young, L. (1990). Depression, self-esteem, and suicidal behavior as sequels of sexual abuse in childhood: Research and therapy. In M. Rothery & G. Cameron (Eds.), *Child maltreatment: Expanding our concept of helping* (pp. 183-209). Hillsdale, NJ: Lawrence Erlbaum.

Bandura, A. (1973). *Aggression—A social learning analysis.* Englewood Cliffs, NJ: Prentice Hall.

Barden, J. C. (1990, February 5). Strife in families swells tide of homeless youth. *The New York Times,* pp. A1, B8.

Barth, R., & Berry, M. (1988). *Adoption and disruption: Rates, risks and responses.* Hawthorne, NY: Aldine de Gruyter.

Bass, D. (1992). *Helping vulnerable youths.* Washington, DC: NASW Press.

Bassuk, E. L., & Gallagher, E. M. (1990). The impact of homelessness on children. *Child and Youth Services, 14*(1), 19-33.

Bassuk, E. L., & Rosenberg, L. (1988). Why does family homelessness occur? *American Journal of Public Health, 78*(7), 783-787.

Bassuk, E. L., & Rubin, L. (1987). Homeless children: A neglected population. *American Journal of Orthopsychiatry, 57*(2), 279-287.

Bassuk, E. L., Rubin, L., & Lauriat, A. (1986). Characteristics of sheltered homeless families. *American Journal of Public Health, 76*(9), 1097-1101.

Bayley, N. (1933). *The California first year mental scale.* Berkeley: University of California Press.

Bellotti v. Baird, 99 S.Ct. 3035 (1979).

Berrueta-Clement, J. R., Schweinhart, L. J., Barnett, W. S., Epstein, A. S., & Weikart, D. P. (1984). *Changed lives: The effects of the Perry Preschool Program on youths through the age 19.* Ypsilanti, MI: High/Scope Press.

Berry, M., & Barth, R. (1989). Behavior problems of children older when adopted. *Children and Youth Services Review, 11,* 221-238.

Besharov, D. J. (1984). Liability in child welfare. *Public Welfare, 42.*

Bierlein, L. A. (1993). *Controversial issues in educational policy.* Newbury Park, CA: Sage.

Biller, H. B., & Solomon, R. S. (1986). *Child maltreatment and parental deprivation: A manifesto for research, prevention, and treatment.* Lexington, MA: D. C. Heath.

Bingol, N., Fuchs, M., Diaz, V., Stone, R., & Gromisch, D. (1987). Teratogenicity of cocaine in humans. *Journal of Pediatrics, 100,* 93-96.

Bishop, K., Rounds, K., & Weil, M. (1993). P.L. 99-457: Preparation for social work practice with infants and toddlers with disabilities and their families. *Journal of Social Work Education, 29*(1), 36-45.

Black Child Advocate. (1989). *Special report: The status of black children.* Washington, DC: National Black Child Development Institute.

Block, N., & Libowitz, A. (1983). *Recidivism in foster care.* New York: Child Welfare League of America.

Bolton, F., Laner, R., & Gai, D. (1981). For better or worse? Foster parents and foster children in an officially reported child maltreatment population. *Children & Youth Services Review, 3,* 37-53.

Boxill, N. A., & Beaty, A. L. (1990). Mother/child interaction among homeless women and their children in a public night shelter in Atlanta, Georgia. *Child and Youth Services, 14*(1), 49-64.

Boyne, J., Denby, L., Kettenring, J., & Wheeler, W. (1984). *The shadow of success: A statistical analysis of outcomes of adoptions of hard to place children.* New Jersey: Spaulding for Children.

Brazelton, T. (1984). *Neonatal behavioral assessment scale* (2nd ed.). Philadelphia: J. B. Lippincott.

Bridge, T. (1988). AIDS and HIV central nervous system disease: A neuropsychiatric disorder. In T. Bridge, A. Mirsky, & F. Goodwin (Eds.), *Psychological, neuropsychiatric, and substance abuse aspects of AIDS* (pp. 1-14). New York: Raven.

Bruno, F. J. (1957). *Trends in social work 1874-1956* (2nd ed.). New York: Columbia University Press.

Bucy, J. (1987). *Testimony before the House Select Committee on Children, Youth, and Families* (February 24, 1987). Washington, DC: Government Printing Office.

Burghardt, S., & Fabricant, M. (1987). *Working under the safety net.* Newbury Park, CA: Sage.

Burke, V. (1991). *Welfare.* Washington, DC: Congressional Research Service.

Butler, A. C. (1992). The changing economic consequences of teenage childbearing. *Social Service Review, 66*(1), 1-31.

Butler, O. B. (1988). Investing in the very young. *The GAO Journal*, Number 3, 35-39.

Caldwell, B., & Bradley, R. (1978). *Home observation for measurement of the environment.* Little Rock: University of Arkansas.

Camp, G. M., & Camp, C. G. (1987). *The corrections yearbook 1987.* South Salem, NY: Criminal Justice Institute.

Cardenas, J. (1990). Political limits to an education of value: The role of the state. In J. I. Goodlad & P. Keating (Eds.), *Access to knowledge* (pp. 273-286). New York: College Entrance Examination Board.

Carlson, G., & Cantwell, D. (1980). Diagnosis of childhood depression: A comparison of the Weinberg and DSM III criteria. *Journal of the American Academy of Child Psychiatry, 21*, 247-250.

Catterall, J. (1987). On the social costs of dropping out of school. *The High School Journal, 71*(1), 19-30.

Center for the Study of Social Policy. (1987). *A framework for child welfare reform.* Washington, DC: Author.

Center on Budget and Policy Priorities. (1988). *Holes in the safety nets: Poverty programs and policies in the states.* Washington, DC: Author.

Center on Budget and Policy Priorities. (1990). *Total income of the richest 2.5 million Americans nearly matches bottom 100 million.* Washington, DC: Author.

Center on Budget and Policy Priorities. (1991). *Two million more Americans become poor as recession hits and wages and incomes decline.* Washington, DC: Author.

Centers for Disease Control. (1987). HIV infection in the United States. *Morbidity & Mortality Weekly Report, 36*, 801-804.

Centers for Disease Control. (1988). *AIDS weekly surveillance report—United States.* Atlanta, GA: Centers for Disease Control.

Chasnoff, I. (1989). Drug use and women: Establishing a standard of care. In D. E. Hutchings (Ed.), *Prenatal abuse of licit and illicit drugs* (pp. 208-210). New York: New York Academy of Sciences.

Chasnoff, I., Burns, K., & Burns, W. (1987). Cocaine use in pregnancy: Perinatal morbidity and mortality. *Neurotoxicology & Teratology, 9*, 291-293.

Chasnoff, I., & Griffith, D. (1989). Cocaine: Clinical studies of pregnancy and the newborn. In D. E. Hutchings (Ed.), *Prenatal abuse of licit and illicit drugs* (pp. 260-266). New York: New York Academy of Sciences.

Chasnoff, I., Griffith, D., Freier, C., & Murray, J. (1992). Cocaine/polydrug use in pregnancy: Two year followup. *Pediatrics, 89*, 284-289.

Chasnoff, I., Landress, H., & Barrett, M. (1990). The prevalence of illicit drug or alcohol use during pregnancy and discrepancies in mandatory reporting in Pinellas County, Florida. *New England Journal of Medicine, 322*(17), 1202-1206.

Children's Defense Fund. (1985). *Black and white children in America.* Washington, DC: Author.

Children's Defense Fund. (1986). *Maternal and child health data book.* Washington, DC: Author.

Children's Defense Fund. (1988). *A children's defense budget, FY 1988.* Washington, DC: Author.

Children's Defense Fund. (1989a). Homeless families: Mired in misfortune. *CDF Reports, 10*(12), 1, 2, 8.

Children's Defense Fund. (1989b). *A vision for America's future.* Washington, DC: Author.

Children's Defense Fund. (1990a). *Latino youths at a crossroads.* Washington, DC: Author.

Children's Defense Fund. (1990b). Maternal and child health worsens; trends must improve for U.S. to meet year 2000 goals. *CDF Reports, 12*(2), 113.

Children's Defense Fund. (1990c). *The nation's investment in children.* Washington, DC: Author.

Children's Defense Fund. (1990d). *S.O.S. America: A children's defense budget.* Washington, DC: Author.

Children's Defense Fund. (1991). *The state of America's children 1991.* Washington, DC: Author.

Children's Defense Fund. (1992). *The state of America's children 1992.* Washington, DC: Author.

Chin, J. (1990). Current and future dimensions of the HIV/AIDS pandemic in women and children. *Lancet, 336*(8709), 221-224.

Cicchetti, D., Cummings, M., Greenberg, M., & Marvin, R. (1990). An organizational perspective on attachment beyond infancy. In M. Greenberg, D. Cicchetti, & E. Cummings (Eds.), *Attachment in the preschool years* (pp. 3-50). Chicago: University of Chicago Press.

Cislowski, J. A. (1988). *Health care for children: Federal programs and policies.* Washington, DC: Congressional Research Service.

Clarren, S., & Smith, D. (1978). Fetal alcohol syndrome. *New England Journal of Medicine, 298*(19), 1063-1067.

Cogill, S., Caplan, H., Alexandra, H., Robeson, K., & Kumar, R. (1986). Impact of maternal postnatal depression on cognitive development of young children. *British Medical Journal, 292,* 1165-1167.

Comer, J. P. (1988). Educating poor minority children. *Scientific American, 259*(5), 42-48.

Committee for Economic Development. (1987). *Children in need: Investment strategies for the educationally disadvantaged.* NY: Author.

Committee on Ways and Means. (1989). *Background material and data on programs within the jurisdiction of the Committee on Ways and Means* (WMCP:101-104). Washington, DC: Government Printing Office.

Committee on Ways and Means. (1991). *1991 green book: Background material and data on programs within the jurisdiction of the Committee on Ways and Means* (Committee Print 102-109). Washington, DC: Government Printing Office.

Committee on Ways and Means. (1992). *1992 green book: Background material and data on programs within the jurisdiction of the Committee on Ways and Means* (WMCP: 102-144). Washington, DC: Government Printing Office.

Comstock, G., & Strasburger, V. C. (1990). Deceptive appearances: Television violence and aggressive behavior. *Journal of Adolescent Health Care, 11*(1), 31-44.

Congressional Budget Office. (1988). *Trends in family income: 1970-1986.* Washington, DC: Congressional Budget Office.

Congressional Research Service. (1987). *Federal programs affecting children.* Washington, DC: Library of Congress.

Congressional Research Service. (1988). *Health insurance and the uninsured: Background data and analysis.* Washington, DC: Author.

Cook, R., & Ansell, D. (1986). *Study of independent living services for youth in substitute care.* Rockville, MD: Westat.

Cordero, L., & Custard, M. (1990). Effects of maternal cocaine abuse on perinatal and infant outcome. *Ohio Medicine, 86*(5), 410-412.

Costello, A., Edelbrock, C., Dulcan, M., Kalas, R., & Kloric, S. (1984). *Report on the diagnostic interview for children.* Pittsburgh: University of Pittsburgh Press.

Crockenberg, S. (1981). Infant irritability, mother responsiveness, and social support influences on the security of mother-infant attachment. *Child Development, 52,* 857-865.

Cummings, E., Lanott, R., & Zahn-Waxler, C. (1985). Influences of conflict between adults on the emotions and aggression of young children. *Developmental Psychology, 21,* 495-507.

Darling-Hammond, L. (1991). The implications of testing policy for quality and equality. *Phi Delta Kappan, 73,* 220-225.

Darmstadt, G. L. (1990). Community-based child abuse prevention. *Social Work, 35*(6), 487-489.

Davidson, C. (1991). Attachment issues and the cocaine exposed dyad. *Child & Adolescent Social Work Journal, 8*(4), 269-284.

Davis, K. E. (1988). Interparental violence: The children as victims. *Issues in Comprehensive Pediatric Nursing, 11,* 291-302.

Davis-Sacks, M. L., Jayrante, S., & Chess, W. A. (1985). A comparison of the effects of social support on the incidence of burnout. *Social Work, 30*(3), 240-244.

Denny, E., Pokela, J., Jackson, J. J., & Matava, M. A. (1989). Influencing child welfare policy: Assessing the opinion of legislators. *Child Welfare, 68*(3), 275-287.

DeShaney v. Winnebago County Department of Social Services, 109 S.Ct. 998 (1989).

DiNitto, D. M., & Dye, T. R. (1987). *Social welfare politics & public policy* (2nd ed.). Englewood Cliffs, NJ: Prentice Hall.

Dobbs, M. (1987, March 13). After suicides, town ponders how it failed 4 teenagers. *The Washington Post,* pp. A-1, 10.

Doe v. Reivitz, 830 F.2d 1441 (September 28, 1987).

Dokecki, P., Baumeister, A., & Kupstas, F. (1989). Biomedical and social aspects of pediatric AIDS. *Journal of Early Intervention, 33,* 99-113.

Dubowitz, H. (1990). Costs and effectiveness of interventions in child maltreatment. *Child Abuse and Neglect, 14,* 177-186.

Edelman, M. W. (1987). *Families in peril: An agenda for social change.* Cambridge, MA: Harvard University Press.

Eisenberg, L. (1989). Public policy: Risk factor or remedy in prevention of mental disorders. In *Alcohol, and other drug use in children and adolescents* (pp. 125-155). Rockville, MD: Office of Substance Abuse Prevention.

Ek, C. A., & Steelman, L. C. (1988). Becoming a runaway, from the accounts of youthful runners. *Youth & Society, 19*(3), 334-358.

Enstad, R., & Ibata, D. (1988, May 21). School rampage: 1 dies, 6 shot. *Chicago Tribune,* Section 1, pp. 1, 4.

Evans, G. L. (1988). School crime and violence: Achieving deterrence through tort law. *Journal of Law, Ethics, & Public Policy, 3*(3), 501-517.

Ewing, C. P. (1990). *When children kill: The dynamics of juvenile homicide.* Lexington, MA: Lexington.

Fagan, J. (1990). Social processes of delinquency and drug use among urban gangs. In C. R. Huff (Ed.), *Gangs in America* (pp. 183-122). Newbury Park, CA: Sage.

Fagot, B., & Kavanagh, K. (1990). The prediction of antisocial behavior from avoidant attachment classification. *Child Development, 61,* 864-873.

Fanshel, D. (1979). Preschoolers entering foster care in New York City: The need to stress plans for permanence. *Child Welfare, 58,* 67-87.

Fanshel, D., & Shinn, E. B. (1978). *Children in foster care: A longitudinal investigation.* New York: Columbia University Press.

Fein, E., Davies, L., & Knight, G. (1979). Placement stability in foster care. *Social Work, 24,* 156-157.

Fein, E., Maluccio, A., Hamilton, J., & Ward, D. (1983). After foster care: Outcomes of permanent planning for children. *Child Welfare, 62,* 485-562.

Festinger, T. (1986). *Necessary risk: A study of adoption and disrupted adoptive placements.* New York: Child Welfare League of America.

Fitz, P., Galanter, M., Lifshutz, H., & Egelko, S. (1993). Developmental risk factors in postpartum women with urine tests positive for cocaine. *American Journal of Drug and Alcohol Abuse, 19*(2), 187-197.

Frank, D., Zuckerman, B., Amaro, H., Aboagye, K., Bauchner, H., Cabral, H., Fried, L., Hingson, R., Hayne, H., Levenson, S., Parker, S., Reece, H., & Vinci, R. (1988). Cocaine use during pregnancy: Prevalence and correlates. *Pediatrics, 82*(6), 888-895.

Frankenburg, W., Fandal, A., Sciarillo, W., & Burgess, D. (1981). The newly abbreviated and revised Denver Developmental Screening Test. *Journal of Pediatrics, 99,* 995-999.

Frisch, L., & Rhoads, F. (1982). Child abuse and neglect in children referred for learning evaluation. *Journal of Learning Disabilities, 15,* 583-586.

Gallagher, J., & Ramey, C. (Eds.). (1987). *The malleability of children.* Baltimore, MD: Brookes.

Gargiulo, R. M. (1990). Child abuse and neglect: An overview. In R. L. Goldman & R. M. Gargiulo (Eds.), *Children at risk: An interdisciplinary approach to child abuse and neglect* (pp. 1-36). Austin, TX: Pro-Ed.

Garmetzy, N. (1979). DSM III: Never mind the psychologists; Is it good for the children? *The Clinical Psychologist, 31,* 3-6.

Garrison, E. G. (1987). The juvenile justice and delinquency prevention act. *Social Policy Report, 11*(1), 1-11.

Gelfand, D., Jensen, W., & Drew, C. (1982). *Understanding children's behavior disorders.* New York: Holt, Rinehart & Winston.

Gemmill, P. (1990). Child abuse management: The role of socialwork. In R. L. Goldman & R. M. Gargiulo (Eds.), *Children at risk: An interdisciplinary approach to child abuse and neglect* (pp. 155-176). Austin, TX: Pro-Ed.

Gershon, E., McKnew, D., Cytryn, L., Hamovit, J., Schreiber, J., Hibbs, E., & Pellegrini, D. (1985). Diagnoses in school-age children of bipolar affective disorder patients and normal controls. *Journal of Affective Disorders, 8,* 283-291.

Gewirtzman, R., & Fodor, I. (1987). The homeless child at school: From welfare hotel to classroom. *Child Welfare, 66*(3), 237-245.

Goodwin, D. (1985). Alcoholism and genetics: The sins of the fathers. *Archives of General Psychiatry, 42,* 171-174.

Grad, R. (1988, Fall). The fight against infant mortality. *The GAO Journal,* Number 3, pp. 31-34.

Grant Foundation. (1988). *The forgotten half: Pathways to success for America's youth and young families.* Washington, DC: Author.

Grant, T. M. (1991). The legal and psychological implications of tracking in education. *Law & Psychology Review, 15*(299), 299-312.

Green, A. H. (1984). Generational transmission of violence in child abuse. *International Journal of Family Psychiatry, 6,* 389-403.

Grey, E. (1984). *Child abuse: Prelude to delinquency?* Washington, DC: Office of Juvenile Justice and Delinquency Prevention.

Gustavsson, N. (1991a). Pregnant chemically dependent women: The new criminals. *Affilia: Journal for Women in Social Work, 6*(2), 61-73.

Gustavsson, N. (1991b). The school and the maltreated child in foster care: A role for the school social worker. *Social Work in Education, 13*(4), 224-235.

Gustavsson, N. (in press). The emotional problems of children. In P. Allen-Meares (Ed.), *Intervention with children and adolescents.* White Plains, NY: Longman.

Guyer, B., Lescohier, I., Gallagher, S. S., Hausman, A., & Azzara, C. V. (1989). Intentional injuries among children and adolescents in Massachusetts. *The New England Journal of Medicine, 321*(23), 1584-1589.

Halmesmaki, E., & Ylikorkala, O. (1988). A retrospective study on the safety of prenatal ethanol treatment. *Obstetrics and Gynecology, 72*(4), 545-549.

Harrington, M. (1963). *The other America: Poverty in the United States.* Baltimore, MD: Penguin.

Hassner, D. W. (1987). *AIDS and adolescents: The time for prevention is now.* Washington, DC: Center for Population Options.

Hawton, K., Roberts, J., & Goodwin, G. (1985). The risk of child abuse among mothers who attempt suicide. *British Journal of Psychiatry, 146,* 486-489.

Hegar, R. (1989). The rights and status of children: International concerns for social work. *International Social Work, 32*(2), 107-116.

Herrmann, K. J., & Kasper, B. (1992). International adoption: The exploitation of women and children. *Affilia: Journal for Women in Social Work, 7*(1), 45-58.

Hewlett, S. A. (1991). *When the bough breaks: The cost of neglecting our children.* New York: Basic Books.

Hochstadt, N., Jaudes, P., Zimo, D., & Schacter, J. (1987). The medical and psychological needs of children entering foster care. *Child Abuse & Neglect, 11,* 53-62.

Hodgson v. Minnesota, 110 S.Ct. 2926 (1990).

Hoffman, E. (1978). Policy and politics: The Child Abuse Prevention and Treatment Act. *Public Policy, 26,* 71-88.

Honig v. Doe, 108 S.Ct. 592 (January 19, 1988).

Horn, W. (1990). Testimony before the Senate Subcommittee on Children, Family, Drugs, and Alcoholism. February 7, 1990.

Houck, G., Booth, C., & Barnard, K. (1991). Maternal depression and locus of control orientation as predictors of dyadic play behavior. *Infant Mental Health Journal, 12,* 347-360.

Howe, P. (1989, August 6). Mayor demands actions on infant deaths. *Boston Globe,* p. 39.

Hughes, D. (1990). Testimony before the Senate Subcommittee on Children, Family, Drugs, and Alcoholism. February 7, 1990.

Hutchison, E. D. (1990). Child maltreatment: Can it be defined? *Social Service Review, 64,* 60-78.

Hyman, I. A. (1990). *Reading, writing, and the hickory stick.* Lexington, MA: D. C. Heath.

In re A. C., 533 A.2d 611 (DC 1987).

In re Baby X, 97 Mich. App. 111; 293 N.W. 2d. 736 (1980).

In re Gault, 87 U.S. 1428 (1967).

In re Michael G., 243 Cal. Rptr. 224 (Decided January 25, 1988).

In re Troy D., 236 Cal. Rptr. 869, 872 Cal. App. Dist. 4 (1989).

Institute of Medicine. (1988a). *Homelessness, health, and human needs.* Washington, DC: National Academy of Sciences.

Institute of Medicine. (1988b). *Prenatal care: Reaching mothers, reaching infants.* Washington, DC: National Academy Press.

Janus, M. D., McCormack, A., Burgess, A. W., & Hartman, C. (1987). *Adolescent runaways: Causes and consequences.* Lexington, MA: Lexington.

Johnson, C. M., Sum, A. M., & Weill, J. D. (1988). *Vanishing dreams: The growing economic plight of America's young families.* Washington, DC: Children's Defense Fund.

Johnson, K. (1988). *Teens and AIDS: Opportunities for prevention.* Washington, DC: Children's Defense Fund.

Jones, D., & McGraw, J. M. (1987). Reliable and fictitious accounts of sexual abuse in children. *Journal of Interpersonal Violence, 2,* 27-45.

Jones, J. Y. (1989). *Child nutrition: Issues in the 101st Congress.* Washington, DC: Congressional Research Service.

Jones, K., & Smith, D. (1973). Recognition of the fetal alcohol syndrome in early infancy. *Lancet, II*(7836), 999-1001.

Kempe, C. H., Silverman, F. N., Steele, B. F., Droegmueller, W., & Silver, H. K. (1962). The battered child syndrome. *Journal of the American Medical Association, 181*(1), 17-24.

Kent v. U.S., 383 U.S. 541 (1966).

Kimmich, M. H. (1985). *America's children: Who cares?* Washington, DC: Urban Institute Press.

King, M., & Yullie, J. (1987). Suggestibility and the child witness. In S. Ceci, M. Toglia, & D. F. Ross (Eds.), *Children's eyewitness memory* (pp. 24-35). New York: Springer.

Kinney, J., Haapala, D., Booth, C., & Leavitt, S. (1991). The Homebuilders model. In E. Tracy, D. Haapala, J. Kinney, & P. Pecora (Eds.), *Intensive family preservation services* (pp. 15-50). Cleveland, OH: Mandel School of Applied Social Sciences.

Knapp, E. S. (1988). *Kids, gangs, and drugs. Embattled youth.* Lexington, KY: Council of State Governments.

Knitzer, J., & Yelton, S. (1990). Collaborations between child welfare and mental health. *Public Welfare, 48*(2), 24-33.

Kotlowitz, A. (1991). *There are no children here.* Garden City, NY: Doubleday.

Kozol, J. (1988). *Rachel and her children: Homeless families in America.* New York: Crown.

Kozel, J. (1991). *Savage inequalities.* New York: Crown.

Lally, J. R., Mangione, P. L., & Honig, A. S. (1987). *Long-range impact of an early intervention with low-income children and their families.* San Francisco: Far West Laboratory.

Lamers, E. (1988). Public schools confront AIDS. In I. Corliss & M. Pittman-Lindeman (Eds.), *AIDS: Principles, practices and politics* (pp. 175-185). Washington, DC: Hemisphere.

Latino dropout rates up, others down. (1992, July-August). *Youth Law News,* p. 6.

Leonard, P. A., Dolbeare, C. N., & Lazere, E. B. (1989). *A place to call home: The crisis in housing for the poor.* Washington, DC: Center on Budget and Policy Priorities.

Levitan, S. A. (1990). *Programs in aid of the poor* (6th ed.). Baltimore, MD: Johns Hopkins University Press.

Lewin, T. (1988, March 20). Fewer teen mothers, but more are unmarried. *The New York Times,* p. E6.

Lewis, D. O., Mallouh, C., & Webb, V. (1989). Child abuse, delinquency, and violent criminality. In D. Cicchetti & V. Carlson (Eds.), *Child maltreatment: Theory and research on the causes and consequences of child abuse and neglect* (pp. 707-721). New York: Cambridge University Press.

Lewis, H. (1980). The battered helper. *Child Welfare, 59*(4), 195-201.

Lewis, K., Bennett, B., & Schmeder, N. (1989). The care of infants menaced by cocaine abuse. *American Journal of Maternal Child Nursing, 14,* 324-326.

Lieberman, A. A., Hornby, H., & Russell, M. (1988). Analyzing the educational backgrounds and work experiences of child welfare personnel: A national study. *Social Work, 33,* 485-489.

L. J. By and Through Darr v. Massinga, 838 F.2d 118 (4th Cir. 1988), cert. den. 109 S.Ct. 816 (1989).

Lockhart, L. L., & Wodarski, J. S. (1990). Teenage pregnancy: Implications for social work practice. Family Therapy, 17(1), 29-47.

Maier, K. (1989). Pregnant women: Fetal containers or people with rights? Affilia: Journal for Women in Social Work, 4(2), 8-20.

Main, M., & Solomon, J. (1986). Discovery of an insecure-disorganized/disoriented attachment pattern. In T. Brazelton & M. Yogman (Eds.), Affective development in infancy (pp. 95-124). Norwood, NJ: Ablex.

Mass, H., & Engler, R. (1959). Children in need of parents. New York: Columbia University Press.

Maza, P. L., & Hall, J. A. (1988). Homeless children and their families: A preliminary study. Washington, DC: Child Welfare League of America.

McCarthy, J., & Hoge, D. (1987). The social construction of school punishment: Racial disadvantage out of universalistic process. Social Forces, 65(4), 1101-1120.

McDonald, T., & Marks, J. (1991). A review of risk factors assessed in child protective services. Social Service Review, 65(1), 112-132.

McGregor, S., Keith, L., Chasnoff, I., Rosner, M., Chisum, G., Shaw, P., & Minogue, J. (1987). Cocaine use during pregnancy: Adverse perinatal outcome. American Journal of Obstetrics and Gynecology, 157(3), 686-690.

Miller, D. C. (1989). Poor women and work programs: Back to the future. Affilia: Journal for Women in Social Work, 4(1), 9-22.

Mohn, S. L. (1988). Testimony before the Senate Subcommittee on the Constitution. December 1, 1988.

Molnar, J. (1988). Home is where the heart is: The crisis of homeless children in New York City. New York: Bank Street College.

Moroz, K. J., & Segal, E. A. (1990). Homeless children: Intervention strategies for school social workers. Social Work in Education, 12(2), 134-143.

National Black Child Development Institute. (1989). Who will care when parents can't? Washington, DC: Author.

National Center on Child Abuse and Neglect. (1980). Interdisciplinary glossary on child abuse and neglect (OHDS 80-30137). Washington, DC: U.S. Department of Health and Human Services.

National Center on Child Abuse and Neglect. (1988). Study findings: National study of the incidence and prevalence of child abuse and neglect. Washington, DC: U.S. Department of Health and Human Services.

National Center for Children in Poverty. (1990). Five million children: A statistical profile of our poorest young citizens. New York: Author.

National Center for Children in Poverty. (1991, Spring). Poverty takes toll on child health. News and Issues, p. 1.

National Center for Education in Maternal and Child Health. (1990). The health of America's youth. Washington, DC: Author.

National Center for Education in Maternal and Child Health. (1991). Adolescent substance abuse. Washington, DC: Author.

National Commission on Children. (1991). Beyond rhetoric: A new American agenda for children and families. Washington, DC: Author.

National Commission to Prevent Infant Mortality. (1988a). Death before life: The tragedy of infant mortality. Washington, DC: Author.

National Commission to Prevent Infant Mortality. (1988b). Infant mortality: Care for our children, care for our future. Washington, DC: Author.

National Council of State Human Service Administrators. (1985). Investing in poor families and their children. *Public Welfare, 43*(3), 5-9.

National Highway Traffic Safety Administration. (1988). *Fatal accident reporting system, 1987.* Washington, DC: U.S. Department of Transportation.

National Institute of Justice. (1986). *Violence in schools.* Washington, DC: U.S. Department of Education.

National Institute on Drug Abuse. (1989a). *National household survey on drug abuse: Population estimates 1988* (DHHS Publication No. ADM-89-1636). Washington, DC: Government Printing Office.

National Institute on Drug Abuse. (1989b). *Overview of selected drug trends.* Rockville, MD: Author.

National Mental Health Association. (1989a). *Final report and recommendations of the invisible children project.* Alexandria, VA: Author.

National Mental Health Association. (1989b). *Invisible children project.* Washington, DC: Author.

National Network of Runaway and Youth Services. (1989). *Runaway fact sheet.* Washington, DC: Author.

National Resource Center on Family Based Services. (1988). *Family based services: A national perspective on success and failure.* Iowa City, IA: Author.

National Women's Health Network. (1986, July/August). Is adolescent pregnancy an epidemic? *The Network News,* pp. 1, 4, 5.

Nurcombe, B. (1986). The child as witness: Competency and credibility. *Journal of the American Academy of Child and Adolescent Psychiatry, 25*(4), 473-480.

Oakes, J., & Lipton, M. (1990). Tracking and ability grouping: A structural barrier to access and achievement. In J. I. Goodlad & P. Keating (Eds.), *Access to knowledge* (pp. 187-204). New York: College Entrance Examination Board.

Office of Management and Budget. (1993). *Budget of the United States government FY 1994.* Washington, DC: Government Printing Office.

Office of Technology Assessment. (1986). *Children's mental health: Problems and services* (OTA-BP-H-33). Washington, DC: Government Printing Office.

Office on Smoking and Health. (1988). *The health consequences of smoking: Nicotine addiction.* Washington, DC: Government Printing Office.

Offord, D., & Boyle, M. (1986). Problems in setting up and executing large scale psychiatric epidemiological studies. *Psychiatric Developments, 3,* 257-272.

Ohio Department of Human Services. (1988). *Child abuse and neglect* (ODHS 1465 [10/88]). Columbus, OH: ODHS.

Ohio v. Akron Center for Reproductive Health, 110 S.Ct. 2972 (1990).

Orshansky, M. (1965). Counting the poor: Another look at the poverty profile. *Social Security Bulletin, 28*(1), 3-29.

Ozawa, M., Auslander, W., & Slonim-Nevo, V. (1993). Problems in financing the care of AIDS patients. *Social Work, 38,* 369-377.

Parham v. J. R., 442 U.S. 584 (1979).

Pearce, D. (1978). The feminization of poverty: Women, work and welfare. *Urban and Social Change Review, 11*(1-2), 28-36.

Pecora, P., Fraser, M., & Haapala, D. (1990). Intensive home based family preservation services: Client outcomes and issues for program design. In D. Biegel & K. Wells (Eds.), *Family preservation services: Research and evaluation* (pp. 3-32). Newbury Park, CA: Sage.

Pecora, P. J., Briar, K. H., & Zlotnik, J. L. (1989). *Addressing the program and personnel crisis in child welfare.* Silver Spring, MD: National Association of Social Workers.

Pecora, P. J., Whittaker, J. K., & Maluccio, A. N. (1992). *The child welfare challenge*. Hawthorne, NY: Aldine de Gruyter.

Pelton, L. (1989). *For reasons of poverty*. New York: Praeger.

Pelton, L. (1993). Enabling public child welfare agencies to promote family preservation. *Social Work, 38*, 491-493.

Pitt, D. E. (1989, April 22). Jogger's attackers terrorized at least 9 in 2 hours. *The New York Times*, pp. 1, 30.

Planned Parenthood Federation of America. (1986). *American teens speak: Sex, myths, TV, and birth control*. New York: Author.

Planned Parenthood of Southeastern Pennsylvania v. Casey, 60 U.S.L.W. 4795 (1992).

Pooley, E. (1991). Kids with guns. *New York Magazine, 24*(30), 20-29.

Powers, J. L., & Jaklitsch, B. W. (1989). *Understanding survivors of abuses; stories of homeless and runaway adolescents*. Lexington, MA: Lexington.

Radke-Yarrow, M., (1991). Attachment patterns in children of depressed mothers. In C. Parkes, J. Stevenson-Hinde, & P. Marris (Eds.), *Attachment across the life cycle* (pp. 115-126). London: Tavistock.

Ralston, E. (1986). Myths and facts about child sexual abuse. *Protecting Children: An American Humane Publication, 3*(1), 12-13.

Regan, L., Ehrlich, S., & Finnegan, L. (1987). Infants of drug addicts: At risk for child abuse, neglect, and placement in foster care. *Neurotoxicology & Teratology, 9*, 315-319.

Rickel, A. (1982). Perceptions of adjustment problems in preschool children by teachers and paraprofessional aides. *Journal of Community Psychology, 10*, 29-35.

Riddle, W. C. (1989). *Early childhood education and development: Federal policy issues*. Washington, DC: Congressional Research Service.

Robinson, D. H. (1989). *Child abuse and neglect: Data and federal programs*. Washington, DC: Congressional Research Service.

Roe v. Wade, 410 U.S. 113, 116 (1973).

Rogers, M. F. (1987). AIDS in children. *New York Medical Quarterly, 21*, 68-73.

Rosenbaum, S. (1989). Recent developments in infant and child health: Health status, insurance coverage and trends in public health policy. In G. Miller (Ed.). *Giving children a chance: The case for more effective policies* (pp. 79-106). Washington, DC: Center for National Policy Press.

Rosengren, J. (1990). Alcohol: A bigger drug problem? *Minnesota Medicine, 73*, 33-34.

Runyan, D., & Gould, C. (1985). Foster care for child maltreatment: II. Impact on school performance. *Pediatrics, 76*, 841-847.

Russell, A., & Trainor, C. (1984). *Trends in child abuse and neglect: A national perspective*. Denver, CO: American Humane Association.

Rutter, M. (1984, March). Resilient children. *Psychology Today*, pp. 57-65.

Rutter, M. (1985). Resilience in the face of adversity. Protective factors and resistance to psychiatric disorders. *British Journal of Psychiatry, 147*, 598-611.

Rutter, M., & Shaffer, D. (1980). DSM III: A step forward or back in terms of the classification of the child psychiatric disorders? *Journal of the American Academy of Child Psychiatry, 19*, 371-394.

Rycraft, J. R. (1990). Redefining abuse and neglect: A narrower focus could affect children at risk. *Public Welfare, 48*(1), 14-21.

Sandberg, D. N. (1989). *The child abuse-delinquency connection*. Lexington, MA: Lexington.

Schorr, L. B. (1988). *Within our reach: Breaking the cycle of disadvantage*. Garden City, NY: Doubleday.

Schweinhart, L. J. (1989). *Early childhood programs in the U.S. today*. Ypsilanti, MI: High/Scope Press.

Segal, E. A. (1989). Welfare reform: Help for poor women and children? *Affilia: Journal for Women in Social Work, 4*(3), 42-50.

Segal, E. A. (1990). *Nowhere to go: Homeless youth adrift in the social service system.* Unpublished manuscript. [Available from College of Social Work, The Ohio State University, 1947 College Rd., Columbus, OH 43210]

Segal, E. A. (1991). The juvenilization of poverty in the 1980s. *Social Work, 36,* 454-457.

Segal, E. A., & Gustavsson, N. S. (1990). The high cost of neglecting children: The need for a preventive policy agenda. *Child and Adolescent Social Work Journal, 7,* 475-485.

Select Committee on Children, Youth & Families. (1984). *Violence and abuse in American families.* Washington, DC: Government Printing Office.

Select Committee on Children, Youth & Families. (1988a). *Opportunities for success: Cost-effective programs for children update, 1988.* Washington, DC: Government Printing Office.

Select Committee on Children, Youth & Families. (1988b). *Youth and violence: The current crisis.* Washington, DC: Government Printing Office.

Select Committee on Children, Youth & Families. (1989a). *Born hooked: Confronting the impact of perinatal substance abuse.* Washington, DC: Government Printing Office.

Select Committee on Children, Youth & Families. (1989b). *Children and families: Key trends in the 1980s.* Washington, DC: Government Printing Office.

Select Committee on Children, Youth & Families. (1989c). *Down these mean streets: Violence by and against America's children.* Washington, DC: Government Printing Office.

Select Committee on Children, Youth & Families. (1989d). *U.S. Children and their families: Current conditions and recent trends, 1989.* Washington, DC: Government Printing Office.

Select Committee on Children, Youth & Families. (1990). *Opportunities for success: Cost-effective programs for children update, 1990.* Washington, DC: Government Printing Office.

Shafer, D., Dunbar, V., Falek, A., Donahoe, R., Madden, J., & Bokos, P. (1990). Enhanced assays detect increased chromosome damage and sister-chromatid exchanges in heroin addicts. *Mutation Research, 234*(5), 327-336.

Shamsie, J. (1985). Violence and youth. *Canadian Journal of Psychiatry, 30*(7), 498-503.

Shaw, D., & Emery, R. (1988). Chronic family adversity and school-age children's adjustment. *Journal of the American Academy of Child and Adolescent Psychiatry, 27*(2), 200-206.

Shostack, A., & Quane, R. (1988). Youth who leave group homes. *Public Welfare, 46*(4), 29-36.

Silvern, L., & Kaersvang, L. (1989). The traumatized children of violent marriages. *Child Welfare, 68*(4), 421-436.

Simons, J. M., Finlay, B., & Yang, A. (1991). *The adolescent and young adult fact book.* Washington, DC: Children's Defense Fund.

Singer, J. L., & Singer, D. G. (1981). *Television, imagination, and aggression: A study of preschoolers.* Hillsdale, NJ: Lawrence Erlbaum.

Smythe, S. M. (1988, Fall). Safeguarding our children's health. *The GAO Journal,* Number 3, pp. 26-30.

Social Security Administration. (1990). *Social Security bulletin: Annual statistical Supplement, 1990.* Washington, DC: Author.

Social Security Administration. (1991). Social security programs in the United States. Social Security Bulletin, *54* (9), 2-82.

Society for Research in Child Development. (1984). *Washington report: The Child Abuse Prevention and Treatment Act, I (1).* Washington, DC: Author

Soobiah, C. (1990). Children: Rights, education and equal opportunity. *Early Child Development and Care, 58,* 23-29.

Spivak, H. (1989). *Testimony in Hearings before Select Committee on Children, Youth, & Families. Down these mean streets: Violence by and against America's children* (p. 29). Washington, DC: Government Printing Office.

Sroufe, L. (1979). The coherence of individual development. *American Psychologist, 34,* 834-841.

Stanford v. Kentucky, 57 U.S.L.W. 4973 (1989).

Star, R., MacLean, D., & Keating, D. (1991). Life-span developmental outcomes of child maltreatment. In R. Starr & D. Wolfe (Eds.), *The effects of child abuse and neglect* (pp. 1-32). London: Guilford.

Starr, P. (1986). Health care for the poor: The past twenty years. In S. H. Danzinger & D. H. Weinberg (Eds.), *Fighting poverty: What works and what doesn't.* Cambridge, MA: Harvard University Press.

Starr, R. H., Jr., Dubowitz, H., & Bush, B. A. (1990). The epidemiology of child maltreatment. In R. T. Ammerman & M. Hersen (Eds.), *Children at risk: An evaluation of factors contributing to child abuse and neglect* (pp. 23-53). New York: Plenum.

Stein, J. A., Golding, J. M., Siegel, J., Burnam, M., & Sorenson, S. B. (1988). Long-term psychological sequela of child sexual abuse: The Los Angeles epidemiologic catchment area study. In G. E. Wyatt & G. J. Powell (Eds.), *Lasting effects of child sexual abuse* (pp. 135-154). Newbury Park, CA: Sage

Stone, N., & Stone, S. (1983). The prediction of successful foster placement. *Social Casework, 64,* 11-17.

Strayhorn, J. (1988). *The competent child.* New York: Guilford.

Strober, M., Morrell, W., Rubboughs, J., Lampet, C., Danforth, H., & Freeman, R. (1988). A family study of bipolar I disorder in adolescence: Early onset symptoms linked to increased familial loading and lithium resistance. *Journal of Affective Disorders, 15,* 255-268.

Stroul, B. A., & Friedman, R. M. (1986). *A system of care for severely emotionally disturbed children and youth.* Washington, DC: CASSP Technical Assistance Center.

Stroul, B. A., & Goldman, S. K. (1990). Study of community-based services for children and adolescents who are severely emotionally disturbed. *Journal of Mental Health Administration, 17*(1), 61-77.

Subcommittee on Human Resources, Committee on Ways and Means. (1990, April). *The impact of crack cocaine on the child welfare system.* Hearing held in Washington, DC.

Subcommittee on Social Security and Family Policy. (1988). *Welfare: Reform or replacement?* (S.Hrg. 100-395). Washington, DC: Government Printing Office.

Suh, E. K., & Abel, E. M. (1990). The impact of spousal violence on the children of the abused. *Journal of Independent Social Work, 4*(4), 27-34.

Taborn, J. M. (1990). Adolescent pregnancy: A medical concern. In D. J. Jones & S. F. Battle (Ed.), *Teenage pregnancy: Developing strategies for change in the twenty-first century* (pp. 91-100). New Brunswick, NJ: Transaction Books.

Task Force on Youth Development and Community Programs. (1992). *A matter of time: Risk and opportunity in the nonschool hours.* New York: Carnegie Corporation.

Taylor By and Through Walker v. Ledbetter, 791 F.2d 881 (11th Cir. 1987), reh'g granted 798 F.2d 431, rev'd in part and aff'd in part on reh'g en banc 818 F.2d 791 (11th Cir. 1987), cert. den. 109 S.Ct. 1337 (1989).

Taylor, C. S. (1990). Gang imperialism. In C. R. Huff (Ed.), *Gangs in America* (pp. 103-115). Newbury Park, CA: Sage.

Teague, J. (1992). Issues relating to the treatment of adolescent lesbians and homosexuals. *Journal of Mental Health Counseling, 14,* 422-439.

Terr, L. C. (1988). Anatomically correct dolls: Should they be used as the basis for expert testimony? *Journal of the American Academy of Child and Adolescent Psychiatry, 27,* 254-257.

Thomas, P. (1984). Unexplained immunodeficiency in children: A surveillance report. *Journal of the American Medical Association, 252,* 639-644.

Thompson v. Oklahoma, 108 S.Ct. 2687 (1988).

Tower, C. C. (1989). *Understanding child abuse and neglect.* Boston: Allyn & Bacon.

Tower, C. C. (1992). *The role of educators in the protection and treatment of child abuse and neglect* (DHHS Publication No. ACF 92-30172). Washington, DC: Government Printing Office.

Tracy, E., Haapala, D., Kinney, J., & Pecora, P. (1991). Intensive family preservation services: A strategic response to families in crisis. In E. Tracy, D. Haapala, J. Kinney, & P. Pecora (Eds.), *Intensive family preservation services: An instruction sourcebook* (pp. 1-14). Cleveland, OH: Mandel School of Applied Social Sciences.

U.S. Advisory Board on Child Abuse and Neglect. (1990). *Child abuse and neglect: Critical first steps in response to a national emergency.* Washington, DC: U.S. Department of Health and Human Services.

U.S. Budget. (1990). *Budget of the United States government.* Washington, DC: Government Printing Office.

U.S. Bureau of the Census. (1989). *Money, income, and poverty status in the United States* (Current Population Reports, Series P-60, No. 166). Washington, DC: Government Printing Office.

U.S. Bureau of the Census. (1990a). *Health insurance coverage: The haves and have-nots* (SB-9-90). Washington, DC: U.S. Department of Commerce.

U.S. Bureau of the Census. (1990b). *Money, income and poverty status in the United States: 1989* (Current Population Reports, Series P-60, No. 168). Washington, DC: U.S. Department of Commerce.

U.S. Bureau of the Census. (1991a). *Children's well-being: An international comparison* (Statistical Brief, SB/91-1). Washington, DC: U.S. Department of Commerce.

U.S. Bureau of the Census. (1991b). *Statistical abstract of the United States: 1990.* Washington, DC: Government Printing Office.

U.S. Bureau of the Census. (1992a). *Health insurance coverage: 1987-1990* (Current Population Reports, P-70, No. 29). Washington, DC: U.S. Department of Commerce.

U.S. Bureau of the Census. (1992b). *Poverty in the United States: 1991* (Current Population Reports, Series P-60, No. 181). Washington, DC: U.S. Department of Commerce.

U.S. Conference of Mayors. (1988). *A status report on children in America's cities.* Washington, DC: Author.

U.S. Conference of Mayors. (1989). *A status report on hunger and homelessness America's cities: 1988.* Washington, DC: Author.

U.S. Congress. (1987). Stewart B. McKinney Homeless Assistance Act. P.L. 100-77. Washington, DC: Government Printing Office.

U.S. Department of Education. (1988). *Youth indicators 1988.* Washington, DC: Government Printing Office.

U.S. Department of Health and Human Services. (1981). *Treatment services for drug dependent women.* Rockville, MD: National Institute on Drug Abuse.

U.S. Department of Health and Human Services. (1990a). *Alcohol, tobacco, and other drugs may harm the unborn.* Rockville, MD: U.S. Department of Health and Human Services.

U.S. Department of Health and Human Services. (1990b). *Characteristics and financial circumstances of AFDC recipients FY 1989.* Washington, DC: Office of Family Assistance.

U.S. Department of Health and Human Services. (1990c). *Child health USA '90*. Washington, DC: Health Resources and Services Administration.

U.S. Department of Justice. (1986). *America's missing and & exploited children: Their safety and their future*. Washington, DC: Author.

U.S. Department of Justice. (1987a). *Correctional populations in the United States, 1987*. Washington, DC: U.S. Department of Justice, Bureau of Justice Statistics.

U.S. Department of Justice. (1987b). *Report on missing and exploited children: Progress in the 80's*. Washington, DC: Author.

U.S. Department of Justice. (1989). *Criminal victimization in the United States, 1987*. Washington, DC: Author.

U.S. General Accounting Office. (1988). *Children's programs*. Washington, DC: Government Printing Office.

U.S. General Accounting Office. (1989a). *Children and youths* (GAO/PEMD-89-14). Washington, DC: Author.

U.S. General Accounting Office. (1989b). *Foster care: Incomplete implementation of the reforms and unknown effectiveness* (PEMD 89-17). Washington, DC: Author.

U.S. General Accounting Office. (1989c). *Head Start: Information on sponsoring organizations and center facilities* (GAO Report HRD-89-123FS). Washington, DC: Government Printing Office.

U.S. General Accounting Office. (1989d). *Homelessness* (GAO/HRD-90-45). Washington, DC: Author.

U.S. General Accounting Office. (1989e). *Special education: Congressional action needed to improve Chapter I handicapped program* (GAO Report No. HRD-89-54). Washington, DC: Government Printing Office.

U.S. General Accounting Office. (1990a). *Drug exposed infants: A generation at risk* (GAO/HRD-90-138). Washington, DC: Government Printing Office.

U.S. General Accounting Office. (1990b). *Home visiting: A promising early intervention strategy for at-risk families*. Washington, DC: Government Printing Office.

U.S. General Accounting Office. (1990c). *Respite care: An overview of federal, selected state, and private programs*. Washington, DC: Government Printing Office.

U.S. General Accounting Office. (1991a). *Drug abuse, the crack cocaine epidemic: Health consequences and treatment* (HRD-91-55FS). Washington, DC: Author.

U.S. General Accounting Office. (1991b). *Foster care: Children's experiences linked to various factors* (HRD 91-64). Washington, DC: Author.

U.S. General Accounting Office. (1991c). *Teenage drug use: Uncertain linkages with either pregnancy or school dropout* (GAO Report No. PEMD-91-3). Washington, DC: Government Printing Office.

U.S. General Accounting Office. (1991d). *Within-school discrimination: Inadequate Title VI enforcement by Education's Office for Civil Rights* (GAO Report T-HRD-91-17). Washington, DC: Government Printing Office.

U.S. General Accounting Office. (1992). *Child abuse: Prevention programs need greater emphasis* (GAO/HRD-92-99). Washington, DC: Government Printing Office.

U.S. House of Representatives. (1990, April). *Federally funded child welfare, foster care and adoption assistance programs*. Hearing of the Subcommittee on Human Resources, Washington, DC.

U.S. House Subcommittee on Human Resources. (1989). *Proposals to improve the foster care and child welfare programs*. Washington, DC: Government Printing Office.

Urban Institute. (1989). Drugs and crime among adolescents: Taking a closer look. *Policy and Research Report, 19*(2), 8-10.

Uribe, V., & Harbeck, K. (1992). Addressing the needs of lesbian, gay, and bisexual youth: The origins of Project 10 and school-based intervention. *Journal of Homosexuality, 22,* 9-28.

Van Dyke, D., & Fox, A. (1990). Fetal drug exposure and its possible implications for learning in the preschool and school-age population. *Journal of Learning Disability, 23*(3), 160-163.

Videka-Sherman, L. (1991). Child abuse and neglect. In A. Gitterman (Ed.), *Handbook of social work practice with vulnerable populations* (pp. 345-381). New York: Columbia University Press.

Vondra, J. I. (1990). Sociological and ecological factors. In R. T. Ammerman & M. Hersen (Eds.), *Children at risk: An evaluation of factors contributing to child abuse and neglect* (pp. 149-170). New York: Plenum.

Wald, M., Carlsmith, C., & Liederman, P. (1988). *Protecting abused and neglected children.* Palo Alta, CA: Stanford University Press.

Walker, J. M. (1988). *Testimony before the House Subcommittee on Human Resources, January 29, 1988* (Serial No. 100-72). Washington, DC: Government Printing Office.

Walker v. Superior Court, 57 U.S.L.W. 3823 (June 20, 1989).

Waters, E., & Sroufe, L. (1983). Social competence as a developmental construct. *Developmental Review, 3,* 79-97.

Watkins, S. A. (1990). The Mary Ellen myth: Correcting child welfare history. *Social Work, 35,* 500-505.

Weissman, M., Gershon, E., Kidd, K., Prusoff, B., Leckman, J., Dibble, E., Hamovit, J., Thompson, W., Pauls, D., & Guroff, J. (1984). Psychiatric disorders in the relatives of probands with affective disorders. *Archives of General Psychiatry, 41,* 13-21.

Werner, E. (1986). Resilient offspring of alcoholics: A longitudinal study of from birth to age 18. *Journal of Studies on Alcohol, 44,* 34-40.

Werner, E., & Smith, R. (1982). *Vulnerable but invincible: A longitudinal study of resilient children and youth.* New York: McGraw-Hill.

Westin, D., Ivins, B., Zuckerman, B., Jones, C., & Lopez, R. (1989). Drug exposed babies: Research and clinical issues. *Zero to Three, 9*(5), 1-7.

Wilensky, H., & Lebeaux, C. (1958). *Industrial society and social welfare.* New York: Russell Sage Foundation.

Wilson, G. (1985). The juvenilization of poverty. *Public Administration Review, 45*(6), 880-884.

Wilson, G. (1989). Clinical studies of infants and children prenatally exposed to heroin. In D. Hutchings (Ed.), *Prenatal abuse of licit and illicit drugs* (pp. 183-194). New York: New York Academy of Sciences.

Wilson, W. J. (1987). *The truly disadvantaged: The inner city, the underclass, and public policy.* Chicago: University of Chicago Press.

Wisconsin v. Yoder, 406 U.S. 205 (1972).

Wise, M. L. (1989). Adult self-injury as a survival response in victim-survivors of childhood abuse. *Aggression, Family Violence and Chemical Dependency, 3*(1), 185-201.

Wodarski, J., Kurtz, D., Gaudin, J., & Howing, P. (1990). Maltreatment and the school-age child: Major academic, socioemotional, and adoptive outcomes. *Social Work, 35,* 506-513.

Wolfe, D., Jaffe, P., Zak, L., & Wilson, S. (1986). Child witnesses to violence between parents: Critical issues in behavioral and social adjustment. *Journal of Abnormal Child Psychology, 14,* 95-104.

Wright, J. D. (1990). Homelessness is not healthy for children and other living things. *Child and Youth Services, 14*(1), 65-88.

Youngblade, L. M., & Belsky, J. (1990). Social and emotional consequences of child maltreatment. In R. T. Ammerman & M. Hersen (Eds.), *Children at risk: An evaluation of factors contributing to child abuse and neglect* (pp. 109-146). New York: Plenum.

Zelizer, V. A. (1985). *Pricing the priceless child.* New York: Basic Books.

Ziegler, E., & Rescorla, L. (1985). Social science and social policy: The case of social competency as a goal of intervention programs. In R. Kasschau, L. Rehm, & L. Ullman (Eds.), *Psychology research, public policy, and practice: Toward a productive partnership* (pp. 62-94). New York: Praeger.

Zill, N. (1991). *Current characteristics of welfare recipients and their families.* Washington, DC: Child Trends.

Zinsmeister, K. (1990). Growing up scared. *The Atlantic Monthly, 265*(6), 49-66.

Zuckerman, B., & Frank, D. (1992). Crack kids not broken. *Pediatrics, 89,* 337-339.

Zuckerman, B., Frank, D., Hingson, R., Amaro, H., Levenson, S., Kayne, H., Parker, S., Vinci, R., Aboagye, K., Fired, L., Cabral, H., Timperi, R., & Bauchner, H. (1989). Effects of maternal marijuana and cocaine use on fetal growth. *New England Journal of Medicine, 320*(12), 762-768.

Author Index

Subject Index

216

About the Authors

Nora S. Gustavsson, Ph.D, approaches social work, both as a practitioner and an academic, from an ecological perspective. In this view, people function in environments that can compromise their achievement and tax their coping skills. The task of the social worker is simultaneously to assess both the client and the environment, noting resources and strengths, and work to enrich the environment and enhance the client system's coping skills.

This approach is reflected in her teaching and scholarly work. Students are encouraged to see clients as partners in the change process who bring strengths and talents to the therapeutic process. Students find this approach refreshing and continue to rate her as an exceptional teacher. Gustavsson's research has been in the area of vulnerable populations: factors that increase negative outcomes and the service needs of at-risk groups. Children and their mothers, especially poor children, are at grave risk for negative outcomes and she focuses on this vulnerable population. She spent many years providing direct services to children and their families and now teaches in this specialization.

Elizabeth A. Segal, Ph.D., is currently an Associate Professor on the faculty of the College of Social Work at the Ohio State University. Her specialization is in Child and Family Welfare, with an emphasis on programs and policies. During 1988-1989 she spent the year in Washington,

D.C., as a Congressional Science Fellow sponsored by the Society for Research in Child Development.

She has most recently conducted research in the areas of child welfare, community programming, homelessness, and welfare reform. Her work includes *A Resource Guide to the Social Welfare Needs of Women, Children, and Families* for the Lilly Foundation; *Early Childhood Intervention* for the Illinois Commission on Intergovernmental Affairs; "The Juvenilization of Poverty in the 1980s" in *Social Work;* "Homelessness in a Small Community: A Demographic Profile," in *Social Work Research and Abstracts;* and "Welfare Reform: Help for Poor Women and Children?" in *Affilia: Journal for Women in Social Work.*

At Ohio State University, Segal has taught at both the graduate and undergraduate levels. Her courses include "Child and Family Welfare Policies and Programs," "Social Work Practice With Children and Families," and "Social Welfare Policies and Programs."

Segal and Gustavsson have collaborated on a number of projects, including "The High Cost of Neglecting Children: The Need for a Preventive Policy Agenda" in *Child & Adolescent Social Work Journal.*